D1030240

Becoming West Indian

Smithsonian Series in Ethnographic Inquiry

William L. Merrill and Ivan Karp, Series Editors

Ethnography as fieldwork, analysis, and literary form is the distinguishing feature of modern anthropology. Guided by the assumption that anthropological theory and ethnography are inextricably linked, this series is devoted to exploring the ethnographic enterprise.

Advisory Board

Virginia Heyer Young

Becoming West Indian

Culture, Self, and Nation in St. Vincent

Smithsonian Institution Press

Washington and London

Copy Editor: Karin Kaufman
Production Editor: Jenelle Walthour
Designer: Alan Carter

Library of Congress Cataloging-in-Publication Data
Young, Virginia Heyer.

Becoming West Indian: culture, self, and nation in St. Vincent
/ Virginia Heyer Young.
    p.   cm.—(Smithsonian series in ethnographic inquiry)
Includes bibliographical references and index.
ISBN 1-56098-211-X (alk. paper)
1. Saint Vincent—History. 2. Saint Vincent—Social life and
customs. 3. Ethnicity—Saint Vincent. I. Title. II. Series.
F2106.Y64 1993
979.844—dc20   92-15902

British Library Cataloguing-in-Publication Data is available

Manufactured in the United States of America
00 99 98 97 96 95 94 93   5 4 3 2 1

75317

Contents

List of Maps and Tables   vii

Acknowledgments   viii

Introduction   1

1 Colonization and Rebellion   17
Vincentian Views of History   18
The Black Carib–British Contest   23
The French Role   31
The War   33
The War's Meaning to Black Caribs and Slaves   36

2 Constructing a Society   45
Conditions of Slavery   47
Small Farming and Large Landholding   52
Popular Political Participation   64

3 Village Culture: West Indian Issues   82
History and Class   84

Working and Consuming   94
Interracial Unions   102
Parental Ties   111
Household Organization   120
Structure of Domestic Groups   132
Childhood and Schools   137
Generations and Genders   149
Funerals and Oppositions   156
Spirituality and Public Ideology   161

4 **Vincentians' Search for Their Culture   168**
Speaking Creole   170
National Carnival   172
Carnival in a Village   179

5 **Discovering Culture and Seeking National Identity   187**

Notes   201

Works Cited   207

Index   223

Maps and Tables

Maps

1. Principal and Secondary Roads of St. Vincent, 1985   11
2. The Island of St. Vincent in the Late Eighteenth Century   21
3. John Byres's Plan for the Settlement of St. Vincent, 1764   22
4. Windward Valley Village   83

Tables

1. Number of Freeholds in Six Colonies   58
2. Windward Valley and St. Vincent Household Headship   125
3. Employment of Female Heads of House   126
4. Household Contributors and Residents   128
5. Households with Resident and Nonresident Daughters   129
6. House Ownership   130

Acknowledgments

My gratitude for the help that made this book possible goes to numerous persons and institutions. A sabbatical from the former Finch College in 1972 enabled me to undertake the first phase of fieldwork in St. Vincent. Mr. A. A. Dennie, then minister of education for St. Vincent and the Grenadines, facilitated my research in several ways. The librarians in the Kingstown Public Library were of much help in locating historical and documentary sources. I am indebted to the columnists, editors, and reporters of the *Vincentian*, the national independent newspaper of St. Vincent. Back home between field trips and while writing this book, its weekly arrival kept me in touch with events and opinions in the country. Particularly informative were Kenneth John's many columns on political history. Anthony Williams's feature reporting offered much insight into Vincentian life and thought.

The 1764 map was reproduced from a drawing made from its first printing by Professor David L. Niddrie, Emeritus, University of Florida. The drawing was published is his article "Eighteenth-Century Settlement in the British Caribbean," Transactions of the Institute of British Geographers, no. 40 (1966). I am grateful for his permission to reproduce it here.

Miss Nesta Paynter, M.B.E. was of inestimable help during my first fieldwork in St. Vincent. The West Indian tourists who flocked to her old estate house (turned into an inn) had been followed by more anthropologists than me, and she knew our objectives well. In any village one was inclined to choose, she would know someone, and it was she who found me a house and a housekeeper, that important first informant.

My family played a large part in this study. On the first trip in 1972, my daughters, Eleanor Young Crowder and Millicent Young, joined me after I had found a field location, and our house became a gathering place for children. My daughters' presence, and their riding the bus daily into Kingstown to attend high school dressed in the school uniform, helped make us all believable and interesting to the village. Millicent at thirteen was still a child and was taken by our self-appointed ombudswoman for many privileged errands. Eleanor at sixteen was in a more difficult position and had to pursue the image of young scholar to deal with the complexities of village teenage life. My husband, James Sterling Young's, brief visit to us in the field broadened my rapport. His conversations with village men, exercising his acuity as a political scientist, gave me my first insights into the functions of political talk in rural St. Vincent. His knowledge of comparative government and society sharpened my political analysis; however, he bears no responsibility for the rudimentary way in which I, as a general ethnographer, have pursued this subject.

My deep gratitude goes to the residents of the village to which I give the pseudonym Windward Valley. Among them many different attitudes toward my stays there were apparent, some hostile, some aloof, some neighborly, some friendly. This diversity of attitudes toward my work was a source of freedom and insight. Vincentians are not people who control an intruder by a united front or by cooptation. Their open expression of opinions was of great value in teaching me about their society.

On my trip in 1984 I boarded with an elderly farming couple whose daughters had sent money from the United States to build a house with that rare feature, an unused bedroom. After a few weeks, when they had tired of this arrangement, I moved in with a large, three-generation family in their house built years ago with an Aruba oil worker's earnings, in which they kept a bedroom vacant for sons returning from abroad. They included me in their family life with the most open spirit. My return visits to old acquaintances from the 1972 trip were some of the warmest and most interesting conversations I had. In 1986 a large and poor family insisted I stay with them, and I did so for five weeks. I had kept in touch with them since 1972, following the school grades, the births, and the marriages by letter. With a small gift from me, and with the salaries of two adult sons, they had installed running water and a bathroom, and this was what they felt allowed them to offer me their hospitality.

My first night there, after traveling all day and catching the last van from Kingstown with my hosts, I got in bed where I was told and did not look around to see where everyone else was to sleep, but on the second night I was glad the woman of the house and one little girl joined me. Four young men shared a bed and three daughters and two grandchildren shared another. The husband made a pallet outside. The house belonged to his wife and her sons. I am grateful for the hospitality and company of all these families. My most reliable insights into family life came from living so closely together.

I am much indebted to Gail Moore and Judy Birckhead at the University of Virginia Word Processing Center for the production of the manuscript. Special thanks go also to Karin Kaufman for her skillful editing of the manuscript.

Introduction

This book is about the present-day culture of the West Indian island of St. Vincent. It assesses the practices and symbols that constitute an adaptive way of life and a shared idea system. The large, loose subject of the culture of whole nations is not a common one in Caribbean ethnology. This book seeks the connection between the whole and the parts, the nation and the ethnography. It includes the local meanings of larger entities, its people's references beyond the time and space of the village to their sense of history and polity. The framework is nation, history, and person—the nation newly transformed from a colony, the history culled from observers, commentators, and tangential inquiries and still awaiting proper historiography. The cultural idea of personhood is depicted through familial and life-cycle practices and in the teaching of the presentation of the self. This ethnography attempts to find the regularities in meaning of social forms and advocated values to Vincentians striving to live in their world as they define it.

In portraying rural life in some of its personal dimensions, the ethnographic sections address two long-standing issues in the study of West Indian cultures: the structure of domestic practices and the ways in which creole cultures resolve the difficulties inherent in the incorporation of broadly divergent values and behavior codes. Village domestic practices reveal more structured forms and values than are often represented in West Indian societies, and I describe relatively consistent modes of behavior and attitudes with regard to household organization, parent and offspring relationships, and the stages of family composition. I found the same general principles of organization in both female-headed and couple-headed families, and in comparing poor households with well-off ones, I discovered the same broadly shared characteristics, thus allowing description of an underlying structure of domestic organization. Because village behavior represents consistent and relatively overt assumptions and obligations concerning the relationships of parents to their young children and adult offspring, household organization and familial relationships allow the delineation of a system of domestic culture.

The issue of value conflict is central to all these relationships, involving the disparity between European-derived familial values, which are well understood and highly respected, and low-respect but formalized extraresidential mating, which evokes a degree of shame and derogation among both low- and middle-class persons. Low- and high-status values are as much a part of current creole cultures as they were part of the dual or multiple traditions brought together in Caribbean societies. The contrast between low- and high-status values sets up a conflict, and value conflicts in the broad areas of mating, households, and parental relationships are an important dynamic in personal development, interpersonal relations, and community relations. These issues have been widely discussed in the literature on the Caribbean. I follow a line of interpretation that stems from Herskovits's introduction of processes of syncretism in the creation of creole traditions in Afro-America and leads to Reisman's perception that individuals "remodel" meanings in playing upon the dual cultural traditions of which their societies are constructed, sometimes using ambiguity to advantage. Among the contributors to this line of thought, Abrahams has described folk models of pairing oppositions and playing upon dualisms. I represent the person as proceeding through the stages in the life cycle by choosing from the range of values and playing out different roles with different meanings.

The playing out of differently valued roles throughout the life cycle, and the self-defense that accompanies some of the roles, demonstrate a personal characteristic—namely, a well-developed sense of self. It is the means of defense against the moral criticism inherent in the respecting of low-valued and high-valued behavior codes. What Herskovits referred to as *socialized ambivalence* places much moral strain on persons. Regularly practicing devalued or ambivalently valued behaviors, as is virtually socially prescribed at certain times of the life cycle, is made possible by a strong sense of self, a form of individualism taught in childhood and evidenced in social interaction.

Individualistic behavior is supported by the family system, the expectations placed on children, gender roles, and practices for resolving the conflicts of principles and values. Mintz ([1966] 1971:37–42) first noted the importance in Caribbean cultures of individualistic modes of behavior and organizational relationships. He discussed institutional factors leading to this social characteristic and drew a relationship between the minimal presence of corporate social group activity, strong Westernization, and the urbanizing characteristics of plantation organization. His analyses of market sellers' social relationships and his discussions of godparenthood networks, which he cited in developing his meaning of individual dyadic ties, remain among the few discussions of interpersonal relations that develop this point. My own work (1970, 1974) demonstrated the teaching and practice of individualism among Afro-Americans in a southern town and in Harlem. Mintz and Price (1976:22) also emphasized individualistic dyadic relationships among slaves, as an early element in the development of creole cultures. In writing of "the relentless assault on personal identity" in the treatment of slaves, they observed:

> Yet, by a peculiar irony, this most degrading of all aspects of slavery seems to have had the effect of encouraging the slaves to cultivate an enhanced appreciation for exactly those most personal, most human characteristics which differentiate one individual from another, perhaps the principal qualities which the masters could not take away from them. Early on, then, the slaves were elaborating upon ways in which they could be individuals—a particular sense of humor, a certain skill or type of knowledge, even a distinctive way of walking or talking, or some sartorial detail, like the cock of a hat or the use of a cane. (1976:26)

Price concluded an assessment of the literature on Caribbean family organization by saying that the individualistic social ties discussed by Mintz may be "the most outstanding feature of rural Caribbean social structure" (1971:49). Ethnographic studies have paid little attention, however, to personal and interpersonal dimensions of social behavior where the sources and modes of behavior would be expected to be observable.

A second emphasis of this study, national identity in Vincentian culture, is assessed through several aspects of history and through expressions of Vincentian opinion leaders and performers. This issue is presented as an introductory historical background for the village ethnography and as a concluding comparison of village and national performances. History and national identity are more, however, than an introductory and concluding context for ethnography. Historical directions and national expressions suggest that Vincentians have long considered their islands a political entity. I suggest that political identification in this society is complementary to individuated, small-scale relationships. In state societies the attenuatedness of kinship and local corporate groups allows for the direct relatedness of individuals and state. Unrestricted by binding local identity, the individual may use larger-scale imagery, either a supernatural world or a political entity, to construct a sense of self.

The two dimensions of this book, the ethnography of the domestic domain and the cultural expressions recorded in history and gestured in national political culture, represent distant relationships. I justify this leap from the domestic to the national by the similarity of pattern on the two levels; furthermore in the absence of kin and nonkin corporate organization, there is no social impediment to this linkage. A leap from the local to the national, and from the present to the past, is part of the villagers' framework of thought, a context they refer to in speaking about their way of life. I was continually reminded, as I worked out my ethnographic analysis, that the villagers thought of themselves in terms of their history, their nation, and the places to which their family members had emigrated. They received the messages of the well-educated members of the society through the media, the schools, the community youth groups, and through their attention to politics. They were farmers and laborers whose context of thought was broader than village life, and they used these broader contexts to shift focus from the prevailing ethics of blame of self and others to subjects that merited respect or held promise of benefits. It was the villagers' orientation to island concepts of history, off-island contacts, and national government that led me to look into these parts of their framework of thought. Although history is represented here as it can be reconstructed from records, I also try to show how Vincentians think about their history, the current meanings of episodes and precedents.

There are many interrelationships among this broad set of topics, and taken together they make up a sketch of a patterned national culture. Placing ethnography in a national context is increasingly significant because most of the former British colonies have become independent nations, and a federation of West Indian nations—a long-standing ideal—is again being pursued. The two goals, of becoming self-governing nations and of creating a federation of the English-speaking Caribbean, were discussed by Caribbean leaders at least as early as 1914, when the Representative Government

Association was formed in Trinidad, with chapters in other colonies, and are familiar to the general public.

Anthropologists have disagreed on whether any integrative social and cultural factors existed even in single colonies. They have stressed the extraordinary histories of merging polyglot elements into agrarian factory societies, histories that set up extreme cleavages and left little time and sentiment for accommodation, let alone for tradition building. The formation of creole cultures was thought to be a necessary precedent to a sense of cultural identity, and national sentiment required a basis in social integration. In the 1960s two opposite views of West Indian societies contended, the plural society and the creole society. Michael G. Smith's plural society model represented the elite, the folk, and the ethnic groups as entirely different cultures sharing no common ideology, without reciprocal interrelationships, and held together only by the colonial political system. This model rejects the idea of creole society and the growth of social and cultural integration. It opposes the interconnectedness characteristic of social phenomena by taking a taxonomic view. Few other scholars have worked with the plural society model in the West Indies, and few have considered its socioeconomic and racial differences to be so great as to constitute separate cultures. A Vincentian specialist in regional planning, Karl John (1974:182), has written that "M. G. Smith's plural cultural model . . . no longer adequately describes contemporary Vincentian culture, in which under the impact of modernization, tourism and the external media, all strata of the society have increasingly come to share a commonality of values and aspirations." To the historian Edward Braithwaite, the idea of a Jamaican creole society was "an historically affected socio-cultural continuum"; among "white/brown/black there are infinite possibilities within these distinctions and many ways of asserting identity." He had a cautious vision "that the 'little' tradition of the (ex-) slaves . . . could well support the development of a new parochial wholeness, a difficult but possible creole authenticity" (1971:310–11). The idea of the growth of creole cultures was developed within social anthropology with models of social stratification, in which social and racial differences among strata may be great, but groups nevertheless share characteristics and modes of interdependency that enable them to cohere into an articulated society. Raymond T. Smith and Lloyd Braithwaite were among the analysts of the West Indian class hierarchies. Smith reporting on Guyana and Jamaica, and Braithwaite on Trinidad, demonstrated shared characteristics within diverse social forms and reciprocal relations across boundaries of social strata and ethnic groups. The integration of other dichotomous elements in these societies, the European and African traditions, was demonstrated by Herskovits (1941) and others. Abrahams showed the creative mixture of these traditions in the important area of the performance arts. Bryce-Laporte, Reisman, and Drummond, among others, described the manipulation of meanings in each tradition in social vignettes more vivid than fiction and with the complexity of real communities. New trends in anthropology have expanded the view of creole cultures as rich and complex. Inclusion of the dimension of culture has brought more investigation of ideological and symbolic aspects of creole societies, and particularly stimulating has been the attention to the ideologies and meaning systems of peasantries, lower-class groups, and the middle classes. I will discuss the contributions of recent scholarship as I develop the various parts of my argument.

The study of Vincentian society was been initiated at a period of questioning and search for new explanatory concepts. The first broad ethnography of the island, the work of Rubenstein, appeared in a series of articles and was published as a detailed ethnography in 1987. Choosing to hold theoretical explanation in abeyance in preference to descriptive analysis, Rubenstein used the minimal explanatory framework of adaptive strategies for coping with poverty (1987a). He employed several analytic devices compatible with this view, such as network systems and situational sociology. He focused on land use and tenure, the effects of migration, and conjugal relationships, and did not include the areas I stress, ideological systems and culture. More recently he has enlarged on an ideological dimension (1987b). In the last pages of *Coping with Poverty,* he rejected both the plural society model and the stratification model as inadequate because he recognized a level of cultural integration: "All Vincentians are united by . . . transcendent interests, understandings, and pursuits. . . . Elite and middle strata mores and values are shared by all members of the society" (1987a:351–52). He briefly identified these shared areas of Vincentian life, noting also that lower-class persons are barred from participation in many high-status practices. Although he did not discuss any of the areas of commonality, he opened the way to the study of a cultural level and elements of national integration.

A second Vincentian ethnography reported on a community on the Grenadine island of Bequia (Price 1988). Price employed the paradigm of a local, normatively based social structure and ideology that included ideological elements imposed on the lower class by the "ex-planter" class. The cultural and structural analysis derived from this geographically isolated community broadly matches lower-class patterns on the main island, but the community's sense of social distance from other entities, detailed by Price, tokens an atypical insularity. Although he derives much of lower-class ideology from the normative systems, Price argues that parts were imposed as instruments of subordination, as predicated in Marx's concept of a dominant ideology. This explanation overlooks many factors, among them the changes in the relationship of classes and the processes of revalidation of ideologies, and it discounts as well significant ideological statements made by Price's own informants (1988:190ff.). Despite these points of disagreement, this ethnology is one of the fullest analyses of a lower-class idea system to come out of West Indian research.[1]

If the reality of West Indian creole culture can be considered well established, the subject of national identities has hardly been broached.[2] *National identity* is a vague expression, but I will discuss its manifestations, leaving to Chapter 5 definitions of the concept and its relation to culture and nationalism. Cogent argument has been made that only the Hispanic culture areas of the Caribbean developed the social basis essential for national identity (Mintz 1974:260; Hoetink 1973). Thus far the only formulations of national identity ventured for the English-speaking Caribbean have been in postindependence political oratory devised by emerging leaders—elite strategies for manipulating votes, not a culturally rooted common sentiment. The argument for national ideology as a product of the educated elite has been made widely for traditional societies and recently developed for postcolonial nationalism in Anderson's *Imagined Communities*. For the British Caribbean, Safa located emerging national identity in the recent recognition by the educated elite of the political necessity of appealing to a mass base. She noted a history of cultural separateness of the racially mixed elite from the black masses:

> By denying their African heritage and emphasizing their cultural whiteness over a nationalist image, the mulatto Creole elite lacked an alternative ideology on which they could build a separate style of life in opposition to that of the colonial power. This elite was frightened by figures like Marcus Garvey, who appealed to black nationalism, and they resisted any appeal to racial solidarity as a basis for national identity. The weak nationalist sentiment of this elite helps explain why the Anglophone Caribbean did not achieve independence until the 1960's. (1987:120)

Safa noted that independence forced the creole elite to seek political backing among the general population and described their invocation of a popular "black" cultural identity, which was reinforced by the black power movement in the United States, and the political leaders' uses of popular styles of music, speaking, and dress, referring particularly to Brodber's work on Jamaican politicians' appeals to popular culture and Rastafarian imagery (1987). Manning also has described political appeals to traditional black culture in Bermudan politics (1981). In St. Vincent similar techniques have been used, particularly in the early period of party politics, and effective use has been made of the display of "talking sense" and "talking sweet," a tradition described by Abrahams (1983:109ff.). This popular practice opened the way for electioneering, with controversy over issues of bread and butter and good government, a type of issue-based political talk now common. My case for national identity is not based on political strategies but on a broadly shared culture. I argue that rural-based culture is pervasive and coherent enough to have been a principal component of the national culture, and that the rural base has been propelled into a national culture by the growth of the middle class out of the village peasantry. Primary and secondary education were means of projecting the culture of the common people into national forms and have been as important as elite education in contributing to the national culture. Most important, I think that many interpretations of West Indian lower-class culture obscure the elements of social and moral order in lower-class customs, and the rural fieldsite exhibits cultural stability and cultural distinctiveness in these customs. It is possible to describe the moral reasoning of persons who practice customs both they and outside observers derogate, and to show the organizational similarity of practices that have often been categorized as different.

In certain respects Vincentian history was more conducive to unified practices than the histories of other Caribbean societies. There have been fewer social cleavages on St. Vincent. Colonized and ruled principally by one nation for most of its colonial period, the island did not have the plurality of colonial languages, religions, and elite identities that divided many other societies. An early four-way contest in St. Vincent—Carib, French, British, and African—was resolved eighty years after the beginning of estate development by defeat in war of the Carib Indians and their French allies in 1795, and by deportation of the Caribs. Although the French had been the earliest European settlers, only Britain established means of governing the colony, and the French heritage remained in little more than place names, family names, and the practice of Catholicism by a minority of the island's inhabitants. St. Vincent early became a dual society, 90 percent African and 10 percent British, both locked in intense sugar plantation development, setting up a simpler dichotomy than in many Caribbean societies. The relative clarity of binary categories is reflected in aspects of Vincentian racial and cultural history. Racial and cultural diversity was introduced by Madeiran and East Indian laborers recruited several decades after the abolition of slavery. The two groups made up approximately 12 percent of the Vincentian population at the close of the nineteenth century, but in 1980 East Indians made up less than 1.6 percent of the population and Portuguese only .5 percent. In 1980 the nation of St. Vincent and the Grenadines, composed of 118,000 people on the main island and 9,000 more on the Grenadines, remained 96 percent black and racially mixed, and the white population had declined from 2.5 percent in 1960 to 1.1 percent. The double origin of Vincentian society and culture, in contrast to the multiple origins of Dominica, St. Lucia, Trinidad, and other Caribbean societies, set up a different historical arena.[3] Dominica, a neighboring island similar to St. Vincent in many ways and recently portrayed as subject to divisive factors throughout its history, had to bring together two European cultures, British and French (Trouillot 1988). On that island the French Creole vernacular was pitted against the administrative and school language of English; the population was divided between a Catholic majority and a small but educated and influential Methodist minority; and the north coast was linked by trade more closely to its French neighbor, Guadaloupe, than to its own island trade. Colonial land use unified St. Vincent geographically. Trouillot portrays disunity through the social use of space, demonstrating "Dominica's spacial dismemberment" and concluding: "The immediately visible signs of dismemberment seem to outweigh the elements of unity. Here space divides" (1988:33, 49). St. Vincent's geographical zones are objectively similar to Dominica's, but their use and organization have been different, incorporating St. Vincent into a single nucleus and periphery. The human geography has resulted in different polities in these neighboring volcanic islands. On St. Vincent an interior mountain chain forms the north to south axis of the island and extends laterally in ridges and valleys toward the coasts. The windward eastern coast has been cut back by the sea and wind to high bluffs; on the leeward side, the steep ridges are less weathered and separate the valleys more precipitously. One large bay on the south coast forms the only harbor suitable for ocean ships, and from the time of the earliest English settlement that bay has been the site of the sole seaport and the only large town. In the northeast third of the island rugged mountains descend steeply into the sea. Scant settlement or cultivation, by either Carib Indians, colonists, or modern Vincentians extended into this area. All commerce traveled southward along the west and east coasts to the single port of Kingstown. Coastwise canoe and sloop transport was supplemented by horse trails, and as early as 1813 by a windward coast road snaking northward along the wind-shaven bluffs and fording the valley streams along two-thirds of the way up the coast to a small, secondary town. The leeward ridges impeded a vehicular road until the middle part of this century. An early road connected the large fertile interior Marriaqua Valley with Kingstown. The cultivated land of the island was threaded together, valley by valley, along the windward coast road and the leeward water route. All travel headed for the port, the site of a shipping beach and pier, shops, and the government. To go from one side of the island to the other, after the abandonment of Carib footpaths across the mountains, one must travel via Kingstown.

The funnel to a single center created a spacial unity, which has been maintained, and the capitol's commercial dominance was enhanced by the introduction of the motor transportation of crops in the early years of this century and by buses for shoppers and commuters after 1945. Although most villagers go to Kingstown no more than weekly or monthly, all of them go there at times for town services and events, as will be described. Kingstown's role as nucleus of the island grows with boat travel to the Grenadines from Kingstown Harbor, the villagers' preference for shopping in town stores over rural stores, employment opportunities increasing in the town area and in the Grenadines, and tourist facilities situated close to Kingstown.

At the opposite end of the island, the periodically active volcano Soufriere symbolizes the uncultivated north. It erupted in 1813, 1902, and 1979, devastating villages and the countryside each time. Many Vincentians tell of climbing the mountain, by either the eastern or western path. People brought back flowers from the edge of the crater lake before the 1979 eruption destroyed it, and they described the clear water and vegetation in words of sacred connotation. Old and young are exhilarated by the beauty and the power of the volcano. A primal place, the young run, the old stride, up the rugged trail, a place for self-expenditure and self-renewal. On the opposite side of the island ellipse is the busy center of government and commerce. Most Vincentians have traveled throughout the island and know its geography well. They speak of the beauty of the cultivated valleys and the mountains in prayers and songs and quote travelers' praise. The island is a shared habitat with one center, one place of urban services. A spacial whole and ethnically undiverse, St. Vincent may have had better prospects than many Caribbean societies for generating cultural and political identity.

Vincentians themselves speak of having a national identity and culture. Their references to themselves include expressions such as "we Vincie," "we kind of people," and "our culture." A few decades ago a sense of culture and history is what Caribbean societies were said to lack. Impor-

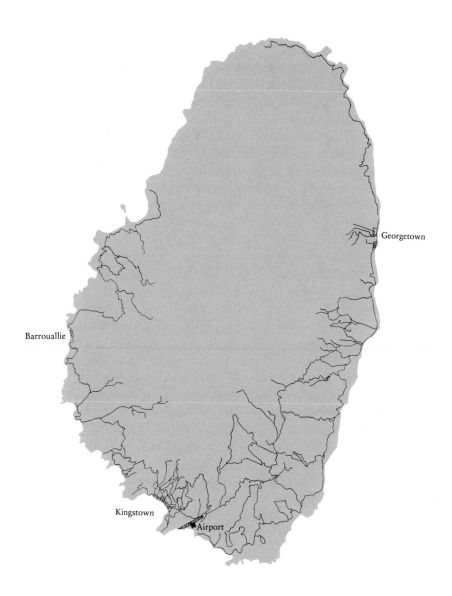

Map 1. Principal and secondary roads of St. Vincent, 1985.

tant episodes in Vincentian history are part of general knowledge, some traditional, some learned in schools. They are keenly aware of their history of slavery and emancipation. Their origin as a people has long been reviewed every August first, the anniversary of the abolition of slavery, with villagers holding meetings to present speeches on slavery and freedom. Their imagery of the island includes the stamp of plantation dominance in the estate names still used for all cultivated areas. Until the last few decades, most land had been held continuously in estates since the slave period; only a few tracts were ever divided and sold to small farmers. Only two or three generations ago most Vincentians were landless laborers employed on estates, and estate employment is still common. As early as the mid-nineteenth century, Vincentians joined the forces of international migrant labor. Their geographical viewpoint includes the places where they and their relatives have been employed abroad: other Caribbean countries, England, and South and North America. Their exposure to other societies and diverse working conditions by means of temporary emigration make up an important component of the Vincentian world view. They gained a comparative social view, helping to define what is Vincentian in contrast to non-Vincentian. An interest in politics contributes to the Vincentians' self-definition as an island entity. Island politics and government are everyday topics of conversation of gatherings and passersby in villages. The heightened sense of cultural identity is partly a result of political independence in 1969, with the ferment of national self-evaluation and the emergence of political roles for leaders and the populace, which preceded and followed the inception of local self-government. The transition to political independence in the whole post–World War II British Caribbean was accompanied by political involvement of the general populace and expanded activity among artists and writers. Among Vincentians, who gained universal adult suffrage in 1951, this stimulated the desire to know their history and to be able to talk about their culture. Vincentians heard Marcus Garvey and T. A. Marryshaw speaking in the Kingstown market square and in the Kingstown library. The educated elite may have been frightened by Garvey, as Safa suggested, but a chapter of the Universal Negro Improvement Association was headquartered in the village of Stubbs. Members of the educated middle class formed a self-government association patterned after Trinidad's, and teachers attended Trinidadian conferences of the Caribbean Union of Teachers. A pharmacist played a role in a workers' tax riot in 1935. A group of lawyers and teachers, educated at the University of the West Indies following World War II, published a quarterly magazine of social commentary. They read and contributed to the literature of Caribbean protest and the nascent ideologies of independence. Several of them researched the working-class riot of 1935, and their descriptions of the episode entered the discourse of village youth groups and village discussion meetings. In the decades after independence, Vincentians participated in the Caribbean growth of scholarship, the arts, journalism, and interisland sports and festivals, and these occasions for self-evaluation heightened the sense of national identity and the knowledge of relations with other societies. Their sense of being a distinctive society is augmented by a great volume of public speaking about themselves transmitted by radio, television, and newspapers, from the church pulpits, from public meetings, from the broadcasting of the annual budget debate in the legislature, and from the custom of talking politics as a form of sociability. Various leaders' evaluations of Vincentianness often echo elitist moralism, but they are also statements of Vincentians' real characteristics and worth, and they maintain an image of a whole society.

Although the idea of a national culture can be promoted for political purposes as a reified and constructed identity, as has been described in the case of Quebec's French-speaking faction, the Vincentian idea is not of this kind (Handler 1988). The idea is more widespread than political rhetoric and nationalist ceremonies, and is heard from many thoughtful persons of low and high status who often speak up about "our society." Vincentians have long heard social critics lecturing in community gatherings; congregations listen as "local ministers" adapt biblical lessons to "we kind of people." Self-consciousness as a collectivity finds expression, but the claims of a Vincentian culture have neither the element of rationalization nor the ring of ungenuineness, nor the confident conviction characteristic of forms of expression termed *cultural reification*. The idea of culture may be seen to be part illusion, but even as illusion it has importance in West Indian societies where social cleavages have long dominated the analysts' schemes. Anthropologists' accounts of culture necessarily have elements of illusion, and popular ideas are likewise part illusion, part reality. Vincentians' cultural claims are listened to with interest by the ethnographer engaged in deciphering a community's customary practices and expressions. What Vincentians cite as parts of their culture are not the rubrics of ethnography, but overt understandings of broad characteristics of their nation and history. Conceptualizations by both the populace and the ethnographer seek a sense of wholeness. The characteristics of nation and history that appear to Vincentians as culture are to the ethnographer sources and context for social and cultural codes. They are a series of selected meanings signifying aspects of the national identity. The historical and ethnographic authenticity of the widespread conviction of a shared culture in the nation of St. Vincent and the Grenadines is the subject of my investigation.

At a University of Florida conference commemorating the fiftieth anniversary of the negritude movement, Aimé Césaire spoke about the desire of Afro-Caribbean peoples to define themselves: "Blacks must create a rehabilitation of our values by ourselves, the re-rooting of ourselves within a history, within a geography, within a culture." Rex Nettleford, in the context of discussing Caribbean festivals, has written:

> The task of nation building looms large, and the manipulation of symbols, festivals included, has become part of the action. Harnessing deeper social forces becomes a continuing challenge in shaping the new society in which values of freedom, equality, and self-actualization, and rehumanization of a policy that had known only slavery and imperialism for most of its existence, are priorities. (1988:183)

The government of St. Vincent and the Grenadines has drawn up a "cultural policy" from the recommendations of a cultural committee:

> The policy has six main objectives: (1) to create and encourage the establishment of appropriate institutions for enhancing cultural development; (2) to instill and develop national pride which will create greater commitment, responsibility, self confidence, discipline and a collective spirit; (3) to identify, stimulate and develop the creative potential of Vincentians so as to improve and enrich the quality of life and to promote the image of St. Vincent and the Grenadines nationally, regionally and internationally; (4) to inculcate an appreciation for the understanding of the cultures of the Caribbean and other countries; (5) to inculcate in the individual an appreciation of and respect for the aesthetic and functional values of our surroundings; and (6) to preserve and conserve our cultural heritage.
> The policy explains that our historical experience has been one whereby colonial tutelage has alienated the majority of our people from a true sense of national pride and self confidence; and this has caused a lack of commitment to and responsibility for national development. This lack of self confidence and national pride is a result of foreign cultural penetration. (*Vincentian*, 18 January 1985)

The value placed on culture, the need to protect it against intrusion from foreign media, the need to compensate for the alienation, the self-denial, imposed by their history indicate a new recognition of self-identity.

Popular use of the word *culture* is owed to generations of anthropologists: they gave the term its broad and integrative meaning. Vincentian intellectuals' definitions of culture could have come from an anthropology book. What a culture is, in a sense broader than arts and history, is traditionally the province of the anthropologist. This book is an attempt to bring the holistic concepts of anthropology, as well as its person-centered traditions, to the analysis of a society that has experienced an exploitative, divisive, and dehumanizing institutional history. I look for a degree of consistency in aspects of personal relationships, social modes, concepts of the self, and concepts and symbols of the society itself, noting the forms of expression and enactment in everyday contexts. This account of Vincentian culture is based on fieldwork and the research of historians and other scholars. The fieldwork was conducted in the coastal village of Windward Valley (a pseudonym) for six months in 1972 and two months in both 1984 and 1986. In Chapter 1 I look to history for choices and adaptive trends that affected Vincentian values. The eighteenth-century war between the British and Black Caribs enacted the fundamental conflict of slave and free society, of English and primitive culture, and I see it as a decisive episode in which slaves, by both choice and inaction, helped to determine Vincentian values. The primary question posed by this episode is, What did the war mean to the slaves, the ancestors of most of today's Vincentians? Chapter 2 inquires into the transition from intense plantation slavery to a currently central occupation of small farming during a long period when estate land was undivided and small farming was maintained through leasing land. The latter part of this period saw the origins and development of popular political participation, which launched postindependence politics.

In this Introduction and in Chapters 1 and 2 the emphasis is on context and large-scale frameworks. In the ethnography of local behavior and thought in Chapter 3, I am concerned with the regularized meaning of social forms to the individuals enacting them. In the West Indies, meaning centers on the advocated values from divergent cultural sources, on "socialized ambivalence," "a covert duality of both cultural and linguistic values," "this competitive and highly contrasting superimposition of voices, ones that speak in different codes and cadences"—phrases devised by Herskovits (1937:299), Reisman (1970:142), and Abrahams (1983:xxx) to describe the merging of different cultural ideas that took place in Afro-America. Their images suggest persons acting and speaking, and yet the ways persons live with conflicting codes and values have not been widely studied. Relevant to these formulations of Caribbean cultures is the perspective of personal character as revealed in the teaching of children and the structure of the life-cycle stages. The regularized forms of behavior in these sectors of culture are individualistic and rest on a sense of self and a projection of individuality. In West Indian cultures, where social groups have been less than collectively solidary, extraordinary responsibility has rested on the individual. Where religion has been moralistically punishing and the social norms are derided, responsibility for meaning devolves more on the person. In a society weak in corporate structures, in which behavior codes and their moralities are asserted by actions and words in the absence of group legitimation, individuals learn self-responsibility. Individualistic qualities become the locus of cultural teaching and dyadic relationships become the form of social solidarity. The importance of the individual projects the phases of the life cycle into prominence. There the diverse directives of the society are resolved by each person, aided by the structured forms for each phase of life, the many different churches and religious sects, and the final rituals at death.

Chapter 4 explores some of the Vincentians' own formulations of their society and culture, first in the intelligentsia's writings and then in popular performance, including the national carnival and a rural carnival. Chapter 5 summarizes this book's construction of Vincentian culture. It compares the elements of Vincentian national identity with formulations of the nature of national identities and disscusses currents of the overarching identity of pan–West Indianism.

I

Colonization and Rebellion

As inspector of army hospitals in the British West Indies for three years, John Davy traveled among all the colonies and keenly evaluated the changes that followed the emancipation of slaves. In St. Vincent in 1848, he noted that a sense of history was present there, unlike in Barbados:

> There is one more point of difference between the two islands not unworthy of mention,—that which relates to tradition and remote times. In Barbados there are no traditions, no vestiges of the remote past; its history is entirely recent. There, there is not a spot which bears other than a modern name. In St. Vincent, not only is there a remnant of the ancient race, but likewise the majority of the more conspicuous spots, and those most resorted to, bear the names which were assigned them before the island was known to Europeans, mixed with French and English names in a very characteristic manner, in themselves as it were a history; and there are objects of like significance, such as rocks, on the face of which rude figures are cut of an unknown antiquity. Even the recent history of the island has a superiority of interest, arising out of the many hard-fought battles and incidents of war that occurred before the island became an exclusive possession by right of conquest. The traditionary

record of the more memorable actions, memorable in a small way as feats of arms, is not yet lost, nor are the localities, the scenes of them, yet forgotten. (Davy 1854:167–68)

Davy was not given to romanticizing; he was appalled by the "want of prosperity of this [higher] class" and foresaw a "decline . . . in point of intelligence and knowledge, art and science, and may it not be added in morals as well as manners" (180). His observations about a sense of history are not to be written off as picturesque. His sense of the presence of the past is as much a part of island places today. Vincentians' tenuous ties to, or consciousness of, the Carib villages, the Carib and French place names, the estate names for almost all cultivated land and villages, and the periodicity and threat of volcanic eruptions constitute a pervasive historicity.

VINCENTIAN VIEWS OF HISTORY

Vincentians' view of their history includes two primary images of themselves: as descendants of slaves, and as participants in British political culture. As contraposed as these two images appear, they are the central Vincentian concepts of self and society. The meaning of slavery in self-imagery extends in the post-emancipation period into the coercive conditions and regulations designed to keep Vincentians estate laborers, conditions from which approximately half the labor force could not escape. Vincentians' image of themselves as participants in British political culture embodies respect for both the institutions of government and hierarchy itself, in which even low-status subjects are elevated by the commanding dignity and power at the top. It is true that Vincentian riots have specifically targeted governors in at least two instances and resentment of colonial government policies is repeatedly expressed; nevertheless, government as a powerful and hierarchical institution is admired and continues to be the society's primary symbol.

Long before the abolition of slavery, the inherent conflict of slavery and respect for the British government was acted out in a dramatic thirty-year episode of Vincentian history, the Black Carib War, in which a Maroon-Indian society waged a diplomatic contest with the Vincentian Colonial Assembly, fought British troops, and in 1795 seriously threatened the existence of the English settlement. That challenge to colonial domination and British institutions increasingly stirs Vincentian historical curiosity in this period of heightened nationalism. For modern Vincentians the war enacted the paradox of their ancestors' British slavery: slave status was a necessary condition to membership in British society. In order to obtain freedom, the Maroons had chosen conditions of life that have appeared inferior and barbaric to modern Vincentians, and, I will maintain, to the slaves. To remain part of the British colonial society, the slaves accepted their status and helped defeat the Maroons. In the late nineteenth and early twentieth centuries, the descendants of slaves staged riots against the colonial system, and after St. Vincent became an independent nation, that first fight against British domination was remodeled from a savage rebellion against civilized society to the first stage of the struggle for a free society.

The themes of a slave origin and respect for the institutions of government are central to Vincentian world views. They emerge in conversations with Vincentians of all walks of life and are a dominant subject of their intellectuals' writings. The humble and the educated explain their society through them, each in their own discourse, for these are collective representations in the minds of thoughtful people, and they are also valid renditions of history. Vincentians who were educated in the island schools learned their history from a secondary school textbook written in 1941 by the prominent citizen and schoolmaster Ebenezer Duncan. This was a competent brief history revised and reprinted five times and read by most secondary school students through the early 1970s. The two dramatic themes—slavery and participation in revered British political institutions—and their representation in the Black Carib War are presented there. Duncan's most extensive discussions concern Vincentian governmental institutions and express the pride of the Vincentians in their English-derived government. The book is a manual for Commonwealth citizenship as well as a history of St. Vincent. The schoolchild and the common people have learned the main themes, but they do not depend on a school book alone.

Vincentians witness a steady round of enactments of their history in many forms: the yearly celebrations of the abolition of slavery; the frequent trials before wigged and robed judges, often with public appearances and newspaper photos of the principals outside the courthouse; the honors of knighthood and membership in the Most Excellent Order of the British Empire conferred on a few persons of black and mixed race; visits from the whole panoply of British-derived offices—"His Lordship Justice," "His Lordship Magistrate," "His Excellency Governour General," "His Lordship Bishop of the Diocese of the Windward Islands," even the Queen herself. Past colonialism is equally evident in the ever-visible symbols of wealth, the white-owned importing companies and the financial institutions based in England and Canada. In between these events and awesome presences, the thematic content of Vincentians' daily thoughts owes much to the news columnists, radio commentators, teachers, and preachers, whose common perceptions of Vincentian history could well have emerged from Duncan's textbook. Vincentians are not passive listeners, and their most common topic of conversation is politics—their British-derived party system, Parliament, ministerial offices, civil service, and judiciary. Political discussion is the daily grist of sociability, and voter turnouts are high. A quality opposite to high-status Englishness has been represented by the remnants of the Caribs, who live in six remote villages and are among the poorest Vincentians. Their presumed exoticness has been viewed with suspicion and fascination. The carnival's use of Carib themes portrays heathen worship and solemn tribal identity, respectfully playing up cultural differences.

This sketch of Vincentian history brings together several early and recent historians' and observers' interpretations and commentaries on several periods of Vincentian history. The interpretation of the war between the Black Caribs and the British attempts to answer a question raised by most recent and contemporary accounts. Observers refer to British colonists' fear that the slaves would support the Maroons and entertain the thought that such an alliance would have driven the colony off the island. None of these accounts, however, attempts to explain the slaves' nonalliance with the Maroons. I take this question as the central purpose of the inquiry into this period. The favorable circumstances for slave alliance with the Maroon-Indian forces and the strength, strategic advantage, and effective fighting methods of that society impose this question on interpretations of the period. The question is not one of military history or the history of power, not of "what if" the two groups together had wiped out the British colony. The question is, What does the slaves' course of action, ununified and undirected as it apparently was, partly choice and partly nonaction, tell about their views, values, and adaptation to plantation slavery under the particular circumstances of the St. Vincent colony? Their actions and nonactions are data on early Vincentian society. Because the war was cruel and prolonged, the casualty rate high for the British and the slaves; because the maroons were powerful, the slaves were numerous, and the British few in numbers yet reinforced repeatedly by shipborne troops and officers; and because a small community of Caribs remained as symbols of the defeated free black challengers, the Carib war has remained etched dramatically into the historical consciousness of Vincentians.

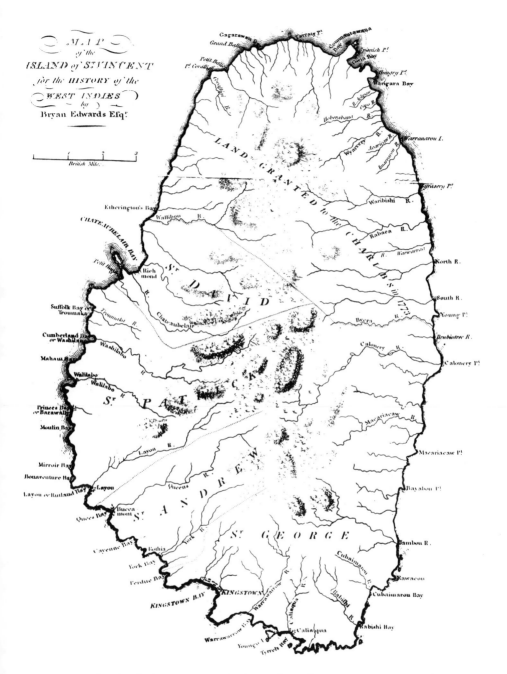

Map 2. The island of St. Vincent in the late eighteenth century. From Bryan Edwards, *History Civil and Commercial of the British Colonies in the West Indies*, vol. 1 (London, 1807).

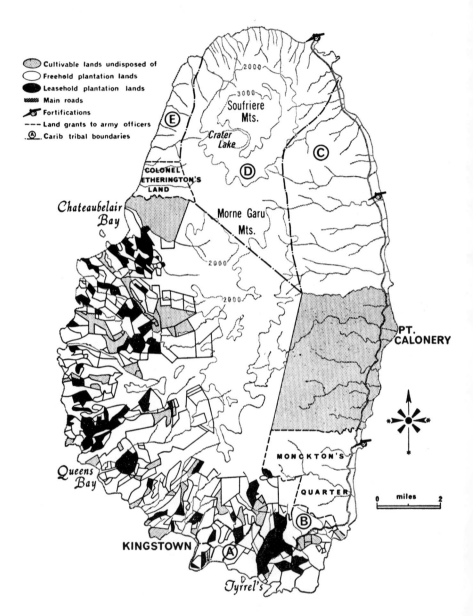

Legend:

- Cultivable lands undisposed of
- Freehold plantation lands
- Leasehold plantation lands
- Main roads
- Fortifications
- Land grants to army officers
- Carib tribal boundaries

Soufriere Mts.

2000

3000

Crater Lake

COLONEL ETHERINGTON'S LAND

Chateaubelair Bay

Morne Garu Mts.

2000

2000

PT. CALONERY

Queens Bay

MONCKTON'S

QUARTER

0 miles 2

KINGSTOWN

Tyrrel's

Map 3. John Byres's plan for the settlement of St. Vincent, 1764. From D. L. Niddrie, "Eighteenth-Century Settlement in the British Caribbean," Institute of British Geographers, publication no. 40, 1966.

22

THE BLACK CARIB–BRITISH CONTEST

The colonization of St. Vincent began a century after Britain began collecting huge revenues from neighboring Barbados and Antigua, and France was enriched by Haiti, Guadaloupe, and Martinique. Occupied with these thriving colonies, Britain and France proclaimed in 1660 and again in 1748 that St. Vincent and Dominica were to be refuges for the Carib Indians, who were numerous there and were being joined by Amerinds forced out of the colonized islands. The Caribs also were joined by Maroons and had become racially mixed before 1646 and continued to incorporate Africans, coming to be called Black Caribs before 1700. Despite British and French declarations, French Jesuit missionization had begun prior to 1700 and colonization in St. Vincent proceeded, beginning in 1719 with French settlers obtaining gifts of land from Caribs in exchange for arms. By 1763 the French settlers numbered thirteen hundred and exported the diverse products of thirty-four hundred slaves. Most of the freehold and leased lands on the leeward, or western, side between Kingstown and Chateaubelair Bay were held in French names, as indicated on Byres's map of 1764 and in lists accompanying it. Britain seized the island and acquired sovereignty by treaty with France in 1763, a treaty that did not reserve the land rights deeded earlier to the Black Caribs. Thereafter English-speaking settlers from the established colonies began to arrive rapidly. The English crown sold land with terms of 20 percent down and five years to pay, requiring purchasers to maintain one white man or two white women in residence on the property. Between 1763 and 1771 the commissioners sold 20,538 acres, or more than half the total acreage eventually brought under cultivation. Included in the acreage put up for sale were lands occupied by the French and the Caribs. Many French owners repurchased their lands, but many Caribs refused to relinquish the tracts purchased by English settlers and remained living on them. Contention among the purchasers, the commissioners, and the Black Caribs continued for thirty years and caused two major episodes of armed conflict.

During this period the hostilities between France and England were played out in seizures and recaptures of Windward and Leeward islands. France armed the Vincentian Black Caribs to harass the British. In 1779 combined French and Black Carib forces obtained surrender from the inept English commander of the small and unprepared garrison. Shephard ([1831] 1971:45) notes that the French did "not appear to have contemplated the permanent possession of the Island. The forms of the British Constitution remained, the Council and Assembly continued their usual sittings, and the Writs were issued in the name of the King of Great Britain." The English residents lauded the French governors' policies. French control was ended by treaty in 1783, although Martinique continued to supply munitions to the Caribs. French assistance to the Black Caribs was clearly no more than a supplement to Carib-initiated opposition to all European incursions in St. Vincent. The British were the main land seekers and displayed greater political and military presence than the French, and against them the Black Caribs became increasingly hostile, assisted by the French but driven by their own determination to hold on to their rights to possession of land. In the last third of the eighteenth century, Caribbean sugar production was profitable, generating a demand for new plantation land. The northern windward coastal plain, which had been ceded to the Indians and was occupied by an estimated two to five thousand Black Caribs, was considered prime cane land.

Whether these possessors of the island prior to the time of earliest European settlement were racially and culturally Indian or African and what kind of amalgamation of these two races and traditions had taken place are questions of interest to the history of marronage. Both contemporary accounts and recent ethnohistory on the racial makeup and history of the Black Caribs agree that the group arose from the joining and intermarriage of Carib Indians with escaped slaves and with the survivors of a slave ship wrecked off the coast of St. Vincent at a time variously stated as 1635 and 1675. The African element in the population was augmented by fugitive slaves from St. Vincent and Barbados. Caribs also are known to have captured and held slaves before 1649 and to have incorporated some of them into their population (Gullick 1985:44). In 1700 the Africans and Indians were observed to be a single, racially mixed people known as Black Caribs, using the Carib customs of body decoration and burial. At the same time a group of Caribs remained politically separate and racially unmixed. The French Jesuit missionary based in Martinique, Père Labat, visited St. Vincent briefly in 1700, a time when the only European residents were two Frenchmen, a priest and his companion. Labat reported a Carib population and a larger group of Black Caribs whose superiority in numbers allowed them to claim the windward side of the island and to "steal" Carib women.

The division between Indian and Black Caribs also was reported in the memoirs of Captain Braithwaite, an Englishman who attempted unsuccessfully to land at and claim St. Vincent in 1723 and whose report to his commander was quoted by Bryan Edwards, the late eighteenth-century British historian of the West Indies. On Braithwaite's first venture onshore he was received by a group of Caribs and carried bodily to meet their chief. A French interpreter for the Caribs was among them. After this meeting and after his return to the beach he was approached by a force of five hundred "Negroes," undoubtedly Black Caribs, armed with muskets superior to the Indians, most of whom used bows and arrows. Edwards observed St. Vincent in 1763 and wrote in 1793:

> The country continued to be a theatre of savage hostilities between the Negroes and the Charaibes, in which it is believed that the former were generally victorious; it is certain that they proved so in the end, their numbers, in 1763, being computed at two thousand; whereas of the red or native Charaibes, there were not left (as hath already been observed) more than one hundred families, and most of these, if I am rightly informed, are by this time exterminated. It is however worthy of remark, that the African intruders have adopted most of the Charaibean manners and customs. (Edwards 1807, vol. 1:420–21)

Recent scholars consider Edwards's population estimate of two thousand low; Gonzalez estimates seven to eight thousand Black Caribs before a severe disease struck and was fatal to many of them in their last months on the island. Gullick quotes two contemporary estimates of two thousand and six thousand, and he suggests that the Carib population may have exceeded the carrying capacity of their lands by 1779 (Gonzalez 1988:17; Gullick 1985:81). The number of Black Caribs held captive after the 1795 war was 4,338 men, women, and children (Gonzalez 1988:21). The Caribs carried off their dead after every engagement, and their casualties were never estimated and may have been light. What is clear is that the size of the group far exceeded Maroon populations in other areas; they also differed in being able to act as a united group in their guerrilla strategies against the colonists. Craton estimated that the Jamaican Maroons numbered less than one thousand at the peak of their armed action in 1723. The Jamaicans were divided geographically and did not coordinate their attacks, allowing the British troops to subdue the eastern and western sections separately (Craton 1982:93; Campbell 1988:251). In Suriname the Maroons also acted as separate bands with separate strategies, and the Dutch subdued them in stages. After the Dutch campaign in 1777, the pacified Maroon population of Suriname was estimated at three thousand and the unpacified Maroons at less than six hundred. Whereas the Vincentian Black Caribs had only one enemy, the Suriname Maroons also suffered attacks from the Amerinds, who sought the bounty given for Maroon hands delivered to the capital. Frequent Dutch patrols sought out the Suriname Maroons, yet the British in St. Vincent did not send patrols and only in the

1795 war did they attempt to destroy the Black Caribs militarily. Black Caribs also had the advantage over the Suriname resisters in munitions. They purchased them from Martinique and St. Lucia in large quantity, whereas the mainland Maroons obtained most of their guns and ammunition by theft from plantations (Hoogbergen 1990:15, 27, 105). Compared to these other rebellious Maroons, the Vincentian Black Caribs had advantages of numerical strength, unified territory, freedom from raids, and a reliable supply line.

That Carib settlement far exceeded the treaty land is clear from the Byres map of 1764, and contemporary commentaries noted the extensive Carib settlement. Byres's map shows four Carib-occupied areas in addition to the ceded northern third of the island: the areas marked Carib Tribal Boundaries A and B; General Monckton's Quarter, which had been ceded in 1763; and the "Cultivable lands undisposed of," indicating that the windward coast was almost entirely Carib occupied. These areas include the Calliaqua Valley on the southern coast and the Coubaimarrou Valley, the modern Stubbs, just north of it, which was the locale of one of the Carib signers of the treaty of 1773. The hills drained by these river valleys lead to the large interior Marriaqua Valley, where Caribs lived during the 1795 war (Coke [1808–11] 1971, vol. 2:201). The Jambou River in Monckton's Quarter was a Carib ceremonial site where petroglyphs have been found. In 1788 Rev. Coke journeyed up the windward coast to visit Carib families living on the coveted plain given the French name Grand Sable, accompanied by a Methodist missionary who was known to the Caribs but who had not yet attempted to teach them. The land was uncleared and barely passable by horseback with Carib guides, but two years later he wrote of the same scene transformed: the cleared land gave views of the mountains, and sugar, coffee and cotton grew in the valleys and cocoa and plantain grew in the hillsides (Coke [1808–11] 1971:260, 268). Alexander Anderson, an English botanist and curator of the Kingstown Botanical Garden from 1785 until after the war, wrote that the

> great part of the island (windward side) was in possession of the Caribs when the planters began to cultivate it. They abandoned it with great reluctance from attachment to the part they had long resided in (and were) born upon. Numbers of them never went beyond the Byera, but moved back into the woods behind the English. Several families were driven off by force from spots the planter wanted for his works and cane land. This was sometimes done imprudently by burning their houses. (A. Anderson 1983:58–59, parentheses inserted by the editors)

It appears that the windward coastal plain had been partially opened only in the late 1780s, the reluctant Caribs still occupying wooded hills between cleared lands, a mixed and contested tenure.

On the southern end of the coast, Tribal Boundary A, located among freehold and leasehold lands, extends to the mouth of the Warrawarra River (now called Greathead River) at the western boundary of Kingstown, includes the east slope of Sion Hill, which directly overlooks Kingstown, and extends far inland along the valleys of the Warrawarra and the Calliaqua rivers. This tribal boundary formed a Carib corridor from the south coast to undeveloped tracts and the northern ceded lands. The map shows that this south coastal area and two river valleys also are divided internally into surveyed parcels, and one small area had been leased even in 1764. In the initial land rush for which Byres's map was prepared, 1,210 acres of Carib lands were sold, apparently located in Tribal Boundaries A and B, and soon a number of estates were established there, including the plantation at Calliaqua of Sir William Young, a member of the Governor's Council. His son's two books describe Caribs frequenting his Calliaqua plantation and camping there; Carib women stopping overnight on trips to and from the Kingstown market; and Carib chiefs coming with gifts, attending Christmas celebrations, and discussing, in English and French, the British and Carib dispositions toward each other. In one critical battle in 1795, a large Carib force lay in ambush for the retreating British forces on the Young estate. Clearly the Caribs treated the Calliaqua estate as Carib territory. Accounts of the war refer often to Caribs frequenting Calliaqua as well as other areas close to estates. Although Coke notes a town of fifteen houses at Calliaqua, the only town other than the larger settlement at Kingstown, and a British encampment was situated there in 1795, the British did not command the valley, as an important battle there indicates. It is clear from the location of the Caribs' strongholds in the war, their places of attack, and the places they frequented apart from military actions that this wide north-to-south strip was a Carib corridor from the shore straight into the fine lands of the interior Marriaqua Valley and the "cultivable lands undisposed of" and to the central mountains and the low-lying paths to land long acknowledged as Carib. These geographical factors gave the Caribs strategic advantages over the British.

A history of the colony's Carib policy was issued in 1795 by the planter and barrister William Young, son of the Vincentian commissioner Sir William Young, based on a series of memoranda from the commissioners to the Treasury Department in London. In the memoranda the colonists defended their objective of obtaining Carib land on the grounds of underuse. They presented a plan that would reduce Carib land to small homesteads, guarantee them access to the shore for fishing, and require them to profess allegiance to the king. The commissioners hoped that the Caribs' developing commerce with them would demonstrate the benefits of coexistence.

In fact economic interdependence between the English and the Black Caribs had proceeded far. Proprietors were dependent on canoes manufactured and operated by Caribs for transporting sugar hogsheads from the shore to the coastwise sloops. Carib canoes were the only means of travel from Kingstown to the plantations on the leeward side, where roads had not yet penetrated the formidable terrain and even the bridle path was hardly passable. Kingstown and the plantations purchased food and goods from Black Carib tradeswomen, and Carib production was stimulated by this growing market. Carib sales reduced proprietors' and townspeople's dependence on slaves' private production, a dependence found widely in the West Indies, where slaves sold surpluses from the plots allotted them. With the free Black Caribs supplying the market, slave labor was fully available for the rapid plantation development and intense sugar production of this period. The commissioners' plan for incorporating the Black Caribs as small homesteaders would not only open the way for sugar expansion on their land but also established an advantageous free peasantry. English recognition of the benefits of a free group of skilled producers in a slave society was reflected in the favorable treatment of Black Caribs in the colonial courts and commissioners' policies and was apparent enough to arouse the resentment of slaves, free blacks, and poor whites (Coke [1808–11] 1971, vol. 2:197; A. Anderson 1983:98).

The Black Carib economy had changed from simple barter of subsistence surpluses to the use of money and the practice of wage labor. The extent of their adoption of European know-how was seen in chief DuVallee's growing cotton with a force of nine slaves. The English proprietors may have contemplated Caribs soon becoming proprietors themselves on their fine sugar lands. It was urgent to persuade them to release the Grand Sable plain, which, because the Black Carib population was concentrated there and the area had been set aside by treaty for them, was not an easy task.

Land speculation was taking place in England and locally on vast, vaguely identified tracts in Carib country, and several individual Caribs had agreed to offer their traditional family areas within the plain for sale. Carib chief Chatoyer sold a large area on the leeward side to the commander of the British garrison in 1776. The excessive speculation in prime wind-ward land was the commissioners' main worry, for they feared incitement of Carib retaliation against intrusion into their heartland and thought that gaining consent of the chiefs to an orderly transfer was possible because they valued their commerce with the English (Young [1795] 1971). Similar speculation on Indian land in the American colonies and by the East India Company in Bengal was fueling parliamentary clamor against the government, and the Treasury Department had been attempting to maintain policies of moderation (Thomas 1983). The local commissioners were the only source of information for the London administrators, and they wanted to determine the Treasury Department land policy themselves. Their recommendations were followed at each key point. Their policy for Carib settlement on small homesteads and relinquishment of the rest of the northern section was approved and was published in French and English in May 1768.[1]

A delegation of forty Black Caribs visited the Board of Commissioners and said that they approved the proclamation but that other Caribs "resist the King's authority." The commissioners interpreted the report of disagreement as a ruse, but they knew there was no centralized authority among the Black Caribs. This delegation included Chatoyer, whom the British considered the most influential chief and the principal Carib strategist, but it had been obvious in many incidents—in Carib land sales, for instance—that local groups acted autonomously. Disagreement among the Black Caribs foiled the commissioners' intentions. William Young commented: "Appearing divided among themselves was a settled design of the Charaibs; and it was the most artful that could be devised. It deferred the plan of entering their country as commissioners to arrange settlements; and it prevented the entering their country with a power, as to control a hostile people" (Young [1795] 1971:40). As a more measured advance, the commissioners called off land sales that had been made, but one year later undertook the survey for the road into Carib lands. The Black Caribs surrounded the troops guarding the surveyors and held them hostage until "the commissioners would give up all immediate pretensions to interfere within their country, or even any attempt to make roads of communication with it" (Young [1795] 1971:47). Two months later a British patrol boat tried to intercept a fleet of four Carib canoes, with twenty men each, carrying ammunition from St. Lucia. Fired on, the Caribs returned fire, killing or wounding three of the crew of nine, and they rowed toward the patrol boat. The commander sank each canoe with gunfire, whereupon the Caribs swam with cutlasses in their mouths and tried to scale the boat as it turned in retreat. The captain reported that all eighty Caribs must have drowned, but the Caribs were renowned as swimmers. Their reputations among colonists and slaves were made by incidents such as this.

After these events the commissioners' memoranda increasingly expressed fear and distrust of the Caribs and called for force. They said, in effect, that they had exhausted all just and equitable means of inducing Carib acceptance of the small homestead policy and the release of their unused land. Vincentian planters residing in London proposed a plan for removing Caribs from the island, and in 1772 Secretary of the Treasury Hillsborough responded, "If necessary demand the removal of the Caribs; do take up such vessels as can be procured, to serve as transports for the conveyance of them to some unfrequented part of the coast of Africa, or to some desert island adjacent thereto" (Thomas 1983:66). With this policy in hand, the commissioners resumed surveying for the road in the fall of 1772. Caribs attacked the surveyors' military guard, and the commissioners requested greater armed strength. Two regiments of British troops sent from North America engaged the Caribs for nine months of fierce fighting. The British suffered 150 killed and wounded, 110 men dead from tropical diseases, and 428 left in the troop hospital.

The cost of the campaign and "the justice and propriety of the motives which gave rise to this expedition" (Shephard [1831] 1971:30) launched an investigation in Britain in which

> it was finally resolved, that the measure was found in injustice, and reflected dishonour on the National Character, a violation of the natural rights of mankind, and totally subversive of that liberty it gloried to defend. This conclusion was productive of immediate orders to suspend hostilities against the Caribs, and to negotiate a Treaty with them on reasonable terms. In obedience to these instructions, General Dalrymple made overtures of peace, which were joyfully embraced by the enemy. (Shephard [1831] 1971:30)

Alexander Anderson (1983:53) said of the Caribs in this first major engagement with the British, "They fought with great courage and resolution, at last obliging a formidable army of regular troops to a cessation of hostilities. We were obliged to give them their terms." Twenty-eight Black Carib leaders signed the treaty of 1773, listing their eight territories by the names of principal rivers and representing tribal areas as far south as the Coubaimarrou and Jambou valleys. In the treaty the British ceded to the Black Caribs the land north of the Byera River on the windward side and north of the Wallibou River on the leeward side. Britain gained an important advantage, however, in that a provision of the treaty acknowledged the sovereignty of the English king over the Caribs. This provision later proved fatal to the Caribs because it was the legal status by which the colonists justified their deportation as rebels against the crown.

THE FRENCH ROLE

Black Carib opposition to the British has been portrayed as an instrument of the French in their contest with that nation. It appears, instead, that the Caribs opposed the power of both the French and the British in St. Vincent and that they took the initiative in all aspects of their political and military actions against the English. As the earliest European settlers, apparently unaided by their government in acquiring land, the French came as small farmers and both Carib groups sold them land. Their crops—coffee, cacao, tobacco, and indigo—did not require as large a work force as sugar, the preeminent English crop at the time of their settlement, or the expensive sugar processing installations, which could grind and refine large quantities of sugar cane and were profitable only with extensive planting. The English sugar plantations tended to drive out the French small holders. French peasant families and Black Carib families both lived in Carib-style houses and socialized with one another (Coke [1808–11] 1971:201), and the Black Carib chiefs had become fluent in French (Young [1795] 1971:37). Alexander Anderson reported close sentiments and social relations between Black Caribs and French, and although, as Anderson observed, relations were not as close with the English as with the French, English planters received Carib leaders in their estate houses and allowed Caribs to traverse their lands (A. Anderson 1983:74).

The rapid arrival of English settlers, their government's survey of lands occupied by the Caribs, and their importation of large numbers of slaves, demonstrated the greater threat posed by the English. Rev. Coke's account of missionizing attempts illustrates Carib suspicions of the English. A Methodist missionary couple built a house at the boundary of the northern Carib territory and offered to teach English. Caribs voiced their suspicion, saying Martiniquans had told them that the missionaries were sent by the king to take their land. When they were assured that the Methodists did not have the support of the king, the sons of two chiefs became students of English. After two years of study they withdrew, and because of the general hostility of Caribs toward them and toward religious teaching the Methodists closed their house and abandoned attempts to missionize (Coke [1808–11] 1971:266–67).

The Black Caribs were in close contact with the French on Martinique and St. Lucia. They had long maintained active canoe trade with these two islands, selling primarily tobacco and also baskets, hammocks, and fishing lines of strong wild fiber, silk grass, in trade for munitions, cutlasses, and sabres (Coke 1816:114). The French on two occasions reinforced the Black Caribs in their attacks on the British. When France threatened to retake St. Vincent in 1793, the English governor called together the Black Carib chiefs for a feast in Kingstown, and wanting to halt Black Carib contacts with the French, read them the treaty that bound their loyalty to the English king, asked them to cease trading with Martinique, and gave them compensation for their loss (Young [1795] 1971:111).

Historians credit Victor Hughes, a St. Lucian free black revolutionary influenced by French ideas, with planning simultaneous rebellions in Grenada and St. Vincent. Although the date was set for St. Patrick's Day 1795, discovery of the plan in Grenada precipitated the French and free black action on that island a week early. The Vincentian Black Caribs apparently learned this on the day the Grenada rebellion began and at the same time as the Vincentian commissioners, for their well-planned attacks began at dawn the next day. Two French officers and an Afro-St. Lucian strategist named Marinier were active in the Vincentian rebellion, as well as thirty-two white soldiers in one battle. However, the Caribs themselves supplied almost all the fighting force and had their own leaders.

The influence of French revolutionary doctrine was dramatically evident in a declaration, written in French, said to have been found on the body of the Black Carib chief Chatoyer when he was slain on the sixth day of the rebellion in March 1795. William Young quoted it in his book published nine months later. It is headed "Chateau-Bellair," a French and Carib leeward settlement, and is dated the twelfth day of March, the day he was killed:

> Where is the Frenchman who will not join his brothers, at a moment when the voice of liberty is heard by them? Let us then unite, citizens and brothers, round the colours flying in this island; and let us hasten to co-operate to that great piece of work which has been already commenced so gloriously. But should any timorous men still exist, should any Frenchman be held back through fear, we do hereby declare to them, in the name of the law, that those who will not be assembled with us in the course of the day, shall be deemed traitors to the country, and treated as enemies. We do swear that both fire and sword shall be employed against them, that we are going to burn their estates, and that we will murder their wives and children, in order to annihilate their race. (Young [1795] 1971:117–18)

Although the language of liberty, citizenship, and brotherhood is French, the Caribs declare their authority over the French settlers in St. Vincent.

That the rebellion was strengthened by French rhetoric, armed and encouraged by the French, and aided by a small number of French soldiers and officers in two engagements does not mean that it was mainly a French-inspired action to harass the British. Seventy-two years earlier Captain Braithwaite had learned of the Caribs' resolve to protect their island against European incursion, and their actions had long demonstrated that resolve. The guerrilla strategy was clearly of the Black Caribs' devising, and they were by far the most numerous combatants. A reading of contemporary accounts shows Carib forces, leadership, and initiative far outweighed French force and inspiration (see also B. Marshall 1973; Gonzalez 1988:34). In Craton's extensive studies of Maroon and slave revolts, he concludes that they arose more from the situations of the rebelling groups than from French revolutionary ideology (Craton 1982:164–65).

THE WAR

The March 1795 launching of a full-scale Black Carib assault to drive the British from the island found the colony militarily weak, unwatchful for Carib rebellion, and concerned only with the productive and profitable sugar industry. Alexander Anderson reported that after the English regained control of the island in 1783,

> they did not repossess the former military posts in Carib country at Rabbacca and Owia [on the north windward coast] and even those within the English boundary were abandoned to the windward of Dorsetshire Hill except for a short time. A few of the military were stationed at Baybou . . . They might as well have been on Kingstown Hill for any awe or check they could have been to the Caribs. Mt. Young had been surveyed for fortifications but none were built. . . . From 1784 to 1795 the White population of the island considerably decreased. This was owing to the rapid increase of sugar estates both in number and extent. Many poor industrious settlers [later identified as French] were obliged to sell their few acres and go to Trinidad and other islands. Several of them having no other title than long occupancy were purchased for little by the proprietors of adjoining estates. . . . The number of English inhabitants capable of bearing arms was scarcely 300 of all descriptions . . . The military strength in the whole island was about 30 invalids of the two flank companies of a battalion of the 60th Regiment, and about 10 artillery men. (A. Anderson 1983:56, 77, 78–79)

The simultaneous Black Carib War in St. Vincent and free black revolt in Grenada are considered the most nearly successful oppositions to colonialism in the British Caribbean (Craton 1982:183). The rebellion opened with a force under Chatoyer's brother, DuVallee, burning an English estate in the windward ceded land. A company of island militia marched up the windward coast into Carib territory upon receiving this news and the news of the outbreak of rebellion in Grenada. The militia was routed, sixteen men were killed, and the wounded and captured were put to death through dismemberment. The men panicked and retreated in disorder to Kingstown, spreading alarm to residents along the coast. The Caribs followed, torching plantations and killing owners and managers, arriving three days later at their lands in Calliaqua just one ridge away from Kingstown. At the same time a Carib force led by Chatoyer attacked on the leeward side, burned houses and fields, killed owners, and joined the windward force in the capture of Dorsetshire Hill, which was considered the last-ditch defense of Kingstown. Two captured cannons were dragged to that promontory. There Chatoyer ordered the execution of three captured "white young men . . . of genteel connexions" by dismemberment (Coke [1808–11] 1971, vol. 3:204). Ships and soldiers arrived in the harbor on the third, fourth, and sixth days and stormed Dorsetshire Hill on the third night after the Caribs took it. There they found Chatoyer wounded, and he was killed by the British commander. The hill was to change hands many times in the next ten months (Kirby and Martin 1972).

Although the Caribs suffered two raids by sea on their northern coastal settlements, one march into their ceded lands, and the burning of many houses, canoes, and supplies, most of the actions took place in the large Calliaqua Valley and surrounding promontories, one of which was the Vigie, overlooking the defenses of Kingstown. Most armed actions were initiated by the Caribs, who, undeterred by the death of Chatoyer, made frequent large-scale attacks all over the island. Only the capital town was held continuously by the colonists. The Caribs captured cannon and dragged them distances that amazed the British, threw up fortifications made of captured sugar barrels, and fired devastatingly into British troops with cannon and muskets. They took advantage of brief lulls to sail to St. Lucia for ammunition and were reinforced after these trips by French officers and soldiers. The British were repeatedly astonished by the amplitude of the Caribs' supplies, which they had to abandon in battle. On May 7, 1795, a force of more than one thousand Black Caribs with a French officer and a few French troops marched from nine directions toward the camp at Calliaqua, which had fewer than two hundred soldiers, and requested their surrender; the Caribs offered to transport them to any other English island they chose. The vulnerable British commander refused, and at that same hour a frigate arrived in Kingstown; sailed for Calliaqua; bombarded the Caribs, who had just made a second demand for British unconditional surrender; and landed 130 sailors. The Caribs retreated but in the middle of the night stormed and took Dorsetshire Hill. The British retook it the next day. Two days later the Committee of Planters and Merchants, chaired by Sir William Young, addressed a memorandum to their agents stating that

> resettlement will not be practical, or cannot be adopted, or pursued, with credit from the British merchants, or with general safety to your Memorialists, if the African negroes (usurping the Indian name of Caribs) are permitted to remain on the island; and they humbly call to the recollection of His Majesty's Ministers, the original plan of transporting them to a part of the world congenial to their origin, temper, and customs, has become indispensable to the safety of your Memorialists. (Shephard [1831] 1971: app., xli)[2]

After disastrous defeats in the first three months of the war, the British saw successes in the Calliaqua area from May 8 to July 4. Attacks far up both windward and leeward coasts followed, but many of these engagements were in response to Black Carib initiatives. With the arrival of a new commanding officer in July a series of botched actions occurred, and the Caribs pursued the routed British, bringing the battle once again to the outskirts of Kingstown. Two other incompetent generals followed leading to continued English defeats from July through January 1796. A succession of generals and other officers accompanied them. The arrivals came at the times of greatest disaster: "This is the third time we have been reduced to the last extremity and as frequently been resuscitated from despair: the Lord is good" (Coke [1808–11] 1971, vol. 2:239). All accounts stress the deep gloom among the colonists and in the island government: "Universal destruction threatened the whole colony and total extermination of the name of English from it" (A. Anderson 1983:75).

The June 8, 1796, arrival of a large British force from England's long Caribbean contest with France secured the British victory over the Black Caribs. The general who had won St. Lucia marched with 3,960 men in six columns on the Black Carib stronghold of the Vigie, just five miles from the capital. Of the 460 men who surrendered some were French and others were free blacks from the island, whereas few of the captured were Black Caribs. The Maroons staged no further attacks. They tried to negotiate a surrender with the preservation of their lands. The planters who for sixteen months had been on the verge of losing the colony, and had received approval of their petition to exile the Caribs for insurrection against the crown, rejected the Carib overtures. They held the few captured Caribs on the small island of Balliceaux and informed the main body of the plan to transport them to Roatán, a small island off the coast of Honduras, with supplies for settlement. Troops pursued the Caribs in the northern villages but captured none of them. With their gardens destroyed, however, and their houses and canoes burned in these forays, and unable to fish safely in the coastal waters, the Caribs began to lose their strength and resolve to resist. A few days after they were informed of the plan for transport to Roatán, six hundred Black Carib men appeared on a beach in their former ceded territory and asked protection, under codes of honorable warfare among nations, against the raiding parties that had been pursuing them and stated their intention to surrender. A son of Chatoyer addressed the Caribs and the English:

> It is no disgrace to us to surrender to a great nation, the subjects of France and all great nations, even of England, are obliged to submit to each other, when there no longer remains the means of resistance. What else is now left for us? have we power to continue the war? No! to-morrow morning I will set you the example of submission, by bringing my family to Colonel Haffey, that he may send us to the General, you may do as you please, I can only be accountable for myself and my family. (Shephard [1831] 1971:164–65)

During the night, however, the orator and all but 180 of the men slipped off. Those who remained and 102 other Black Caribs who were captured from their encampments nearby, apparently indecisive in their predicament, were taken to Balliceaux. Several of the prisoners were later brought to their compatriots to attest to good treatment and to British preparations for supplying them on the island of Roatán. In October many more surrendered, weakened by starvation and illness, and by the end of that month 4,338 Black Carib men, women, and children had been assembled on Balliceaux. Stricken by an epidemic, 2,248 survived the three months of captivity (Gonzalez 1988:36). In February 1797 they were taken to Roatán, and from there they soon crossed to Honduras. They settled over a long distance of the coast, and their adaptive success there has been the subject of commentary and study.

THE WAR'S MEANING TO BLACK CARIBS AND SLAVES

The surrender appears to have included almost all of the Black Caribs, except for a small community that remained in hiding in the upper reaches of the Massarica River and the few families of unmiscegenated Caribs who had remained independent of the Black Caribs and had been allowed to stay in several north coast settlements. In their unified surrender action they did have a margin of choice. They acted as a group and stayed together.

They had fought for their homeland and lost it, but they had preserved their society.

Recent research has sought out the sources of adaptive abilities and cohesive identity of the Black Carib people on the Honduran coast in their Vincentian period, as well as in their later history (Macklin 1986; Gonzalez 1988), but their actions in the war and the surrender have not been thoroughly assessed as a source of their cohesion, and the meaning of the war to the slaves has not been queried. Although sentiment at this period can only be a subject of conjecture, it is possible to partially reconstruct the two groups' intentions through inferences that can be made about traditions and contexts of actions.

As their final action, the Caribs attempted to negotiate a surrender in which they could remain on the island as protected citizens and reminded the British of their codes of honorable treatment toward surrenderers, representing themselves as the same as European nationals, whose codes of war they had ample opportunity to observe. They thus tried to undermine the colonial government's determination to deport them, a plan that the whole colony knew had been attacked in several British magazines as unjustifiable and designed to allow confiscation of Carib land. In declaring that they could no longer wage war and asking the British for protection from the army's mopping-up action, the Caribs were appealing to British codes of war. The Colonial Assembly, however, met on July 13 to agree on the plans for deportation, the ministers in London having already approved transporting the Black Caribs. Unable to shake the determination of the colonists, the Caribs surrendered for deportation to free lands with equipment for building, farming, and fishing. The prospect of dispersing into the mountainous Vincentian interior and hiding from raiding parties was probably far from attractive to people used to the freedom of the whole island. Their trade in Kingstown would have been cut off, and trade by boat with other islands would have exposed them to attack. It is probable that an important motive in the eventual surrender was to reunite with the captured Caribs, numbering at least 210. By reuniting, they gave up their homeland but preserved their society.

For the slaves it was difficult to aid the Black Caribs and easier to remain on the plantations, as most of them did. Shephard noted "disaffected Negroes and Mulattoes of the island" in the Black Carib forces of one assault, not identifying them as slaves or free men. They were probably slaves; Alexander Anderson observed, "Not one English coloured man or free Black ever joined the enemy." Shephard also remarked that individual slaves were recognized in Carib ranks on several occasions and that slaves supplied Carib forces under siege (A. Anderson 1983:76; Shephard [1831] 1971:92, 109).

Both slaves and colonists saw the Black Caribs as holding the offensive throughout most of the eighteen-month war, continually attacking the capital town and the island's most developed plantations from their commanding positions. English losses in battle and from tropical diseases were extremely heavy, whereas Carib losses from guerrilla actions appear to have been light. The Caribs eluded every English assault and recaptured strongholds a few days after each English victory. Knowledge of the mother country's military power sustained the faith of the English, but the slaves must have doubted English strength as they observed the course of the war. With crops burned and sugar works destroyed, production ceased. With their housed torched, owners and overseers left for town or for other islands, leaving the slaves unguarded, without work, and in Carib country. Why the slaves did not join the Maroons and help complete their take-over of the island is a difficult question whose answer can only be inferred. Reconstruction of the elements of nonalliance between these two victims of colonialism opens up the social views and experiences of early Vincentians.

The time for choosing freedom through marronage may have been in the early years of Carib resistance, when a Carib victory would have been considered unlikely. It is possible that during the war the majority of the slaves decided to wait out the defeat of their masters, although joining the Maroons would have appeared to assure that defeat. More than opportunism and inertia, the slaves' decision against defection was in part a choice between plantation life and marronage. The Maroons were in close contact with the plantations, escape was easy, and the subsistence conditions of the slaves were inferior to those of the Maroons. In considering this question, a few facts can be assembled that show the actions of the slaves in the contest and indicate relations among the slaves, the Maroons, and the British. It is possible to make conjectures concerning the slaves' view of the Caribs' way of life.

At the outset of the war, both the British and Black Caribs took measures to enlist slave military support, but control over the slaves allowed the British, with trial and error, greater facility in this purpose, whereas the Caribs abandoned their earlier inducements for slave escape and killed many of them. Upon the first intelligence of the impending rebellion, two hundred slaves were put under arms and sent out to round up Black Caribs who, along with poor French settlers, had raided a French estate. They returned without a single Carib and only with French peasants, most of whom were women and children, and plundered French and British property alike. The governor then prohibited this practice unless properly directed (Coke [1808–11] 1971, vol. 2:208). In April 1795, after the British had reversed their initially disastrous situation, a battalion of the Island Rangers was raised from the slave population by quota from each estate, the estate being held responsible for their good conduct. Five hundred strong, they were armed and led by British officers and sergeants and served through the end of the war. They are commended many times in Coke's and Shephard's accounts. In his general orders at the close of the war, the commander in chief expressed his "fullest approbation of the good conduct, intelligence and courage of the Island Rangers" (Shephard [1831] 1971:157).[3] The British were thus able to command the services and loyalty of a battalion of slaves. The Black Caribs encouraged defections of slaves to join their forces. A 1771 address to the king from the St. Vincent council and assembly asking protection of their purchases of Carib lands stated that the Black Caribs were "daily enticing their slaves to join them" (Thomas 1983:66). The Black Caribs were bound by the treaty of 1773 to return runaway slaves, but in the absence of contemporary commentary that they performed this service, it is probable that they seldom did so, especially as they must have sought increased strength when preparing for their major actions in 1795. It is certain they never played the role of "policemen for the slave regime," as the Jamaican Maroons had (Geggins 1987:245; Campbell 1988:13).[4] Writing of Carib overtures to the slaves, Shephard reported that few joined them:

> Hitherto [before the Carib reverses in May 1795] they had carried themselves toward the Negroes in a very wily and politic manner, they had offered them liberty and exhorted them to receive it; but happily for the inhabitants, the proposal, however flattering, was rejected with disdain, comparatively few espoused their interests, while a considerable number opposed them well armed. . . . The great scarcity of provisions which prevailed among the number pent up in town, impelled them to adventure beyond the lines to search for subsistence, these excursions of necessity proved fatal to many, as numbers were taken and destroyed. (Shephard [1831] 1971:94–95)

Because Black Caribs occupied the whole central and windward parts of the island and brought quantities of diverse products to the Kingstown market, many women and men doubtless frequently passed by slave housing, which was usually in the steep hills above the cultivated fields and contiguous to the Carib mountain paths from north to south. Policing of estate boundaries could not have been effective, and no attempts are described. In their regular passings, Black Caribs and slaves had opportunities to converse. The slaves saw the ample produce of the Black Caribs; in fact, they were said to resent Carib competition in the market, and with the extreme demands on their labor during crop production, slaves could not have been as productive in their own cultivation and husbandry as the Caribs were. Caribs consumed and sold chickens, turkeys, cassava bread, fresh fish, and pineapples. Slaves had inferior diets, allotted only dried fish by the proprietors, and had little time to work their gardens and prepare their meals. Slave and Black Carib houses were much alike in construction and size.[5]

Material factors, as well as the Black Caribs' freedom of travel and freedom of occupation, would have encouraged marronage, but the great differences between Black Carib culture and African traditions probably deterred flight from the plantation. Differences in gender relations and in-group aggressiveness were marked. Carib women were subservient and abused. Labat's observations, as well as those of Coke and William Young, reported wife beating and wife killing. Gullick considered the reported incidents of wife murder probably true, because men's authority over their families was unchecked in the absence of community authority, and the scattered settlement pattern allowed abuses to go unrestrained (Gullick 1985:104). The Black Caribs' symbolic body paint, infant head deformation, menstrual seclusion, and concepts of spirit (implied in a seated position for burial) may not have influenced decisions about marronage, but did make the Black Caribs exotic to the slaves, as well as to the English (Young 1807, vol. 3:255; Coke [1808–11] 1971:193; Coke 1816:115). Marronage not only held risks but also required crossing a cultural boundary. Perhaps the most effective deterrent to marronage may have been the reluctance of men and women torn from one culture to uproot themselves a second time, even from a life of slavery. The factors that held slaves to the plantations must be weighed against the dilemmas faced in marronage.

Some aspects of plantation life may have been what held slaves to the plantations, outweighing the severe conditions of slavery depicted (see Chapter 2). Most important among these aspects were the kin networks developing on plantations. Research on the slave registration records colonial governments and planters were required to assemble after the end of the slave trade in 1807 has found that the residential groupings reflected in these records are composed in familylike age and sex groups, and kinship within groups and between contiguous groups was sometimes recorded.[6] Vincentian plantations, most of them with more than one hundred slaves, and some with more than five hundred, brought together numbers large enough for exogamous and age-matched marital unions.

The slaves were allowed to cultivate garden plots as well as raise poultry and small livestock, and their use of these resources was well developed prior to 1795. As for clothing, the customary yearly allotment of cotton cloth for each slave provided clothes more familiar than the grass aprons worn by Black Carib women and the pubic covers worn by men. The Scottish plantation owner Mrs. Carmichael (1833, vol. 1:142–60) noted the importance field slaves, as well as house slaves and slaves in supervisory ranks, attached to clothing. William Young (1807, vol. 3:258) described the fine Christmas clothes of field slaves who danced at his estate house. Ashton Warner, a slave whose chronicle is described in Chapter 2, complained of inadequate allotments of cloth and blankets, and he commented on how important these supplies were to slaves (Cameron [1929–34] 1970:74).[7] The large concentrations of slaves, typically one to three hundred on each plantation, must have fostered a community structure (Higman 1986:381).

Celebrations brought all ranks of the estate together. At Christmas on the Young estate, the proprietor danced a minuet with one of his slaves to open the ball, and the two fiddlers and tambourine player were estate slaves. When an African instrument was brought in and played, "about a dozen girls, hearing the sound, came from the huts to the great court, and began a curious and most lascivious dance, with much grace as well as action; of the last plenty in truth" (Young 1807, vol. 3:259). At Carmichael's balls slaves danced in a room adjoining that of the proprietors and their guests, and some owners gave over the great room entirely to slaves' balls (Carmichael 1833, vol. 1:45, 286). Welcoming the proprietor on visits from England, as he rode from the shore on horseback and distributed gifts, was another special event that humanized plantation relationships. Occasions such as these, moments of high celebration and the lowering of class and race barriers, defined slaves' participation in a hierarchical culture. The plantation hierarchy would have seemed a proper society to people as preoccupied with status differentiation among themselves as Afro-Vincentians were said to have been (Carmichael 1833, vol. 1:282).

Plantation society eventually became the source of cultural identification for black Vincentians, and settling into a new mode of life took place rapidly under slavery. Through the plantations the slaves participated in British society. Slaves in estate houses and in supervisory positions had amenities and opportunities for improving their lot and had reason to make the best of these advantages. It is apparent that most of the field slaves also accepted plantation slavery, preferring it over the dangers of flight and the uncertainties of life with the Black Caribs. The Vincentian slaves had more of a choice than slaves on islands where Maroons lived far from plantations and had little power. Many chose marronage, but many more chose the British plantation society.

The slaves also may have had a vision of Britishness, a sense of civilization, that transcended plantation life. Colonial government was one of the few institutional dimensions of slave culture beyond everyday life. Government had the accouterments of rank, office, and costume to hold the imagination. The Government House, office of the governor, was in view on a hill in Kingstown. Proprietors made up the Governor's Council and the Assembly. There was a frame courthouse in town. Decisions were made in the name of the king of England, and his ships anchored in the harbor. The uniforms of the officers and men were displayed in the planters' houses, and a ship's band sometimes provided the music for balls. Besides government, Britain brought a religion that was attractive to Afro-Vincentians. They had observed the Anglican church only from the outside, but in 1787 Methodists came to evangelize the slaves. In that year five proprietors allowed Methodist preaching on their plantations and in the town, and a missionary was allowed to preach at the courthouse. On his first trip, Rev. Coke reported that he overheard a slave "informing his companions with simplicity and pleasure, 'These men were imported for us'" (Coke [1808–11] 1971:257). The Governor's Council was alarmed by the slaves' enthusiasm for Methodist preaching and in 1703 passed a law that enabled them to imprison a missionary:

> Through the iron gratings of his window, he repeated the crime which brought him to that condition. The serious negroes, affected with this situation, continued to throng round the prison, to receive his instructions, and weep over his calamities. . . . Before the above iniquitous law was enacted, no island afforded a more pleasing prospect of the prosperity of religion than St. Vincent's. About a thousand of the poor slaves were already stretching forth their hands unto God; and multitudes more attended constantly the preaching of the word. The negroes throughout the island appeared, in general, ripe for the gospel, but the door was shut against it. (Coke [1808–11] 1971, vol. 2:272, 275)

The law was annulled in England seven months later and the mission continued to gain converts, having 1,522 "Colored and Negro" and only 32 whites in 1794 (Southey [1827] 1968:74). Preaching went on in town, on plantations, and in houses of blacks (Coke [1808–11] 1971:284–85). No matter that "they had acquired those hypocritical forms . . . had learnt at chapel to groan, turn up their eyes," as Carmichael, an Anglican, wrote (Carmichael 1833, vol. 2:282–83). The attention the Methodists directed to the slaves was in itself important; church was a place of assembly and of hearing the doctrine of equality.

Anglophilia in the British Caribbean is entirely familiar. Ebenezer Duncan's widely read history lauds all things English—the English language, which united multitongued slaves and opened up English learning; the Magna Carta, to which Vincentians owe their rights and citizenship; Queen Victoria, who was deeply loved throughout the island; the judiciary and the police, which uphold right and punish wrong; the Commonwealth. It is only for nostalgia, the reader soon realizes, that Duncan began his book with the Caribs' love of their beautiful island and depicted their freedom. As the story of the contest proceeds, Duncan's Caribs murder and plunder, whereas the British kill and sacrifice their lives. In Duncan's account of British military maneuvers, the arrival of general after general on warships with regiments, marches, and sieges on the hills every Vincentian has walked over, frontal attacks in six columns of six hundred soldiers each, the valiant Caribs serve only to call up British military pageantry. They were at least a worthy enemy, no small status in British values, and in the end the British accepted "officers of submission." Who would be on the Carib side thereafter? The nation of 12,000 black slaves and 1,450 white masters had stood together and defended civilized life.

The small Carib population that remained was restricted to several villages in the remote north. The English inspector Davy visited these communities in 1845, noting that "in complexion they reminded me of the Malay. . . . In features they might pass for Europeans" (Davy 1854:195). This information confirms that the Caribs who did not accept deportation had not intermarried with Africans, upholding the view of the separateness of Indian and Black Carib societies held by eighteenth-century observers. They retained their role in boat building and shipping: "Most of the boats of St. Vincent are made by them, formed of single trees scooped out . . . They are useful not only in making canoes, but also in the management of them and in shipping produce, a thing of difficulty and of some danger on that wild coast" (Davy 1854:195). The 1844 census listed 273 Caribs and the 1851 census gave a figure of 167, and the author notes that the governor placed little confidence in the returns (Davy 1854:196). Population estimates made by Gullick (1985:1) for 1970 are 2,125 persons living in six villages; however, in the 1980 national census only 43 persons identified themselves as Carib. The few words of the Carib language, said to be spoken by one old woman in 1955, when Le Page did linguistic work in the island, were found to be French (Le Page and Tabouret-Keller 1985:55).

Carib ancestry is thought to show in preferred physical features of straight hair, thin noses, and light skin, and in volatile temperament.

In the Vincentians' recent search for their history and cultural definitions, they have reconsidered the significance of the Black Caribs. Carib identity has more positive value now than two decades ago, and the carnival bands depict Carib mythological views, art styles, and resistance to colonization. Residents of the Carib communities have recently participated in pan-Carib overtures from Belizean Garifuna. They have taken a lead in reviving Carib dances and themes and have taken over the roles of portrayers of the Carib past. Audiences watch these enactments of sun worship and stone worship with the tolerance of Protestant fundamentalists. Their slave ancestors decided long ago for Britishness.

Duncan gave Vincentians a historical view of their society. His slave ancestors saw Vincentian destiny in British rule; he saw it in statehood modeled on British principles. Through chronicling Vincentian history he taught the superiority of British values, and, like the slaves, he saw the Black Caribs as enemies. But by telling the Carib fight he reclaimed the defeated Caribs as part of Vincentian history and made their adamant fight a symbol of defense of autonomy. As national identity grows at the expense of emulation of Britishness, the Black Caribs are emerging as a political model and the message of the colonial period school master is being transformed. Duncan portrayed Chatoyer as a savage, but in 1990 Chatoyer was called "our nation's first National Hero" and one of "three outstanding political leaders" (R. Gonsalves, *Vincentian*, 28 March 1990). Duncan, a political leader before the British allowed offices for black Vincentians, was not named among the three. In his position Duncan could not have been as free in conferring honor. National heroes are sought only when the nation has been won. Before that, values and directions were too dependent on immediate objectives and changing circumstances to allow easy symbolization. A black and white alliance against the Black Caribs assured white power into the next two centuries. Gradually, white elites lost legitimacy and racially mixed descendants moved into formerly white statuses. They claimed, and eventually gained, control of the society.

2

Constructing a Society

The costly war against the Caribs had been waged to secure a potentially rich colony at a period of prosperity and growth in the Caribbean sugar industry. As soon as the Caribs were removed, the commissioners sold their lands and with the proceeds paid the war debt to the British treasury and expanded the colony's funds for public improvements. Even thirty years after the war, sentiments about its sacrifices were so high that Vincentian planters commissioned the English historian Charles Shephard to write a history of the Black Carib opposition to British occupation. He particularly was requested to include the names of war heroes and war dead, and the planters dedicated the book to "the survivors of the Carib War." Shephard's explanation of how he received his commission to write the history conveys the colonists' commitment to the war: "The Proprietors of St. Vincent are conscious of the exertions, the sacrifice, the devotedness of the Inhabitants in 1795, although they were a small scale, yet they were made for their existence and their property" (Shephard [1831] 1971:xiii). At stake had been not so much the planters' homes and homeland, for many of them

45

were absentee owners or intermittent residents, but their investment in expensive sugar installations, for much of which they were in debt to their factors in England. In the wake of the destruction of plantations and the cessation of production, "British merchants serving as factors for the planters [in Grenada and St. Vincent] suddenly found themselves called upon to bear advances made in anticipation of consignments for 1795 and stood upon the verge of bankruptcy. . . . Many estates were sold to meet the demands of creditors, often for less than the debts against them" (Ragatz 1928:221, 308). For those who rebuilt, twenty years of prosperity followed, and then fifteen years of severe decline preceded emancipation.

The price of sugar increased steadily after the war until 1813–18, when a decline in price and profit began; but sugar production continued to increase until 1828. With the debts of most plantations, and the decreasing margin of profit, the labor force was under pressure to increase production. In 1829 the estimated annual expenses of a Vincentian sugar estate exceeded the profits by £280, a loss amounting to 6 percent of the receipts for the sale of sugar (Shephard [1831] 1971: app., xxix). Higman's study of the slave registration records compiled from the cessation of the slave trade in 1807 to the Abolition of Slavery Act in 1834 shows the intensity of plantation development on St. Vincent equal to that of any colony in the British West Indies during these years. In some respects more like the old sugar colonies of St. Kitts, Nevis, and Antigua than the other Windward islands or Trinidad, which developed at the same time, more than 70 percent of St. Vincent's slaves were in large holdings, that is, holdings with more than one hundred slaves per plantation (Higman 1984:105, table 5.2). Because St. Vincent was more exclusively devoted to sugar than any other Windward colony, the proportion of Vincentian slaves in sugar production increased steadily from 60 percent in 1810 to 68.5 percent in 1830, and the proportion of slaves working other crops declined (Higman 1984:55; 68, table 3.8). The rate of manumission was low, and the proportion of African-born slaves was high. For the two years data was adequate for Higman to figure manumission rates, 1820 and 1834, St. Vincent had the lowest rates of manumission in the British Caribbean save the late-colonized Demerara and Berbice (Higman 1984:381, table 10.1). In 1817 38.8 percent of St. Vincent's slaves were African born, a far higher proportion than in the old sugar colonies, higher than Jamaica, with 36.6 percent African born, and equal to Tobago. Only Trinidad and Berbice had higher proportions of African-born slaves, both more than 50 percent at that time (Higman 1984:458, table S 3.6; 464, table S 4.1).

The colonists voted for funds for public building immediately after the war. A fine stone courthouse was completed in 1798, with an upper story "for lectures, concerts and other public entertainment." The road up the windward coast was improved in 1813 by a 250-foot tunnel blasted through a coastal bluff. A large, ornate Anglican church was completed in 1820, replacing the frame structure leveled by a hurricane thirty years earlier. Stone jetties and aqueducts on the plantations impressed Shephard in 1829 as signs of proprietors' investments in their estates. Although as late as 1833 the Kingstown harbor had no wharf or pier, more than a ship a day steered outward from the port in 1829 (Shephard [1831] 1971: app., xxxiv; Alexander 1833:270). The number of ships and the ship tonnage departing in 1829 was triple the numbers in 1787 (Edwards 1807, vol. 1:430). England's trade rivalries with the United States in 1812–15 left St. Vincent and other islands with a severe lumber shortage, dependent as they had become on imported wood for construction and sugar casks (Ragatz 1928:343).

CONDITIONS OF SLAVERY

Several representations of slavery in St. Vincent, both early and recent, have depicted conditions as relatively benign. Charles Shephard, no critic of slavery, wrote that "while slavery exists, it is no doubt an evil, but the most prejudiced Abolitionist must admit that it exists in this island in a very mitigated form" (Shephard [1831] 1971:191). Recent writers on Vincentian history have considered Shephard's comment correct. Earlier William Young had written of slavery in St. Vincent in the years just preceding the Carib war. He had watched the bare shoulders of slaves as he traversed the road on horseback in St. Vincent and Tobago and reported that almost none had scars from lashings. Bryan Edwards comments on this passage with a footnote stating that lashing was directed to the buttocks and unscarred shoulders proved nothing. Young's vision of happy, healthy slaves extended to slave ships in the harbor, which were "as clean as a Dutch cabinet. We visited every part of the ship, in the hospital there was not one sick, and the slaves mustered on the deck were to all appearances, and uniformly, not only with clear skins, but with their eyes bright and every mark of health . . . [There was] not a scent that would offend and was indeed sweeter than I should have supposed possible in a crowd of any people of the same number in any climate" (Edwards 1807, vol. 3:259). A man who enjoyed the personal presence of slaves, who danced at the slaves' balls in his several estate houses, whose pride was served by providing adequate resources for slaves' welfare, he wrote about their contentment and good cheer.

Two descriptions of Vincentian plantation life in the 1820s were written, one by a proprietress and one by a slave. One was a portrayal of just and caring owners and contented slaves happy at their work, absorbed in their own interpersonal status discriminations and finding enjoyment in deceiving their truth-telling masters; the other depicted endless assaults on the body and spirit. Mrs. Carmichael, an upper-class Scottish woman, took up the duties of proprietor's wife in St. Vincent in 1821. She lived there for five years and published her detailed and seemingly factual observations about the lives of all classes on the island, an account frequently quoted by scholars. Less widely read, although familiar to Vincentians through reprints in the quarterly magazine of essays and literature, *Flambeau*, is Ashton Warner's account of his own slavery. He lived his first ten years free in Kingstown, but he was seized and returned to the plantation from which his mother had been bought and freed, by her own freed aunt, when he was an infant. He worked in slavery on the Cane Grove estate in the leeward Buccament Valley from 1820 to 1830, then escaped and made his way to Grenada, then to Trinidad and England, where his story was recorded by an English abolitionist and published in 1831 (Cameron [1929–34] 1970, vol. 2, bk. 1:62–85). Carmichael's most shortsighted and prejudiced statements are generally recognized as such, but many of her observations appear to be reliable. Her account of the way of life in estate houses and her view of her relations with house slaves afford much insight, and many other details in her observations are undoubtedly valid; but scholars have not always recognized that she had limited familiarity with field production, slave provision grounds, and slave quarters. Warner's observations from the opposite side of a plantation at the same period are interesting not only because his interpretations are directly contrary to some of Carmichael's statements, which should alert the scholar who would try to pick out neutral and unprejudiced data from Carmichael's account, but also because he gives data on central issues of slave adaptation.

Impressive in Warner's testimony are his words of deep feeling and reflection, impressive because slaves' thoughts were so seldom preserved. The man who recorded and published Warner's account, S. S. Strickland, adds a footnote about Warner's compelling language: "Such is the impressive language in which Ashton speaks of slavery, The above are his own expressions; for, though an uneducated, he is a very intelligent negro, and speaks remarkably good English. Any reader, who wishes it, may see and converse with himself, by making application through the publisher" (Cameron [1929–34] 1970, vol. 2, bk. 1:75).

When Warner was claimed as property by a new purchaser of the estate he had been born on, which Strickland notes was probably legitimate under slave law, his case was pleaded by his freed mother and aunt as high up as the governor, who was said to have agreed to intervene with the proprietor who claimed him. The governor did not intervene, and private attorneys never completed the documentation of his manumission, which his aunt had paid them to do. After ten years as a slave on Cane Grove, he planned his escape, reluctantly leaving his wife and infant, and left the island by means of a pass issued to him by the governor's secretary on the basis of the papers attesting to his free status but still incomplete and unsigned by the estate owner. He had set his mind on seeking out the owner in England, and finding him deceased, the executors told him they would look into the matter. He died without hearing from them. Like experienced English subjects, the two freed women used law and lawyers. The runaway slave obtained a clerk's authorization of his flight, citing the ambiguities of the law.

An artisan slave himself, Warner wrote of field labor, "It is a dreadful state of slavery. I have often seen it. I may say I have felt it, though never in my person . . . When the manager threatened to send me to the field, I felt so ill and so desperate that I did not care for life" (Cameron [1929–34] 1970, vol. 2, bk. 1:69). The field gang on Cane Grove worked twelve hours a day, from five in the morning to seven in the evening, with two respites of half an hour and one to two hours, during which each had to pick a bundle of grass to carry back in the evening for cattle fodder, a task consuming the whole rest period during the dry season's paucity of grass. The work day was two hours longer than most slave laws set. If they arrived in the field later than 5:00 A.M., they were flogged with a cart whip. In crop time when they left the fields at 7:00 P.M., they had to work at the boiling shed until 10:00. Warner wrote: "After this the slaves have to prepare their suppers, for, if they have no very aged parents or friends belonging to them, they must do this, which occupie[d] them another hour." During crop time, that is, half of each year, "certain spells of them . . . work half the night also, or three whole nights in the week." Carmichael declared that in her many walks into the cane fields at all times of day she had never seen a driver use a whip, yet Warner's account of field cultivation observed that "the driver keeps forcing him with the whip." Carmichael wrote that carrying wet manure in baskets on the head "appears disagreeable work; but in so far as cleanliness is concerned the Negro is perfectly indifferent." Warner, on the other hand, said, "This is most unpleasant as well as severe work . . . the manure drips constantly down upon the faces and over the body and clothes of the slaves. They are forced to run with their loads as fast as they can; and, if they flag, the driver is instantly at their heels with the cart-whip." Although Warner tells of managers occasionally easing up on a harsh course action, relief is rare (Cameron [1929–34] 1970, vol. 2, bk. 1:70–72; Carmichael 1833, vol. 1:105; Carmichael 1833, vol. 2:4). Carmichael complained of malingering among slaves, and it is defended by scholars as legitimate, but there are few accounts of the sick-house for slaves. Warner wrote:

> The sick-house is just like a pen to keep pigs in. If you wish to keep yourself clean and decent you cannot. It is one of the greatest punishments of the slaves to be sent there. When we were hard pressed, and had much sugar to pot, the manager would often send to the sick-house for the people who were sick or lame with sores to help us. If they refused to come and said that they were unable to work, they were taken down and severely flogged by the manager's order with the cart-whip. There is nothing in slavery harder to bear than this. When you are ill and can not work, your pains are made light of, and your complaints neither listened to nor believed. (Cameron [1929–34] 1970, vol. 2, bk. 1:73)

Caribbean studies have recognized the stimulus that slaves' subsistence gardening provided for the later growth of peasantries (Mintz 1974: 146ff.). Mountainous islands such as St. Vincent are generally credited with ample forest land for slave provision grounds, land unsuited to sugar cultivation and remote from the attention of managers, and both Carmichael and William Young wrote of slaves' private production and marketing of their produce. Slave cultivation of provision grounds was described by Mintz as ordinarily forced and supervised production, although some accounts emphasize the independence allowed in provision grounds, depicting it as alleviating the conditions of slavery (Olwig 1985:135). Warner describes the land for provision grounds as

> such as has been over-cropped, and is no longer productive for canes. This is taken from them the next year, when, by manuring and planting with yams and other things, it has been brought round and recovered strength for the cultivation of sugar. The slaves are likewise permitted to cultivate waste pieces of ground, and the headlands of fields, that are unfit for planting. They work on this ground every Sunday. It is generally given to them in March or April, an it is taken away in December or January.
>   Besides the Sunday, they get part of twenty six Saturdays, out of crop-time, to cultivate their grounds. What I mean by saying they get only part of these Saturdays is this—that they are employed in their master's work, such

as carrying out trash, etc. from five to ten o'clock in the forenoon; and in the evening they must bring each his bundle of grass to deliver as usual at the calling of the lists, so that about seven hours, even of the day which is called their own, is occupied with their owner's work. They are obliged to work on these days at the provisions ground if they wish ever so much for a holiday. If they are absent when the overseer inspects the grounds, they are flogged or put in stocks. (Cameron [1929–34] 1970, vol. 2, bk. 1:73–74)

Warner's report of worn out sugar land, of use rights lasting only eight to ten months, of too short a time to grow long-season crops such as cassava or to repay improvements, of not enough time to work the gardens, and of punishment for being absent from the grounds suggest caution in assessing the benefits of provision-ground rights during slavery.

Warner's account also provides insight into slave family life:

Among the field slaves there was a very respectable young woman called Sally, for whom I had long felt a great deal of regard. At last I asked her to be my wife; and we stood up in her father's house, before her mother and her uncle and her sisters, and, holding each other by the hand, pledged our troth as husband and wife, and promised before God to be good and kind to each other, and to love and help each other as long as we lived. And so we married. And though it was not as white folks marry, before the parson, yet I considered her as much my wife, and I loved her as well, as though we had been married in the church. (Cameron [1929–34] 1970, vol. 2, bk. 1:75–76)

Warner's wife was put in stocks for being late to the fields when she was far advanced in pregnancy and when she was nursing their child. Much is written about planters' attempts to encourage slave reproductivity by favorable treatment of pregnant and nursing women. Warner gave his view of fathering slave children: "To be the father of a young family of slaves, who must grow up to endure the same sad lot was very bitter to me and I often repent my thoughtlessness in marrying a poor unfortunate slave, though I loved her dearly" (Cameron [1929–34] 1970, vol. 2, bk. 1:82). Warner died in a London hospital February 25, 1831, approximately four months after he arrived in England and soon after he dictated his account of his life. Carmichael's book was published two years later. In these years the debate on abolition reached its height. One wonders if Carmichael, who then lived in Britain, read the slave's testimony about the institution she portrayed as being so benign.

Although the availability of slave provision grounds and the production of surpluses on them allowed during slavery a measure of adaptation to the methods of peasant farming and marketing, this adaptation was restrained in St. Vincent by the intensity of plantation development and demands on slave labor in the final decades of slavery. Claims that slavery was practiced in a mild form there originated in the writings of two estate proprietors, and possibly others who influenced Shephard's views. This opinion cannot be upheld in the face of Ashton Warner's account of plantation practices and Higman's study of slave population records. These factors reduce the significance of pre-emancipation adaptation as a contributor to the relative success of small farming in St. Vincent after emancipation.

Slaves' loyalty to British political institutions was eventually recompensed by their government. Duncan instructs his students at length in the parliamentary process of the passage of the Abolition of Slavery Act. He goes on to describe the eve of freedom. The Methodist Chapel in Kingstown was "overcrowded with the black folk who began to assemble in the evening of the 31st July, some time before midnight. Service began; and as the clock struck twelve, . . . a whole congregation of newly freed people leaped to their feet and sang with joy and thankfulness Charles Wesley's hymn: . . . This glorious triumph in a fight for freedom is an example of what can be accomplished by trust in God and the employment of constitutional methods" (Duncan 1941:33). These two resources, faith and the constitutional method, were the best St. Vincent was to have for the next hundred years.

SMALL FARMING AND LARGE LANDHOLDING

Emancipation was much more than the inconvenient legal fact which could be circumvented and even nullified by legislative action as some of the planters' attempts to limit its operation seemed to imply that it was. To its beneficiaries, the Negroes, it represented both the opportunity to re-possess the manifestations of human dignity and the possibility of realizing their still surviving aspirations toward independent, self-respecting existence outside the capricious control of their former masters. Since, as the event proved, they were obviously determined to exercise their freedom in their own interests, they would no longer answer as mere economic units in the production of the staples or as mute subordinates in the social system. Despite the planters' continuous efforts to limit their freedom, they created a situation, largely through the emergence of a substantial peasant class, in which their social and especially their economic status was enhanced . . . (W. Marshall 1965a:235)

Studies of particular colonies and surveys of the whole British West Indies area demonstrate wide variations in the course of action of planters and freed slaves. This variation raises questions concerning the different post-emancipation experiences. In seeking generalities within the variations, Bolland has argued that ratios of availability of land to population density are too simple to account for differences in the incidence of small-land holding among the emancipated populations and in the effectiveness of planters' coercive measures to retain labor on the plantations. Instead he reconstructs the dialectical "dynamics of domination," the particular social relationships of authority whereby elites controlled or failed to control labor power (Bolland 1981:614). Commenting on the effects of coercion, Riviere indicates the great range of situations in the West Indies in this period:

> It was not unusual for a common tactic [of plantation owners] to provoke varying responses, or for different tactics to secure a common response [from the emancipated population]. Coercion, for example, secured adequate plantation labour in St. Kitts and Barbados, but tended to alienate labour in Jamaica, Tobago and St. Vincent. Conciliation similarly provoked an exodus of plantation labour in Trinidad, Guiana and, to a lesser extent, in St. Lucia and Montserrat, but a retention of labour in St. Lucia and Dominica. (Riviere 1972:9)

In attempting to reconstruct the particular factors in St. Vincent that characterized the development of agriculture after emancipation, I consult recent histories and nineteenth-century sources. Constructing a consistent account of one island's development allows attention to certain problems of local interpretation.

In St. Vincent plantation owners' absenteeism was the highest and most persistent in the Windward Islands. According to the figures of John Davy, 88 percent of estate owners were nonresidents in 1848, and according to Woodville Marshall's citation of Colonial Office records of 1854, absenteeism was 80 percent (Davy 1854:184, W. Marshall 1965a:240). Absenteeism can not be considered in all cases as worse than a resident proprietary (see especially Hall 1964). The managers and attorneys left in charge of estates were not necessarily less capable in confronting the problems of estate management than the absent, and presumably indifferent, owners. They were an emerging creole elite, and they had an island identification. It is likely, however, that owners who remained on their estates were in a better position to take initiatives. The absent owners' usual priority of profit over reinvestment, the lag in communications between managers and absent owners, and the divided authority left the managers without incentives to change the abysmal conditions of sugar estates. Colonies where absentee proprietorship was lower than in St. Vincent showed more response to local demands by reforming labor laws, as in Antigua and St. Kitts, or introduced more technological improvements, as in Barbados and

Guiana (Hall 1971; W. Marshall 1987). Coercive labor policies were typical throughout the region, but in St. Vincent the early measures that attempted to bind labor to estates as effectively as slavery were not reformed in the face of workers' abandonment of plantations, and they remained unusually harsh. In 1847 one Vincentian resident proprietor introduced machinery with the capacity of a centralized sugar processing factory, but it went unused by neighboring estates (W. Marshall 1965a:244). Indifference and inertia were high under extensive absentee ownership.

Much of the Vincentian labor force was lost in the first decade after emancipation. In 1835–37, fifteen thousand persons worked in plantation labor; after the end of the apprenticeship period, 1839–41, the labor force had declined to eight thousand, and in 1845 it declined further to sixty-eight hundred, a loss of more than half the pre-emancipation laborers.[1] Only Tobago had a comparable decline in this period, and the loss of estate labor in St. Vincent was much higher than in St. Lucia, Dominica, Barbados, Trinidad, or any of the Leeward Islands (Riviere 1972:9–15; Hall 1971:32ff.). The planters' and attorneys' response was to use colony funds for the importation of workers who would work for wages less than the freed slaves would accept. Between 1846 and 1851 approximately thirty-four hundred contract laborers entered St. Vincent, or half the existing plantation labor force at the time importation began. Among them were twenty-four hundred Portuguese from Madeira; the rest were Africans freed by British intervention in the slave trading still being conducted. From 1861 to 1882, East Indian contract laborers were brought in. Among the Windward Islands, Grenada and St. Lucia received similar numbers of Madeirans and free Africans in the early importations, and only Tobago, lacking public funds, took in few contract laborers. Tobago resorted instead to the share system known as *metayage*, which proved to be a boon (W. Marshall 1965b). Most imported laborers left the plantations as soon as their contracts were over and brought no lasting alleviation of the planters' labor problems.

The working conditions imposed by St. Vincent's proprietors caused the laborers' widespread rejection of plantation employment. The Vincentian wage was lower than in Barbados, but taking the planters' point of view, Davy considered it higher because no rent was charged for houses, provisions grounds and rights to make charcoal on woodlots, as was charged in Barbados. He does not take into account the fact that most workers' houses cost the planter nothing, unlike in Barbados, where planters built post-emancipation laborers' houses. In St. Vincent the typical laborers' houses both during and after slavery were built out of poles the occupants cut themselves, wattle and daub, and roofed with thatch of "trash." Barbadian planters were building workers' houses out of stone and roofing with shingles (Gibbs 1987:33). Not only in Barbados but also in Guiana, houses were built by proprietors in an attempt to keep former slaves on the plantations (Riviere 1972:9). When Vincentian estate owners did build new workers' housing they charged 30 percent of the 1845 weekly wage for rent, higher than Barbados and Tobago but less than in Grenada (Riviere 1972:7). The planter who built housing in Windward Valley built barracks, not the preferred separate houses. Vincentians also found they did not have the right of a one-month notice before eviction, which was common in other colonies. Although Riviere was surprised to find no evidence of evictions in St. Vincent, it did occur in the twentieth century: "In the benighted days of the first half of this century, peasant farmers had no security whatever on lands rented from the Estate. Their wattle-and-daub would be thrown willy-nilly in the road to enforce eviction, as happened on Dos Santos' Colonaire Estate, among others, in the 1950's" (Kenneth John, *Vincentian*, 24 May 1991).

Conditions such as these, persisting without the impetus to more equitable terms that resident proprietaries initiated in some other colonies, led to the decline in the plantation labor force. Low wages in lieu of rent was a major cause of dissatisfaction (W. Marshall 1965a:219). Writing of the Leeward Islands, Hall describes the meaning of these conditions:

> The calamity of sudden ejectment was one thing; the system by which security of housing and continuous labor for the landlord were tied together was another fundamentally greater misfortune . . . The basic point at issue was simply that if a labourer received housing and provision-grounds as part of his wage he would be subject to pressure from his landlord who was also his employer. He would, as tenant-employee, be unable to offer his labour to any but his landlord. If rents and wages were completely separated, his greater freedom would follow. (Hall 1971:48)

In the Leeward Islands, terms that prevailed in St. Vincent were replaced early by conditions allowing more free choice. Legislation and court actions in St. Vincent continued to be punitive. Managers were either more rigid or less interested than resident proprietors, who in other colonies tried through local legislatures to respond to the problems that drained labor.

Trinidad solved its labor shortage, felt only in 1843, by attracting other West Indian labor with high wages and free houses, the very conditions that had allowed Trinidadian labor to move off the estates onto freehold property available in undeveloped parts of the island. Guianese planters offered even more attractive wages and charged no house rent, and agents from Guiana and Trinidad went to the other territories to advertize their terms and recruit workers. Along with other West Indians, Vincentians took temporary labor contracts in Trinidad and Guiana. Migration from St. Vincent continued throughout the nineteenth century, and by the early twentieth century many other Caribbean areas attracted them as well (D. Marshall 1986, 1987). Although some of this early emigration was permanent, many contract and seasonal laborers brought their wages back to St. Vincent and undoubtedly contributed to the beginnings of a peasantry there.

In many British West Indian colonies an increase in small-land holdings in the decades after emancipation indicates the alternative to estate labor that was coming into being. In St. Vincent, however, the number of freeholds was the lowest in the whole area, and the meaning of this fact has not been examined in any of the comparative histories of this period. The anomaly that freeholds were rare and yet prosperity was reported in the first few years after 1838 among Vincentian small farmers presents another variation in West Indian postemancipation adaptations. The Vincentian experience is of particular interest because a strong peasantry appears to have developed without access to land ownership and on the basis of leaseholds. Contemporary observers, Davy and others, reported large peasant production of the export crop arrowroot on freeholds and leaseholds, but also reported a small number and acreage of freeholds. We must thus conclude that small producers were cultivating primarily rented land. The slaves had learned methods of growing and processing arrowroot from the Carib Indians, and, well suited to cultivation in small plots, it was grown for sale on slave's provision grounds. In the 1840s it was still grown mainly on small plots, having become a major export crop second only to sugar, with a rising market in Britain and favorable prices until an oversupply caused prices to plummet in the early 1850s. From 1847 to 1851 one-quarter to one-half million pounds of arrowroot was exported each year. Most of it, Davy noted (1854:183, 185), was produced by small growers, although he observed that by 1848 one or more of the large estates had begun growing it. Estate entry into arrowroot production caused the oversupply and the subsequent drop in prices. By 1868 four estates operated by one absentee owner produced equal quantities of arrowroot and sugar (Beachey 1957:17). They could profit from the fluctuations in price for the two crops, whereas peasants relied on arrowroot alone as a cash crop.

Arrowroot could be processed by the Carib methods still seen occasionally and described below as practiced for cassava; however, large quantities for export came to be processed in estate factories, where the roots were crushed by rollers and the starch washed several times in pans and then dried on large cloths. Estate ownership of the processing equipment reintroduced the peasants' dependence and took some of their profit, although as a customer of an estate mill they were less dependent than they had been as employed laborers. St. Vincent was the foremost producer of arrowroot, favored by many small rivers that supplied the water for processing this crop and operating the mills. Jamaican arrowroot production was high until 1835, and by 1847 it had declined far below that of St. Vincent's (J. Handler 1971:69, table 3). The boom years were brief, but production remained high as estates turned increasingly to arrowroot. In 1892 the value of arrowroot exports surpassed sugar, and the crop continued to be the most valuable export until after World War II. Because they owned most of the land, it is not surprising that by 1940 estates were producing 71 percent of the colony's arrowroot crop, although it continued to be an important peasant crop (Spinelli 1973:153).

The arrowroot prosperity of the 1840s has led to inferences of extensive small-land holdings in St. Vincent. When the data are read carefully, however, the inference is not supported. The problem in interpreting Davy's figures in this regard is that he did not distinguish the area owned by small holders from the area they rented:

> At the present time whilst the number of large estates has continued much the same [as in the time of slavery] many small holdings have been created. In 1845 there were not fewer than 158, varying in extent from 11 acres to spots no more than sixty feet square obtained at purchase at the ordinary rate of about 27 pounds per acre . . . It is believed that there are now not less than ten to twelve thousand acres under cultivation in [arrowroot], and for growing provisions; land *either the property in fee of the labouring class, or rented by them* at the rate of about sixteen dollars the acre. (Davy 1854:183, emphasis added)

Riviere cites another source from the same period that gave the number of freeholds in St. Vincent as 178. The same source stated that 11 of the holdings were in excess of 10 acres, 1 in excess of 5 acres, 7 in excess of 1 acre, and 159 of lesser area (Riviere 1972:17). Considering this data along with Davy's data on plot size, the small holdings probably covered less than 230 acres. Using Riviere's figures, Table 1 compares the number of freeholds in the Windward Islands, Barbados, and one of the Leeward Islands with the fewest freeholds. Note that St. Vincent had far fewer freeholds than these other colonies,[2] in spite of Riviere's comment, based on citation of a letter of 1842, that in regard to St. Vincent "leaseholding was, generally speak-

Table 1. Number of Freeholds in Six Colonies

Year	Colony					
	St. Vincent	St. Lucia	Grenada	Tobago	Barbados	Montserrat
1844						150
1845	178	1,345	1,947	658		
1846						
1847					1,630	
1848						
1849		1,920				
1850						260
1851						
1852						
1853		2,343	3,571	2,367		
1897	1,360					

Source: W. Emanuel Riviere, "Labour Shortage in the British West Indies After Emancipation," *Journal of Caribbean History* 4(1972): 17.

ing, a practice of secondary importance . . . In St. Kitts and Montserrat though, where planters showed great reluctance to surrender landed property, it was the basis of petty farming . . . In other territories the tenure of land on the basis of leaseholds was exceptional . . . In St. Vincent . . . the majority of ex-slaves reportedly preferred purchasing land at a price of £ 30 per acre to leasing it at £ 3 6s per acre annually" (Riviere 1972:19).

Arrowroot, Riviere observed, brought a measure of early prosperity to small cultivators:

> Jamaica and St. Vincent are the only British West Indian territories which can lay claim to having a recognizable, if small, body of such small-farmers in the decade or so following the inception of the free-labour system . . . In St. Vincent where "industrious" ex-slaves reportedly netted £ 20 annually from the sale of surplus provisions, small farmers of arrowroot gained even more . . . The "pressure of want" was said to be "entirely unknown" among black settlers in the island whose cottages were furnished with tables, chairs, a sideboard displaying decanters, wine glasses, and tumblers, and where many men rode horses, and their wives sported silks and satin. (Riviere 1972:21–23)

The reports Riviere quoted are from 1842 and 1843, and Riviere noted that after 1846 hard times set in. Even before that date, however, an annual profit of £20 was not as high as impressed observers in St. Lucia, where sharecroppers in sugar had netted £24 in 1845, and in Tobago where an acre of yams could produce a profit of £30 in 1850 (W. Marshall 1965b:52–53). This level of success in independent small farming must have boosted the commitment of the recently freed Vincentian slaves. The decline in arrowroot prices after 1850 was, however, a greater blow in St. Vincent than in Jamaica, because it was the only widespread crop small cultivators produced. Cotton was exported, but so far as is known it was produced mainly on estates until 1902, when a small-land settlement program encouraged cotton cultivation on small farms. As early as 1843 Jamaican small farms produced "one or other of the minor export crops . . . farinaceous roots, fruit, poultry, pigs, fish, honey and wax, sugar, starch, ginger, allspice, and dyewoods"; cacao and coffee became important export crops of small farmers by 1850 (Hall 1959:182). Diversification protected them from the hazards of specialization in a single crop and sustained small farming in Jamaica better than in St. Vincent.

Peasant landholding has been suggested also by the presence of "free villages." Marshall noted the establishment of new villages and cited the figure of ten thousand residents of independent villages in St. Vincent and Grenada combined (W. Marshall 1968:256). Davy (1854:178) noted "the thriving villages reared by them." Free villages indicate the rejection of tenency on estates and probably the purchase of residential land, but do not necessarily imply the ownership of agricultural land. On the contrary, the concentration of residences in villages suggests that cultivation was not on owned land but on rented land. Rural houses in St. Vincent are situated typically in densely settled residential villages, not as separate homesteads on family fields, such as are found in some parts of Jamaica. In St. Vincent cultivated plots and fields are some distance from the village cluster, and house lots are large enough only for a kitchen garden. Early independent villages thus do not suggest ownership of small farms but rental of farm plots. Early independence and prosperity among some small farmers and an increase in nonestate residential clusters demonstrate a decisive departure from the conditions of slavery for some of the people. Although this departure was not common, it pointed the way for others to follow. Davy (1854:177, 185) commented favorably on the emancipated slaves:

> Of the people of color constituting the great majority of the whole, their condition unquestionably has vastly improved since the time of slavery, and is improving. Very many, even of the labourers, can read and write, and the number of such is daily increasing in consequence of the attention paid to their education. Compared with the same class in Barbados, perhaps on the whole they are more independent, and more disposed, being more able to enforce their own terms. . . . The difficulty of obtaining continued labour is very much greater, the interests of the working class so much interfering.

Davy quotes Lieutenant Governor Campbell writing in 1851:

> Where a body of what may almost be termed yeomanry has associated in a village, they have sometimes acquired too free ideas of liberty and independence, which lead them occasionally to make some attempts at resistance to lawful authority. These attempts, it is however right to remark, are made against officers of the law, or constables of their own color, often inferior to themselves in intelligence and generally when employed in the distasteful business of enforcing the collection of taxes. (1854:178)

Education for black people was available to a limited extent in parochial schools, and a school had been established by free blacks during slavery in Kingstown "for the education of the coloured poor, which with very limited means ha[d] been productive of great advantages" (Shephard [1831] 1971:209). Throughout the nineteenth century, however, the small allocations from government and the churches for education were repeatedly eliminated. Schools were established and within a few years closed (Keizer 1967). Becoming literate, successfully resisting estate employment, resisting tax collection, considered a yeomanry with too-free ideas of liberty and independence, former Vincentian slaves in the first decade after the apprenticeship period rapidly put their freedom and capabilities to use.

Throughout the nineteenth century, almost all cultivable land was held by the estates and remained undivided. The steep slopes of much estate land and the mountainousness of all uncultivated areas left almost no usable land outside estate boundaries. One estate was sold soon after 1838 to a group of free blacks who divided it into small farms. It appears that no other estate was divided into small plots throughout the century. The decline in land value, estimated as tenfold for one Vincentian estate from 1834 to 1845, discouraged sale or division (Davy 1854:193). Heavily indebted estates with high subventions legally due their heirs could not meet their costs, and as a result one-quarter to almost one-half of Vincentian estates were left idle between 1854 and 1859 (Spinelli 1973:113). The particularly acute problems in St. Vincent initiated the enactment of the Incumbered Estates Court Law in Parliament to decide claims against West Indian estates so that they could be sold and brought back into production. Between 1858 and 1864, a period of relative profitability in sugar, thirteen Vincentian estates were sold through this estates court as well as sections of two other estates on the island (Cust 1865:313). By 1888 thirty Vincentian estates had been sold under this act, a number exceeded only by the estates sold in Jamaica. In all the colonies these sales "tended to concentrate estates in fewer hands than prior to the existence of the court" (Beachey 1957:36). Most of the sales of Vincentian properties took place in London, and most of the purchasers were merchant companies. Only three estate sales took place in the island court where sales to residents were transacted. The agglomeration of estates also had taken place among resident proprietors; John MacFee, for instance, had accumulated seven estates between 1856 and his death in 1862 (Cust 1874:9). Among the large merchant companies, Porter and Company owned twenty estates, and another large owner in St. Vincent also had extensive estates in British Guiana, Trinidad, and Barbados. These large merchants responded to the 1880s sugar crisis brought on by European sugar beet competition by ceasing cultivation and holding the land for a better market. By 1886 two-thirds of the sugar-production area had been left idle (Beachey 1957:38, 39). In moving from high absentee proprietorship to merchant agglomeration of estates, Vincentian land was removed further from local control.

Several factors thus explain why small farming continued more on rented land than on freeholds. The nondivision of estates appears to have been contrary to the interests of impoverished owners, who were needful of capital, and may have been a spiteful refusal to deliver to former slaves the control of resources. Merchant owners who bought cheap could hold the land. The unavailability of divided land was only one impediment, and it is probable that small producers could not accumulate enough capital for land purchase. The rapid boom and bust in arrowroot would have reduced savings, and the low wage for estate labor would not have allowed it. Vincentians who worked abroad, however, returned with savings. In 1897, 1,360 acres were in holdings of less than twenty acres each, much more than in 1850 but much less than in the other Windward Islands, as Table 1 indicates. Trouillot's findings concerning current peasant production in Dominica—that small owners do not fare better than small renters in their total income from banana production—suggests another factor in the small number of freeholds.[3] If a similar factor was operating in early independent farming in St. Vincent, land ownership may not have been considered more advantageous than land rental, and in general small cultivators may not have sought to purchase land.

Social conditions of this period led to a riot in 1862. Citing the governor's report, William Green said it was a major riot: "Although the riot began as a protest against wage reduction, it quickly assumed racial overtones. Whites and coloureds took refuge in the capitol as bands of blacks, especially inflamed against whites, travelled about seizing and beating their victims" (Green 1976:379). Ten years later the governor banned the Lenten carnival, fearing the disorder of the parades. The ban was kept in effect but was defied in 1879 when revelers took to the streets for the first time in seven years. Arrests were made for two days, and on the second evening a Kingstown crowd drove off the police with sticks and stones. The following day three to four hundred people massed and the governor was stoned (see Chapter 3).

Before the end of the century, the Colonial Office sponsored a wide-ranging investigation into conditions in its Caribbean colonies. The report of 1897 recommended land reform in St. Vincent, and in response the Colonial Office's Peasant Land Settlement Scheme was initiated on abandoned estate lands. As part of the program, a credit source for small loans was opened in 1913, processing factories were built near the divided land, and an agricultural school was established. By 1915, 7,527 acres had been divided into small holdings and assigned to lessees who could acquire freehold title after a period of restrictions on the conditions of use. Much of this land is said to have been of poor quality, but the demand for it far exceeded the acreage available. The commitment to farming is evidenced in the repayment of loans to the Agricultural Credit Society—in excess of £35,000 with interest by 1926—whereas the debts defaulted amounted to £345, a repayment ratio considered favorable by the agricultural economist Wright (1929:249).[4]

In this program a cotton ginnery was built for the first time on the island, and sea island cotton exports rapidly increased in the strong international market, to the benefit of small and large growers. In 1920, 20 to 50 percent of the total acreage in cotton was in the hands of peasant proprietors (Wright 1929:254). The Colonial Office's program was carried out by three English agricultural specialists assigned to the newly created Vincentian Department of Agriculture. A Vincentian intellectual's observations on island problems published in 1966 under a pseudonym because the article was a leftist critique, commends this reform and the three English specialists: "In this age of anti-colonialism I want to go against the grain and say that the early efforts of these Englishmen go a long way in explaining the superiority of our small farmers when compared to those of other Eastern Caribbean islands" (A. F. Idiot, "Random Reflections on St. Vincent," *Flambeau* 1 [1965]:5). Not only this social critic's commendation of a Colonial Office program should be noted but also his impression, which many Vincentians share, that small agriculture is successful in the island.

The Vincentian economy continues to depend on the export of agricultural products, and small farms have an increasing share in production for export. Land holding continues to be concentrated among large owners. In 1972 the .4 percent of all farms that exceeded one hundred acres each held 59 percent of the cultivated land, whereas 85 percent of the farms held under five acres each, and close to half of these small farms held under one acre each. However, estate labor has declined and the number of small owners has increased. In 1972, 73 percent of those engaged in agriculture were farm operators and their dependents who worked with them, up from 43 percent in 1961 and showing a sharp increase in farm ownership. Holdings under five acres were worked more frequently by their owners than by a tenant, as indicated in the tenure on holdings under five acres each in 1972: 66 percent ownership, 17 percent use rights without rent, 12 percent rented, and .4 percent share tenancy (St. Vincent Department of Agriculture 1975:1, 24–29, tables iii, viii).

The principal estate crops of the past have been abandoned or markets for them have sharply declined. Cotton was abandoned when the ginnery burned down in 1959 and was not rebuilt by the owners or the government. Sugar cultivation and refining had ceased throughout St. Vincent and the Grenadines by 1970, and exports of arrowroot have declined. In the last decade the coconut market has shrunk with decreased use of tropical cooking oils. Bananas, grown on both small and large holdings, became the largest export crop in the late 1960s. Dependency on export agriculture leaves the economy vulnerable to competition among exporting countries for limited markets and depression in prices. Compared to the U.S. dependence on exports for approximately 10 percent of the Gross National Product, St. Vincent depends on exports for about 75 percent of its Gross Domestic Product (GDP) (Deere 1990:22). Tourism, important in some Caribbean economies, contributes only about 2 percent (St. Vincent Department of Agriculture 1975:24, 29; Digest of Statistics 1982:52, 58; World Bank 1985:13). With the lowest GDP of seven small Caribbean states from 1967 to 1982, the Vincentian economy nevertheless grew in that period. From 1982 to 1987 the growth rate averaged 5.7 percent per year, and in 1988 the economy grew by 8.4 percent (Worrell 1987:164; Eastern Caribbean Central Bank Report for 1988, quoted in *Vincentian*, 12 January 1990).

The large share of agricultural exports consisting of bananas poses a threat to the economy, particularly when the European Community abolishes national tariffs in 1993. Windward Island bananas have been protected in Great Britain by tariffs on the cheaper plantation-grown bananas from South and Central America, which supply parts of Continental Europe. The Windward Islands and England are attempting to persuade the members of the European Community to continue this tariff agreement and extend it to the whole community until the year 2000, but the outcome is in doubt. Although the banana crop is the mainstay of agricultural exports, traditional food crops exported to Caribbean countries account for a large share of total exports. Although bananas made up 52 percent and 43 percent of the value of all exports in 1981 and 1982 respectively, root crops and plantains, exported to Caribbean countries, made up 21 percent and 25 percent in the same years and rose to 37 percent of the total in 1985, declining thereafter because of depression in Trinidad, a major buyer. Small livestock is also exported, principally to Trinidad. Regional trade has been promoted since the 1972 formation of the Caribbean Free Trade Association (CARIFTA) and its successor the Caribbean Economic Community (CARICOM), and the smaller Organization of Eastern Caribbean States (OECS). These organizations have promoted internal trade and parallel occupational organizations that confer on common problems.

The first land resettlement program since the 1932 Three Rivers resettlement was initiated in 1986 on the fertile Orange Hill estate, formerly Black Carib land. By 1991, 229 farms had been settled and an equal number were ready for settlement. Former laborers on the estate and local people, many of whom are descendants of the Caribs, were favored in allotting the divided land. This project has entailed building access roads, settlers' houses, and crop processing facilities, and it includes an agricultural experimentation station in which new export crops are being developed. Several other former estates have been purchased by the government for resettlement. In another area a Department of Agriculture program enlisting established small farmers has developed a locally adapted type of onion, thus supplying the island with a product that formerly had to be imported. The diversification of export crops and the reduction in food imports are major government objectives. Food imports, however, are not the main contributor to the imbalance of trade (merchandise and autos contribute heavily) and in 1989 amounted to half the value of food exports. New export crops have been successfully grown, but obtaining reliable markets for them has been problematic. Agriculture is the keystone in the economy at present, and government policy supports agricultural development.

POPULAR POLITICAL PARTICIPATION

In this section I will review several aspects of Vincentian political action: the early political organization and views among educated persons; a political demonstration by lower-class people in the capital; a brief political history from the beginning of ministerial government, parties, and universal suffrage in 1951; and the type of popular political involvement practiced in Windward Valley. What follows is a selection of indicative episodes and illustrations. I drew the history from Vincentian political commentators' newspaper columns and *Flambeau*, which was published from 1964 to 1969 by a group of the intelligentsia. I simplified political history to an outline only full enough to provide context for my points about political action. A full political history would require the reader to follow a detailed chronology, be familiar with many persons and party labels, and comprehend it all unaided by party platforms, because policy has been uncertain and undifferentiated in this small nation with limited possibilities for social improvement. A fuller history would be a rendition of political maneuvers and constant resorting of public postures and private alignments, all enacted before a populace following every move, aligning with leaders, and tending toward party loyalty by districts. I attempt both less and more than a political history—an ethnography of popular political actions.

All West Indian colonial legislatures requested administration directly from Britain as Crown colonies. These requests came and were accepted between 1865 and 1868, and nine years later St. Vincent asked for Crown colony rule. This significant choice and change in colonial status has been seen differently by historians of different territories. Woodville Marshall, for instance, writing of the Windward Islands, saw colonial legislators as so narrowly self-interested that better government was to be found in the rationality of professional British administrators (W. Marshall 1972). Hall's comments, based on the Leeward Islands and Jamaica, are more critical of Crown colony rule; for example: "The imposition of a common constitutional form, perhaps, stifled any small local germ of creative political thought which might have begun to stir" (Hall 1971:179). In St. Vincent the small number of resident estate owners and elite persons, to whom voting and office holding were restricted, suggests that local political talent and motivation had become, after the vigorous legislatures of the eighteenth century, insufficient to govern. Creole nationalism emerged, however, and nurtured the first political leaders.

St. Vincent participated in the crosscurrents of black Caribbean protest in the first part of the twentieth century. The West Indian Regiment sent to Europe in World War I to fight for the motherland, Vincentians among them, returned embittered, and less insular, by the racist discrimination they had experienced. Their lessons were to be relived through news coverage of the Ethiopian War. In 1914 the Representative Government Association was established in Trinidad, and soon in other colonies, with the mission of ending Crown colony status. It was an organization of professionals and middle-class persons. The Vincentian leadership came from historian and teacher Ebenezer Duncan and others who were active in the Caribbean Union of Teachers, the oldest trade organization in the area, dating from the 1890s. An important figure in the Representative Government Association was the radical George McIntosh, a Kingstown pharmacist who had his professional training in Grenada. He was influenced by Marcus Garvey, socialist opinion in the *Sentry* (published in Trinidad), the World War I regiment's experiences, and the promises of the Russian Revolution. He wrote, "Working people awake from your slumbers and be not satisfied to live in misery and squalour. The change of conditions lies in the hands of the working people." He called for "a more equitable distribution of land," identifying planters and capitalists as exploiters (Kenneth John, *Vincentian*, 11 November 1988). His mix of international communism and English socialism was radical compared to his fellow member, Ebenezer Duncan, the admirer of British government, and the general membership, which is said to have been made up of middle-class reformers. Yet he worked through the Vincentian chapter of this organization and sought labor representation in it because he thought a trade union was unsuitable for organizing agricultural workers. To enlist rural people he organized political discussions in the larger villages, and the idea of self-government roused so much enthusiasm that the district in which the village of Windward Valley was situated petitioned the island administrator for local self-government. McIntosh was to play an important role in the 1935 riot, and in the aftermath of that riot he organized St. Vincent's first political party.

Before 1925 the resident administrator of St. Vincent was advised, under Crown colony rule, by an appointed legislative council (above the administrator was the nonresident governor of the Windward Islands). Election to the council became possible only after that year, when, partially in response to the Representative Government Associations, the Colonial Office recommended that three members of the Vincentian Legislative Council be elected rather than appointed. Even after a 1937 increase to five elected councilors, appointed members exceeded elected members. Property requirements for voting were high until 1937 and ensured election of conservatives in those few posts. The lower classes throughout the area were impoverished to an extreme degree. In St. Vincent in the 1930s there was a chapter of the Universal Negro Improvement Association in the windward village of Stubbs; Marcus Garvey and T. A. Marryshaw were speakers in the public library. Ebenezer Duncan published a newspaper, the *Investigator*, which featured reports on the Italian-Abyssinian War, and George McIntosh posted news and photographs of that war on a bulletin board outside his Main Street shop. A wave of unrest in the English-speaking Caribbean led to spontaneous riots and union strikes in Trinidad, Guiana, Jamaica, and St. Kitts from 1933 to the Vincentian riot in 1935. The larger colonies had long experienced trade union organization and labor disturbances, and St. Kitts plantation workers had formed a trade union that functioned illegally (Hart 1988:65). St. Vincent had no trade union or union organizer before the 1935 riot. Most incidents of the labor unrest of this period took the form of strikes at industrial or plantation work sites. Several spontaneous demonstrations occurred; for instance, in Trinidad four to five hundred unemployed laborers marched from an oil field to Port of Spain shouting protests of hunger. Police fired into each of these strikers' and demonstrators' groups, and in each episode rioters were killed (Hart 1988; Lewis 1939).

The Vincentian riot of October 21, 1935, occurred one week after the governor arrived on the island to announce and enact a proposed tax on the luxuries of the poor: beer, ale, spirits, tobacco, cigarettes, and matches—exempting automobiles, the luxury of the few rich. On the morning the governor was to meet with the Vincentian Legislative Council to pass the tax legislation, a crowd gathered at McIntosh's store. They learned that McIntosh was at the courthouse, where the governor and councilors were meeting, seeking an audience to present protests to the tax, and that the governor refused to see him until after the session had ended. The crowd at McIntosh's store that morning soon came under the leadership of a popular spokesman among the groups accustomed to gathering at Market Square and talking about the state of the country, a man named Sheriff Lewis. He had served as a volunteer in Ethiopia and upon his return was called Haile Selassie, the name of the Ethiopian emperor. This man credited the mass sentiment for public demonstration to a very old mentor who used to lead the conversations at the square with the motto, "St. Vincent needs a riot." Lewis took leadership along with a woman called Mother Selassie, a laborer for the Agriculture Department. The crowd moved to the courthouse where the governor, administrator, and council were meeting. The police closed the high iron gates, but the crowd pushed into the courtyard. The administrator came outside and spoke to the crowd but failed to disperse them. The rioters were said to have shouted, "We have no work!" and "We are hungry!" They overturned council members' automobiles, hurled rocks through courthouse windows, and stoned the administrator. One researcher was told that the police left the scene to get arms from their barracks and returned with unloaded guns, the bullets in their pockets (DeBique 1982). A rioter, however, described police fire in his recollections to a reporter fifty-five years later; like a legend the episode is told with variations in details (*Vincentian*, 19 October 1990). The rioters left the courthouse and looted a white importer's store; beat the white owner of another large store; and marched to the jail, beat the warden, and freed several prisoners. Looting continued throughout the day. A warship with troops arrived in the harbor that evening, and the troops and militia were used in beatings and mass arrests. Reports of casualties differ from one to three killed, with twenty-six reported injured. The next day Kingstown was quiet and arrests continued, but other, smaller centers took up the demonstrations and staged minor looting for three days.[5] In the trials of the arrested rioters, thirty prison sentences were meted out. Sheriff Lewis was sentenced to the longest term, twenty-one years, and served five years before being pardoned (*Vincentian*, 19 October 1990).

The governor's extreme response in summoning a battleship, imposing a state of emergency for three weeks, and requiring strict censorship of the press was followed by treason charges against McIntosh. His trial was "so ridiculous that at the preliminary hearing the magistrate threw out the case without calling on the defense. The reaction of the general public throughout the West Indies, even as far as Jamaica, was amazement and deep resentment against the repressive measures adopted" (Lewis 1939:13). The governor's response was a measure of the rioters' direct challenge to the colonial government. Most previous and later West Indian rioters used the strategy of the strike and presented negotiable demands; however, the Vincentian crowd had not learned trade union methods. They acted in the bold spirit of market square oratory and not by rules of unionization. They marched directly to the building where the government was in session and attacked the person and property of the heads of government. They challenged a central right of government, the power to tax, and went on to challenge the government's right to imprison. The issue of excessive taxation could unite the lower and middle classes and the governor considered the riot instigated by a middle-class leader. Experienced union leaders, although middle class, controlled strikers. In Jamaica, for instance, "the tenor of leaders' appeals to the workers in the critical moments helped to defuse the crisis . . . Far from emboldening the combative side of the workers' sensibility, both [Bustamante] and Manley sought a submissive and quiescent consciousness. The repeated appeals for order, good behavior, and conformity disclosed the convergence of these leaders' views with the colonial stereotype" (Gray 1991:30). Barbados' only riot in this period protested the government's infringement of the rights of a single labor organizer, a cause less unifying than the one that rallied the Vincentian crowd (Belle 1988; Hart 1988). McIntosh emerged from the treason trial a symbol of anticolonialism. He organized the Workingmen's Cooperative Association in 1936 and registered it not as a union but as a political party. In the election of 1937, with liberalized property qualifications for holding office and voting as a peace offering from the governor, McIntosh's party won four of the five elective seats on the legislative council. W. A. Lewis's commentary (1939:14) continued: "In three years this association has become the focus of radical opinion in St. Vincent and a body of great political influence. . . . It has attracted wide middle class support. . . . It is one of the new organizations which is changing the orientation of West Indian politics." Change under colonial government could not be rapid or smooth. McIntosh and the three other members of his party on the legislative council eventually won a token land settlement scheme and legislation on a minimum wage and work hours, although "such laws for the most part have been more honored in the breach than in the observance." After 1946 McIntosh himself "became a convert to elitist politics and won the blessing of the planter class" (Kenneth John, *Vincentian,* 11 November 1988). Ebenezer Duncan remained conservative. His history explains the 1935 riot with a quotation from the governor's speech given soon after the end of the state of emergency when he announced passage of the tax law: "The causes of the riot . . . are still obscure, but . . . one contributing cause was a misunderstanding of the Governments' policy in introducing the measure which we have just passed into law" ([1941] 1970:52). In spite of Duncan's outspokenness on the issue of race in his newspaper, his ideals disallowed popular rebellion. He quoted the governor as recommending in the same speech political representation of the working class.

The radicalism represented in the riot and in McIntosh's political program continued to inspire many Vincentians. Ebenezer Joshua, the leader whose party won every election from the first under universal adult suffrage in 1951 until 1966, spoke as radically as the early McIntosh. On the eve of political independence in 1969, *Flambeau* published a detailed reconstruction of the riot and an evaluation of its meaning. This article is the main source for my description of the event. In their summation, the article's authors stressed the racial antagonism that stemmed from whites' monopoly of resources: "The most significant aspect of the episode was the hostile attitude of the masses toward the white section of the community . . . The blacks felt they had been cheated and oppressed by a small white class which jealously paraded along the corridors of power. They owned the lands, they owned the business-houses, they ran the Civil Service, and they controlled the legislature" (Peters and John 1967:31).

Once independence had brought about a more firmly settled view of nationhood, an interpretation of the riot stressed the emergence of political consciousness and national identity: "McIntosh tried to abort the 1935 riots with advice to the hot headed, but is the hero of the move to initiate a consciousness of their rights and their dignity in the people of St. Vincent" (Nora Peacock, Editorial, *Vincentian*, 14 November 1986). To another writer the episode signified the unification of social classes: "It was the 1935 Riots that blasted the colonial straight jacket, calling the bluff on the whole system and exposing it for the farce that it was. The disturbances represented a general movement from down below, but there were members of the articulate middle class which inspired and informed it" (Kenneth John, *Vincentian*, 27 March 1987). After becoming a nation, the episodes that enacted popular aspirations and expressed a shared ideology were sought out and recognized, becoming symbols of the national past.

National identity and Caribbean identity were linked from the beginning in the aspirations of the leaders. Throughout the Caribbean political parties representing laboring interests "had come into being to harness the flood of political energy released by the disturbances, strikes and riots of the 1930s" (Springer 1973:193). The Caribbean Labour Congress, representing these parties, was conferring in the same time and place—Montego Bay, 1947—as delegates from the West Indian governments and the Colonial Office were meeting to set in motion the process of political federation of the English colonies. Including some of the same representatives, and expressing similar views on political development, "these two conferences thus signified that the decision to seek national independence for the West Indies through federal union had been arrived at both by the government of the United Kingdom and by the peoples of the West Indies themselves" (Springer 1973:194). The principal Vincentian proponents of federation were Duncan and McIntosh, who strove to give a sense of the island's common history and interests. They presented nationalism and pan-Caribbeanism as allied ideas. Duncan in his newspaper and classroom, and McIntosh in his speeches to the rural and town gatherings, advocated locally the ideas circulating throughout the area. Opposition to federation in many colonies was a result of different size and levels of prosperity and influential Hindu and Moslem minorities in Trinidad and Guiana. But the small islands were strong supporters of federation, particularly the Windwards, which had been administered under a single governor, were poorest, and foresaw advantages in economic cooperation. In federation they sought to overcome the weakness of small size. After the high hopes of the 1947 conference, the ten years spent drawing up a constitution for the West

Indian Federation was "a period during which the West Indian leaders, instead of being involved in unifying activity of demanding independence from Britain, found themselves engaged in long drawn-out and self-regarding negotiations with one another" (Springer 1973:195).

The large mainland colonies of British Guiana and British Honduras had not been strong supporters and withdrew early. The leaders of Trinidad and Jamaica had been prominent in promoting union, but in both islands opposing interests caused their withdrawal in 1961, and the federation was dissolved. Soon thereafter eight islands—the Windwards, the Leewards, and Barbados—began discussions of a federation. The St. Lucian economist W. Arthur Lewis played a key role in the three-year talks. His arguments concerned the economic and political advantages of federation, and although he appeared a masterful strategist in conferring with the Colonial Office, he did not, like Duncan, cite heritage or common sentiment:

> Federation is the only framework which will guarantee law and order, good government, financial stability, the recruitment and retention of good technical staff and the ability to attract financial assistance from outside, including the power to borrow and including also the kind of stability which attracts private investment.
>
> Jamaica is out forever; and should never have been in, since sentiment for federation was never strong in that island. But it is the inescapable destiny of Trinidad, British Guiana and the other British islands to link their fortunes together. (Lewis 1973:232–33)

"The Agony of the Eight," as Lewis titled it—the rocky road of planning for giving up local high offices, cooperating on currencies, representation by island although each had different populations, the opposition of political rivals and the leaders' own advisors—together thwarted working commitments, and the leaders' momentum was lost. In 1966 the Colonial Office proceeded to plan the transition to independence for each colony. St. Vincent was allowed only eight months to elect a government to take charge of an independent state. Since 1951 two parties had emerged and alternated in winning the majority of the thirteen legislative seats, thereby occupying the cabinet ministries and the chief minister's office. The two parties were the People's Political party (PPP), led by the populist Ebenezer Joshua and his wife, Ivy, also an elected representative in Parliament, and the St. Vincent Labour party (SVLP), led by lawyer Milton Cato. In the rush to independence, the 1966 election was followed by party realignment among the winning candidates, resulting in loss of a legislature majority. The Colonial Office then allotted another three years before statehood.

The Labour party won the election of 1967 and was in office when St. Vincent became an independent state in association with Great Britain, a relationship that lasted ten years and was followed by full independence.

The political context preceding statehood was described with dismay and irony in 1966 by the Vincentian political scientist Kenneth John. His depiction reflects the sense of colonial ruin and local powerlessness that loomed over attempts to control and order newly opened governmental processes. A governor and appointed members of council were still able to tie up the programs of the elected representatives. John, with a Ph.D. from Manchester University, was educated in the strategies of English elective power, and in an article that soon became a classic among scholars of Caribbean local politics, he derided the scene of gaucheries in the Vincentians' race into politics:

> With the advent of the universal franchise in 1951 our main story begins. The flood-gates of pent-up frustrations were unlocked and the people channelled all their released emotions into politico-economic movements. Everyone had to be a party man and a unionist in a fashion bordering on the fanatic. A political vacuum was created which sucked in the charismatic leader to offer a "Father figure" image to a people still afflicted with the slave mentality of Massa Day. Political meetings spiced with meaningless sloganising and empty promises became the chief form of entertainment in a culturally benighted region. Following their local hero to whom they were often bonded by the spell of persuasive oratory and social identification or by the more compulsive strangle-hold of economic dependence, the people shifted their support with every move he made. And the politician, newly arrived, and bewitched by the intoxicant of freshly-won laurels, gyrated between parties, crossed the floor, and performed all sort of incredible political gymnastics in the haunting desire to consolidate his acquisition of power. Thus has the political situation in St. Vincent remained fluid, even amorphous . . . The obstinate conservatism of an inefficient Civil Service aggravates the problem; and the intrasigency of the Employer-class in dealing with irresponsible Trade Unions adds to the troubles. . . . Precisely because they had been denied a place in the political process the people got themselves to believe that politics held the key to all problems and offered the panacea to every ill . . . Further, the face-to-face relations of our very intimate and compact society has led to the practical personalization of politics . . . Feuds and quarrels as well as personality problems are hammered out and settled on political platforms when not in the Council Chamber . . . The net result is that anyone with pretensions to introducing a rationalistic and intellectual approach to St. Vincent's problems is more likely than not to be hounded out of the political arena, as indeed was the fate of "son" Mitchell when he threatened to launch a third force and revolutionize politics.
>
> If we retrace our historical development we can easily account for some of the inter-party animosities and personality conflicts. The parties are

based on no ideology or, in so far as they stand for anything, they stand for the same thing. Since one cannot attack the other side's programme in as much as manifestoes all preach the same story, personalities are assailed.

There is a lot of talk in St. Vincent that the parties are divided on class lines. This is sheer nonsense. In terms of educational qualification, shade gradation, or economic indices, the country is about eighty per cent lower class. And since both parties share the country evenly it is obvious that both are supported by a substantial portion of the working class. (Kenneth John, *Flambeau* 5 [July 1966]: 1–9)

Caribbeanists have differed in their assessments of patronage politics, and several have documented the early 1970s practices in St. Vincent and, more recently, Bonaire politics.[6] The study in Bonaire is of particular interest. In considering machine politics and patronage practices there, and in reviewing the criticism of similar systems elsewhere, Klomp discerned many positive effects of this kind of politics. She pointed out social integration and a modification of the stratification system through increased personal contact and recognition of shared interests. Bonaire's system drew the populace into politics "quickly and intensively . . . and len[t] a great deal of vitality to the politics-derived integration" (Klomp 1986:177). It appears that there was a change in local patronage practices in St. Vincent, but I have not researched this subject locally. I suggest, however, a hypothetical interpretation of one aspect of recent political changes based on my long-term attention to the national newspaper. This hypothesis concerns local political organization only and does not concern other factors contributing to political changes—for instance, the important influence of the characteristics of current leadership. I suggest that the power of the local leaders has been bypassed by the decline of the two dominant parties and the emergence of a new majority party without the benefit of a local network of leaders. The transitional history shows that the Labour party, which had the support of professionals and the middle class as well as a strong grassroots base, increased its elective margin and patronage rewards from 1972 until 1984, while Ebenezer Joshua, the leader of the People's Political party, was reduced to coalition and opposition politics in the same period. His PPP was disbanded after its 1979 loss to Labour. Labour sustained its local leaders through small patronage until its defeat in 1984 by the former Independent, James F. Mitchell, who led the New Democratic party (NDP). Although the NDP had been contesting elections since its formation in 1975, it appears to have been unable, or to have declined, to replicate the old system of local power brokerage in most areas, and its emergence as front-runner in 1984 can be attributed to the national focus of its leadership. Although Joshua ordered his tattered ranks to support Mitchell's NDP in

1984, that election appears to have been won in most areas without local leaders dependably delivering the vote. The Labour party was left with only three seats in government in 1984, forecasting a lean five years for local party men, and in the next election in 1989 their party lost all districts. This landslide turned into a political liability for Mitchell and the NDP. The early outcry against the sweep concerned fear of dictatorship because of the opposition's loss of representation. Effects of this landslide crept into the commentaries many months later when allusions were made by several opposition spokesmen to a decline in local government. As the two older parties were defeated and declined, their inability to deliver the spoils decimated the local party networks. The NDP had won two elections without a developed local patronage base.

Not only are St. Vincent's early politics now viewed benignly by numerous newspaper contributors, but an appreciation for the heady days of vigorous personal loyalties and for the charisma of Joshua has become part of the conjuring up of a significant past, a past with heroes and legends. Five years after his retirement, Joshua was dubbed a hero by Calypsonians; ten years after, the airport was named for him. When he died on March 14, 1991, the eulogy, the editorials, the letters to the editor and the newspaper columnists looked back over his career as a vital thread of recent history. The eulogy of Joshua, delivered by Kenneth John, departed from his 1966 assessment. Honorific for the occasion, it could become the new nation's origin legend, giving explanation of the emergence of popular leadership from indigenous roots. By 1991 the truculent populist whose politics embarrassed the well educated was seen as a hero of the struggle to make a nation out of a colony:

> Comrade Joshua had been a colorful and controversial figure from morning, the sort of personality to whom no one was indifferent, the kind of man who evoked strong feelings one way or another. . . . Taken within the context of his times, E. T. Joshua must be seen as a colossus that bestrode the political centre stage at a critical time of our development, and as one who made a positive contribution in that crucible to mould the shape of present-day St. Vincent . . .
>
> In 1951 Joshua returned home to St. Vincent from Trinidad where he had had a dry run in electoral politics on a Butler Party ticket. Joshua was appointed treasurer of the United Workers and Rate-Payers Union and selected to contest the North Windward constituency under the banner of the newly-formed 8th Army of Liberation which swept the polls, all eight candidates being returned with over 70% of the popular vote. It was a resounding mandate for change given by an electorate voting in elections for the first time. . . . Within weeks the 8th Army was split right down the middle with Joshua leading the more radical faction. . . .
>
> Joshua continued to mesmerize the crowd with a spell-binding rheto-

ric. According to a Press Report of the day: "He ranted and raved about Imperialism as usual. At times he attempted to soar to Churchillian eloquence and would then power-dive to soap-box oratory, to the delight of the masses." . . . He had become the tribune of the people championing their every cause, seeking to redress for all their grievances, real and imagined. The disprivileged and down-trodden identified with Joshua who appeared to eschew all social pretensions, living the simplest of lives as he rode his bicycle around town or with his wife, Ivy, walked from village to village preaching the gospel of anti-colonial politics and spreading the word of militant trade-unionism. . . . In thunder, lightning or in rain, Joshua held his regular Wednesday night meetings in Kingstown, and on other nights wherever two or three were gathered in his name, hammering home his message by constant repetitiveness fired from a voice-box of gravel. From that time until recently the Market Square became a political institution, the People's Parliament.

The message was often underscored in black-and-white personally by Joshua who largely wrote, edited, and sometimes stencilled and rolled off "The Voice," Bulletin of the P.P.P. on a regular basis. An enthusiastic student of English literature and devoted disciple of Shakespeare, Joshua often threw in a quotation or two by mouth or print to the elation of his admirers. . . .

What ever he did, Joshua made sure that he kept in constant touch with the grassroots, taking the pulse of the people and keeping his ear close to the ground. . . . When he became overbearing to the island's entrenched interest Joshua was twice voted out of the Executive Council on the ground that he was a fellow-traveller of the communists and was importing a foreign way of life to the country. But such official harassment only served as a badge of colonial respectability endearing Joshua all the more to the mass of the people as well as earning the respect of a sizeable slice of the anti-colonial intelligensia. . . . Probably to placate private industry, Joshua publicly denounced socialism and leaned over backwards to entertain private enterprise. . . .

But for all his faults, weaknesses and short-comings, Joshua has left us a monument more lasting than bronze. In the terminal stage of colonialism he bestirred the ordinary man out of his lethargy by the use of shock therapy, making him alive to his dignity as a worker and assertive of his rights as a person. Joshua in effect awoke a slumbering giant who will never go back to sleep. For that we owe him an eternal debt of gratitude. (Kenneth John, *Vincentian*, 22, 28 March 1991)

Also in the *Vincentian* was an editorial entitled "A Legend Passes":

He was tutored in the rudiments and esoteric finer points of politics by another political giant, the late Tubal Uriah Butler, flamboyant leader of the Butler Empire Workers and Home Rule Party in Trinidad. Like Butler, who was born in Grenada, Mr. Joshua was also a trade unionist and agitator for the rights of the working class, the underprivileged, the poor, the downtrodden and the dispossessed. Joshua's struggles for the under class are well documented: for the record he was responsible for the abolition of child labour and rescinded the ban on "Shakerism." (Jeff Hackett, *Vincentian*, 22 March 1991)

These comments come from a politically middle-of-the-road press, certainly not unionist or leftist. A Vincentian wrote from London:

> I have always admired the man. To me he was the archetypal politician; he was the master who brought political awareness to ordinary folks in St. Vincent and the Grenadines. These days when I hear the words: plantocracy, guillotine, railroading, veto and other political jargons, I know where I first heard them—at Joshua's political meetings in St. Vincent during the fifties. Listening to Joshua's rousing speeches with a quote or two from the Bible or Shakespeare was pure theatre. The man had no equal in St. Vincent. (*Vincentian*, 12 April 1991)

On the night he died, Joshua was overheard in his hospital bed praying continuously. An elegiac news story quoted passages from his prayers: "I approach thee nearer God. Please be merciful to me dear Father. I know you are at my side every second, every minute, and every day Lord. Now we are ready to walk together God" (Anthony Williams, *Vincentian*, 11 March 1991). The spiritual journey of death is a prominent image in island religious thought, and particularly in the Shaker church to which Joshua and his wife belonged. Joshua died on the 196th anniversary of Chatoyer's death, augmenting the heroic status of both men. Joshua was not only linked with the recently elevated Black Carib leader but also was given status equal to the highly respected Ebenezer Duncan, the conservative constitutionalist (Clem Iton, *Vincentian*, 3 May 1991), and George McIntosh, the shopkeeper instigator of the 1935 riot (Ralph Gonsalves, *Vincentian*, 28 March 1991).

On the first anniversary of Ebenezer Joshua's death, and the 197th anniversary of Chatoyer's death, celebrations of the Black Carib chief dominated the day. Only Kenneth John, the preeminent chronicler and analyst of Vincentian political history, returned to the story of Joshua. No longer constrained by the format of the eulogy, he added to his funeral oration the darker side of Joshua's leadership. Of his thirty years in politics, Joshua could be lauded for only the period from 1951 to 1960, "when he lifted the level of political awareness of the man-in-the-street" and "behaved responsibly" in office. After 1961 "Joshua denounced Socialism and his government became more business-oriented, self-centered, even corrupt . . . Joshua became . . . repressive . . . and resorted to unfair control of the streets for purposes of demonstrations. . . . He began to see a Communist under every bed. . . . He cast aspersion on the . . . burgeoning movement of Black consciousness." The tactics of his political coalitions threw into confusion long-standing alignments and lost him the backing of formerly loyal followers. John evened out the ledger, however, quoting his tribute to Joshua for "bestirring the ordinary man, making him alive to his dignity as a worker and assertive of his rights as a person" (*Vincentian*, 13 March 1992). John saw this dignity as a worker and assertion of rights as a person as political accomplishments in the days of transition from colonialism. Dignity as a worker and assertion of rights as a person were, as John wrote, bestirred. Would he agree with the anthropological formulation, which I am presenting in this book, that these self-concepts were part of the culture of the ordinary people, learned and practiced in daily interchanges and actions and evident in their history? As "a man of the people," a black man, a Shaker "living the simplest of lives," Joshua possessed qualities and abilities that allowed him to mobilize the people's culturally embedded characteristics into national power. He catalyzed the individualism of the country and town people and mobilized their desire to transcend local colonial indignity. This indignity, so overtly acknowledged by ordinary people, consisted of not only the insults to them of power and profits garnered by the estate owners but also the insults, which I will describe, cast among contesting neighbors as they manipulated the ambiguous village moralities. Joshua captured these sources of political energy in the culture and showed Vincentians the uses and power of national rhetoric. What he lacked was a vision of a nation and a program for a nation. He could not invent a governmental program to begin transforming the exploited colony into an independent nation in a competitive regional and international arena. After Joshua's political downfall, the lawyers who made up the Labour party leadership struggled with this task in their two decades in power. Vision and program were also elusive to them, and the task was exceedingly complex. After the Labour party's loss of all parliamentary seats in 1989, the party remains organized, holds conventions, contests local elections, and uses the press to speak in opposition to the New Democratic party government in power. The NDP and its leader, James Mitchell, represent a new phase in Vincentian national politics. I have hypothesized this party's absence from local patronage practices; in many ways its course has been a new political departure.

The Vincentian prime minister since 1984, Mitchell has been on the political scene since he won the Grenadine district for the Labour party in 1966. His position on national problems was commended as "rationalistic and intellectual" in Kenneth John's account that same year. He was elected as an Independent in 1972, an election that divided the other twelve seats evenly between Labour and the PPP. Appointed prime minister in this uneasy coalition government, the alliance was kept together for two years. He remained in Parliament and organized the New Democratic party in 1975. He became a highly visible leader of the opposition, and "by 1982 Vincentians had already identified Mitchell as their new leader" (Kenneth John, *Vincentian*, 29 December 1989). After winning twelve seats in an expanded fifteen-seat Parliament in 1984, his government launched its program centered on fiscal soundness, land reform, and improved external funding.[7] The change in electoral politics that brought him into office represented increased attention among the electorate to the national image and a turn from local bosses.

According to John, "Mitchell has put St. Vincent on the political map of the world and vastly enhanced our overseas image." This has been a home-education and home-reform mission as well as a diplomatic mission. "The many trips abroad bring results. Mitchell and his Ministers are committed to giving a public blow-by-blow account on their return, as well as straighten out all financial business with the Treasury. Indeed prudent financial management as well as probity in all financial matters are a trademark of the Mitchell administration" (*Vincentian*, 29 December 1989). He has also been the chief proponent in the Eastern Caribbean for a renewed attempt to achieve federation of the Windward Islands. Before his party's sweep of all districts in 1989, most columnists usually commended his government, but after the disarray of the political opposition in that election, the continuing accomplishments of his program received minor acknowledgment, and a barrage of personal criticism followed. News coverage concentrated on the hopeful politicians who hammer away at Mitchell, looking forward to the next mandatory election in 1994.

It may be too simple to say that once it became clear that there was no contest, because there were no opponents, politics as a demonstration of authority was perceived as awry, but certainly this is part of the reason the public's role degenerated into clamor. The massive outcry for a political opposition was more than fear for the threat to democracy. It also had an echo of tradition in it, dismay at the loss of the public confrontation of opponents. The contests of the best among "men-of-words," in Abraham's phrase, was what held the public. The purpose was less to have a winner than to have a contest.

The public's views of what the political process should be, and how that process serves basic cultural patterns, is a matter that links national and local society, elite political behavior and lower-class habits. The high level of interest in politics and voter turnouts averaging more than 80 percent of the electorate, is due to the respect for hierarchy and government cultivated by colonial society and invigorated by suffrage rights, party politics, and independence. Village manifestations of this interest are readily apparent. Comments about government members and national issues are the regular subject of rural house-to-house visits and chats in chance encounters on the roads. Talk about politics is a social convention, and most of the rural people I knew were informed and well able to pursue this form of sociality. Village social relations promote attention to politics, and, moreover, politics is used to deflect personal conversation. A focus outside the community and away from the self is necessary and protective, because of the malicious gossip and ever-present slurs on behavior, as I will discuss more fully in connection with village culture. The social use of political talk enlarges the desire to be up on current topics.

The media and traditional speech meetings are the models for popular political talk. Information comes via newspapers, radio, and, lately, television. Newspapers are eminently political, and information is detailed. Newspaper reading is a habit of long standing; only recently has radio given adequate time to news broadcasting and cut into rural newspaper reading. Although the rural literacy rate in 1972 was low, newspaper reading was surprisingly high and is still quite common—this despite the sale of newspapers only in Kingstown and the Friday afternoon appearance of the main weekly after many rural people have left town. In recent decades there has been only one weekly newspaper published regularly; several other newspapers sponsored by political parties publish irregularly and for short durations. All give much space to opinions by columnists and letters to the editor. Diverse and vehement opinions are expressed about prominent persons and public issues. Divided viewpoints and an argumentative and provacative style demonstrate the enjoyment of controversy, which is important in the society. Traditional oratorical contests, celebrating Christmas, Easter, and emancipation, were staged until recently in village events called *tea meetings*—the name derived from the bush and bark teas served. The more oppositional the speeches the better, and the more excessively stated the more admired. The principles of talking sense and talking sweet are employed in these events:

> That confusion and contest rule this occasion is important in order to understand why this ceremony has developed. This uproarious meeting differs from similar occasions for eloquence in European and Euro-American cultures because of the various attempts made to "confuse." The battle of wits is so organized because the Vincentian would see little value in the demonstration of the coolness (or lack of confusion) of the orator if it were not tested, contested, surrounded by a heated-up audience. Although the speeches are calculated to obtain the attention of the audience, attention does not mean

quiet. Indeed, if the speaker is not able to obtain the "hot" responses of laughter, rapping, clapping and continuative words (like "fact, fact" or "proceed"), he regards his performance as a failure. And well he must, because the alternative to this guided response are louder noises, generally of a derisive nature. Thus learning to talk sweet is calculated not just to show an ability to speak a code effectively; far more important, it provides an occasion to perform, edify, entertain, and demonstrate, through the aesthetic of the cool, the highest values of the group. By this, the group and the performing individuals achieve a sense of fulfillment—the group because it has come together and celebrated its overt values; the individual because his abilities have been utilized and tested in a manner that allows him to achieve status. (Abrahams 1983:120)

Tea meetings were described to me in 1972 much like Abrahams's accounts of them, but are not known to have been held since then. Close in program and purpose to rural electioneering, they must have loaned style and enthusiasm to the early decades of universal suffrage and political party campaigning.

A district council meeting held in the village of Windward Valley in 1972 carried over some of the entertainment value of the tea meetings and showed the contest form in its political adaptation. A local Portuguese man was attempting to gain office, and he and his son addressed a district council meeting, proposing his nomination for district chairman, a post he had held for one year. He said that withholding renomination at the end of his first term had been unconstitutional, because the council members could do so only if they found fault with the incumbent, and this they had not done. Reading the constitution aloud disproved his interpretation to the other councilors' satisfaction, but he and his son persisted, becoming louder and more accusatory, he chain smoking in his nervousness as they kept up the decorous phrases proper in public address. Opposed by all the speakers, he burst out with the accusation that two council members present had promised him their vote, promises witnessed by his son in certain places and times, and at the voting had "turned Judas" against him. The accused council members were much embarrassed at the accusations of vote rigging and denied it, but the revelation so amused the gathering of public-spirited citizens that the meeting broke out in laughter and one old man gleefully tapped his cane and said, "Oh, sweet meeting!" The councilors slowly and deftly brought order, one acknowledging that the rumors that things had not been done entirely right appeared to be true, and one declaring he was due an apology for this public insult, which brought more roars of laughters. The councilors themselves were in turn laughing and insulted, using the free-for-all atmosphere to make innuendos against one another. The laughter at others' expense succeeded in generalizing and multiplying the irregularities and obfuscating the case of the Portuguese candidate. One motion after another to adjourn was protested by the Portuguese man, but when the hilarity subsided the "floor people" began to drift out. The Portuguese man and his son had been compromised so much more than the other men, who took their embarrassments stonily, that their case was clearly defeated. I left also, my arrival having been greeted with scowls, teeth sucking, and prolonged minor topics, reluctant to miss the leave-taking of the battered insurgents and their deft manipulators but ready to give a little to remain tolerated. The next day the old chairman was as cordial as usual and commented only, "People don't want him." It had been a democratic process. Its likeness to the orchestrated tea meeting of the recent past did not diminish its political accomplishment. Although the speech contests were falling into disuse, the style and purpose of talking sense carried over into talking about incumbents' achievements and political platforms. In election contests candidates do not meet or debate, but the contest is staged in the wine shops and in shouts from porch to porch. I viewed the 1984 election in the village of Windward Valley. An entirely orderly day of voting was followed by an all-night blackout of electricity and media all over the island caused by a severe storm. The news of the election results came to most villagers in the form of a dawn parade of young carnival-costumed villagers carrying a mock coffin and chanting, "Labour dead," with the Labour supporters shouting invectives from their yards. The parade duplicated others in all the large villages and in the capital, where the marchers carried a coffin for the Labour party and the new prime minister.

Contests create the Vincentian sense of political entity. It is not a sense of commonality, national mission, or community that gives this conviction, but individualistic and strong-minded ordinary people taking different views in skillful verbal performances. When local performance shifts to the national scene, the contest is enhanced with high-status incumbents and challengers and governmental words, acts, and controversies. The popular tradition promotes enjoyment of the acts of government and politics. Enjoyment combines with the tendency to talk about politics as a foil for village hostilities, which gives government an essential role in personal life. Government itself is the focus of an identity outside the self, and it is the primary signifier of national identity.

3

Village Culture: West Indian Issues

The village in which fieldwork was conducted, called Windward Valley in my account, is situated on the south windward coast. When the first plantation was established there, Carib lands lay to the south and north. The valley was one ridge of hills south of Fort Dalrymple, the main army encampment on the windward side and the site of the signing of the 1773 treaty with twenty-eight Carib leaders. The valley is known to have been brought under sugar cultivation by 1779, and at that time a cannon installation overlooking the shipping bay was in place to deter Carib harassment of the sugar shipments. As this bay was the only one suitable for shipping on the rough south windward coast, a small dock was maintained for coastwise shipment to the main port in Kingstown. Carib-built and -manned canoes plied between the dock and the anchored sloops, carrying forty hogsheads a day in crop season, one per canoe. The cane grinding mill was powered by the valley stream.

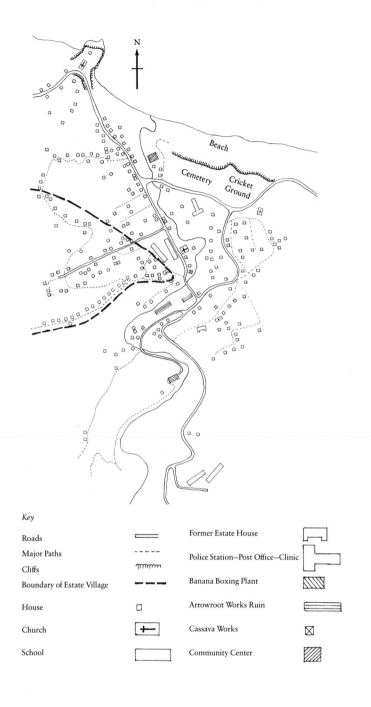

N

Beach

Cemetery

Cricket
Ground

Key

Roads

Major Paths

Cliffs

Boundary of Estate Village

House

Church

School

Former Estate House

Police Station–Post Office–Clinic

Banana Boxing Plant

Arrowroot Works Ruin

Cassava Works

Community Center

Map 4. Windward Valley village.

HISTORY AND CLASS

The first estate owner's name is still the name of the oldest part of the village, although the origin of the name is not recognized by villagers today, and only the names of the most recent estate owners, going back to about 1900, are remembered. This section, which I will call Old Village, was apparently the site of slave quarters. Located on a steep hillside, the area's lower boundaries were marked on later maps, but its hilltop boundaries were unmarked. The only land owned by non-whites at the turn of the century were two narrow strips on the edge of the main road, which were the locations of black-owned shops. Another old area is called "Barracks" and was the site of postemancipation estate laborers' housing. Other than the area for slave quarters and the Barracks, all the land was reserved for cultivation, sugar works, and the estate house, which looked out across the valley to the ocean. It is not known whether the estate house was occupied by owners in early days; as far back as memory goes white managers lived there until the mid 1930s when a white owner and his family lived there. This estate appears on Shephard's 1827 list and was one of the largest on the island, consisting of 666 acres and worked by 511 slaves. Bordering this large estate were smaller estates with their own slave-housing areas. The 1891 census lists the Old Village as having a population of 368 and 79 occupied dwellings. No other documents of village life are known. Elderly residents were interviewed by both me and a village schoolteacher, Robert Fitzpatrick, who published a brief history of the village in 1976. Some villagers recalled the 1898 hurricane that leveled many of the buildings on the island, and along with them the old Windward Valley estate boiling sheds and shipping dock. By that time arrowroot had superseded sugar as the island's leading export, and old-timers remember arrowroot as the main crop on both the estate and small holdings. The estate arrowroot-processing factory withstood the hurricane. It was operated by water power until 1942, and by diesel power until it closed in 1979. In the share-rent system in use in arrowroot in 1920, the estate owner provided the seed, fertilizer, and land, and the grower was obliged to take his crop to the estate factory and pay the planting costs and rent in arrowroot starch. The grower received a small amount of starch, which he could sell, and the edible by-product, which was consumed at home and fed to livestock. In this period estate labor paid a maximum of twenty-four cents per five- to six-hour task for men and half that amount for women. The economist Walker, who wrote of "the abject poverty of a great part of the Negro population outside Kingstown," found the actual wages much lower and the hours longer. A skilled carpenter earned sixty cents per day. In this way estate owners continued production, small farmers operated little above subsistence level, and cash purchasing was at a minimum. Transport to the market was available only for large producers, which was one of the conditions that enforced use of the estate processing facility. Estate owners sent their casks of molasses and arrowroot starch to Kingstown by donkey carts on a coastal road, which was improved in 1914 by several bridges, one of which crossed the Windward Valley stream. Old-timers recall the slow caravan moving north three times a week and returning toward the seaport each following day, lighted at night with torches. A large estate owner began using trucks in the 1920s, "so slow a man could walk beside them."

Community organization was a particular interest of the local village historian and schoolteacher, who had been a member of a village youth circle in the 1960s and 1970s that promoted a community study group and local political initiatives. Calling themselves the Young Agitators, they were only one of a sequence of entirely local organizations promoting similar purposes. The earliest village leader in memory was a black school teacher, brought, as were many teachers in the island, from Barbados to teach students in the Methodist school, which, like a small Anglican school of the same period, was conducted in a churchyard, this one located in the Old Village. In 1907 this teacher spurred the Diocese to put up a separate school building. The same year the Barbadian teacher organized the Windward Valley Social Union, which served as a savings bank and death-benefits society. The island legislature had voted in 1830 to encourage "friendly societies," even before emancipation, placing on individuals responsibility for the proper disposal of their own remains. It is probable that Windward Valley had such a society before the 1907 organizational phase. It has been in existence continuously since then, with factioning and reuniting in 1918. The society went beyond the intentions of the legislature, however, and built a structure that served as a civic center. There the records of individuals' fortnightly ten-cent funeral payments were kept, and there the officers and the public held meetings.

Fitzpatrick noted that there was a black middle class at this time, describing them as four owners of village shops and one owner of a sweet drinks factory. Each occupied one or more house lots in the former slave quarters. This land was estate owned, but house lot boundaries were recognized. One estate overseer in that period was black and several were white.

From 1898 to the 1920s the largest Windward Valley estate, with three of the four major estates along a ten-mile section of the windward coast and adjoining interior lands, were owned by one absentee landlord.

At his death his white Vincentian attorney obtained the northern part of his land, including Windward Valley. In 1931 the mountain estate and part of the valley estate were surveyed into small lots and offered for sale on share-rent and share-purchase bases. The main sources for purchase money were the remittances and savings of émigrés, especially those who worked in oil refineries in Curaçao and Aruba. Lots remained unpurchased after World War II, and at that time additional areas were surveyed and put up for sale. In his history, Fitzpatrick (1976:8) observed that the owners made a fortune from the land.

During World War II the owner of the undivided part of the valley estate lived in the village, and his three children attended the village elementary school. He renovated the old stone estate manager's house, and he reserved from sale the valley land across which his house looked out to the ocean. Several villagers recall working for this family or teaching their children in school.

The surveyors' map of 1931–33 prepared for the sale of these lands shows that aside from the Old Village, the original housing for slaves and laborers, two narrow roadside strips and a small area near the beach where the stream flows into the sea, were owned by local residents. The roadside strips were the site of the early shop residences and the sweet drinks factory. The bridge took some of the beach land and the friendly society also built its meetinghouse there. The division and sale of the estates transformed the community. The local residents took estate land to cultivate on a share-purchase basis and when their crop was is went to Kingstown to the office of the owners' attorney to make their payments. Share renters became landowners, and male and female squatters became house lot owners. "Pieces" of mountain land were bought, and the fruit trees on it—both cultivated and wild mangoes, cocoa, and breadfruit—became the property of village residents. Most of the land was bought by the resident villagers. The few owners who are known to have come from outside were from nearby. Many of the purchasers were émigrés and returned émigrés. Even the share-rent method of purchase appears to have been difficult without the help of savings from employment abroad. A local man, Wheatley Williams, wrote a poem in the 1960s using the imagery of a change from cash crops to subsistence crops to convey the meaning of the transition from estate ownership to small farms. He wrote looking back on the period of his youth, and then went on to comment on 1960s governmental relationships, the lack of attention to the local small producer from the government-owned Banana Association, and attention to the needs of rural children from "tho' dem come big civil servant":

Nobody Remember

From Brighton to Cedar's boundary,
Nobody remember.
From Greggs onto Hopewell Village,
Nobody remember.
Friend, you ask me, "remember what?"
Ah go tell you de whole story.
Dem people dey too ungrateful
Nobody remember.
Long time in de early 'Twenties'
De estates plant groundnut.
Dem plant up dem cane an' cotton
An' den de coconut.
Yam an' tannia, dey didn't like dat.
Arrowroot is de thing dey wanted.
In dem days we bin glad to know dat
Simon ha de breadfruit.

Not only de breadfruit bin dey.
Tannia an' plantain, too.
Remember de golden apple,
Breadnut an' de orange.
So much mango from ridge to ridge,
Ripe banana, an' grindey, too.
In dem days we bin glad to know dat
Simon ha de breadfruit.
Up here in de middle 'Twenties' since the estate sell out,
Ahwe ah de Simon people,
De record will tell it.
First we bin in de group to plant
Lacatan[1] fo' de 'sociation'
Now dem say we too small fo' dem.
Nobody remember.

Friend, yo' ask me, "remember what?"
Same ting ah jus' tell yo'
Some more other tings dem fo'get—
All pickney ah de same.
Dem who live ah town an' city,
An' dem who live ah country village,

All ah dem want dem school an' water;
All ah dem want play-ground.

Some who used to come ah Simon,
Dem still ah remember.
Tho' dem come big civil servant,
But still dem nuh fussy.
So lay ahwe fo'get dem proud one
An' do all ahwe bes' fo' Simon.
Ge dem pickney dem school an' water,
Because we remember.

The elderly poet and his wife now live in a comfortable house provided by their children, and they have small banana fields, but when they were young they had only a subsistence garden plot. The family were Seventh-Day Adventists, and the children were educated at the church college in Trinidad. They made their way from there, one to a clerical job in the United States and one to an elected member of Parliament. A man who also wrote poetry in standard English, he chose to use Creole for his recollection of the transition from estate to peasant ownership.

The community staged two contests with the sellers over areas they had come to consider public lands, the cemetery and adjoining cricket ground and a road. The cemetery was on a high bluff between the beach and the coastal road, the most prominent location in the village yet unsuitable for cultivation and exposed to storms. The resting place of the village dead, it was estate land, like all land. A playing field had been leveled off on one end of the cemetery bluff. The contested road connected the Old Village with the coastal road, the original road from the sugar works to the pier. It was one-quarter of a mile long, also estate land. Both areas were surveyed and put up for sale. In the case of the cemetery and cricket field, the councilor for the district, an appointive office, obtained a government grant to purchase both and hold them for their traditional uses. In the case of the road, when the estate owners blockaded it, the local branch of the Representative Government Association tore the barriers down. Three times the blockade went up only to be torn down. The island administrator, the chief appointee of the British Colonial Office for the island, inspected the right-of-way and decided the road should be acquired for public use.

The village chapter of the Representative Government Association was led by the Barbadian schoolteacher who had been a village leader since 1907, and by a younger man returned from agricultural employment in

Trinidad and in the United States, son of a poor village family, returned to become a small farmer and, later, a shopkeeper. This local chapter "demanded local government status" for the village, a demand not supported by the Windward councilor (Fitzpatrick 1976:10). After the 1935 Kingstown riot, during which Windward Valley was quiet, the association chapter "died." Fitzpatrick wrote, "With [the Barbadian teacher] frailing with age, the government used subtle measures to disunite the villagers," one of them being the replacement of the old schoolmaster activist with a new head teacher. "The upheavals of the 30's revealed the strength of a united working class. The government embarked on building a powerful police force to deter any future workers' uprisings" (Fitzpatrick 1976:13). This is a fair evaluation in view of the government building of rural police stations in the 1940s. In Windward Valley a tract of land that had been selected by the councilor and Representative Government Association for a projected clinic and post office was now to include a police headquarters. The clinic was to have had in-patient beds and to be staffed by a resident doctor and nurse, but after the police station took part of the space, the clinic was reduced to an out-patient service and was staffed by two nurses. The police station is staffed by nonvillagers.

The village population in 1980 was 1,530. Three other communities, situated north, south, and inland of Windward Valley, are closely affiliated with the village and have a combined population of 1,215. These four communities, with a total population of 2,745, share a clinic, schools, churches, police office, and post office and are densely related by kinship ties.

Ethnic differentiation in Windward Valley is as slight as it is island-wide. The population is composed predominately of blacks and persons of mixed descent. Several Portuguese families live in Windward Valley and satellite villages. There is a large concentration of rural Portuguese in a nearby village, but most Vincentian Portuguese live in or near Kingstown, where they are engaged in urban businesses. Several of the Portuguese families in Windward Valley work fifty to seventy-five acres of land, or more than most non-white farmers, and several families have members in the civil service. Their economic level and light skin color elevate their status. No nearby Catholic church serves them, and most of them remain outside the religious practices of the village. Although Portuguese men sometimes marry non-white women, and frequently father children with non-white women, they often do not recognize their illegitimate racially mixed children. In one case a Portuguese father disinherited legitimate children by his legal Afro-Vincentian wife. Illegitimate children of Portuguese and Afro-Vincentian unions have the advantage of light skin but often have the disadvantage of a reduced kin network, unlike illegitimate Afro-Vincentian children, whose paternal kin usually give social recognition. These factors bring about marked social distance and an undercurrent of antagonism between Afro-Vincentians and Portuguese in the village. East Indians are also often socially distant from Afro-Vincentians, but antagonism is not usual. East Indian families employed as schoolteachers and an East Indian Seventh-Day Adventist preacher have lived in the village as well as several laboring East Indian families. Differing in some of their practices, and within easy distance of several large East Indian villages, they tend to be aloof from and be held aloof by Afro-Vincentians.

Economic differences among Windward Valley families are great enough that it is useful to consider two strata present and to refer to them as a lower class and a middle class.[2] The middle class is made up of the families who own the two main shops, farmers owning approximately five or more acres, several families of town office workers, several families of schoolteachers, and several skilled craftsmen. Many of these families also have income from more than one source. Members of both strata may have savings from employment abroad or receive remittances from emigrated members. Standard of living differences are apparent in house size and furnishings, clothing, diet, and occupation. Middle-class women do not do manual work for wages as lower-class women do. The children of all families have their elementary education in the village, but most middle-class children attend secondary schools in town, whereas relatively few lower-class children do so. Some aspects of village life do not correspond to social class, such as church affiliation and political party preference.

Along with these differences in consumption and social status, a shared rural life-style is characteristic. Economic differences bring little separation, because housing is randomly situated and kinship links many of the poor and well off. Deference is shown to higher-ranking persons and employers, and employees recognize their status differences. Mobility through emigration and school achievement has placed many persons born poor into better circumstances. Schoolteachers, for instance, were almost all raised in the village, many in families of low status. Thus the lower and middle classes are thoroughly knowledgeable about both statuses and often closely linked through mobility within the village. The returned emigrants who become farmers narrow the distance between occupational groups because of their experience as wage workers. The "proletarian peasant" is joined by a new type of farmer, schoolteachers, and white-collar worker who cultivate in addition to holding salaried jobs. These "salaried peasants" also bridge social strata.

The gamut of European and African values characteristic of West Indian culture is itself a bridge between different economic statuses. Elite values are familiar to all statuses, and a generalized acknowledgment of and partial adherence to elite values is characteristic of low-status persons. Few observers would deny the sharing of elite values; how deeply the elite values motivate lower-class people is more controversial. I think the poor are genuinely concerned with some elite values. Schooling, for instance, is endowed with middle-class anglophile connotations, bringing that set of behavior and values to the experiences of Vincentian children. Parents work and sacrifice to keep even the lowest achievers in school, where they are at least pursuing respectableness and where parents hope they will achieve employability. People of both low and high status associate race characteristics with value judgements. Lightness of skin color is associated with economic opportunity in rural lower-class thought. Skin color differentiates family members no less than it differentiates economic strata. People perceive fine gradations of skin color and expect a child's performance and opportunities to be closely related to racial appearance. "I the darkest in my family," commented a girl when speaking about having recently dropped out of school. Others are told they have "that little clear" in their skin that makes everyone expect them to do better. A slight lightness of skin enables some of the poorest villagers to reiterate, "Me no like black people." The embedding of originally white symbols in West Indian creole values is expressed also in the respect for government, the strong identification with Christianity, and the prestige of marriage. These very general attitudes and values held by, and familiar to, the average villager make up a set of assumptions that is found in both the lower and middle classes.

Cultural similarity does not bring about marked social cohesion. Indeed there is little sense of cohesion, little social solidarity, and much practice of social avoidance—setting oneself apart from others except for a few close relatives and friends. Neighbors have no obligation to be friendly or cooperative and are often hostile. Yards are marked by carefully kept boundaries, often with hedges; have only one point of entrance, called the *gate;* and are defended by small dogs. Friends call out when they pass, whereas the passersby who are not friends remain silent and both occupant and passer ignore each other. The need for privacy is considered very great in this village where everyone knows each others' personal history and where moral judgments of other people's behavior are freely made. There is little village solidarity in political action, the defense of the road remaining the outstanding exception. Although cultural systems, thoughts, and values are shared, there is low social cohesion, marked differences in living standards, and recognition of status differences.

The relevance of the village to the nation, and village culture to national culture, can be posed in terms of village and town relationships. Kingstown has throughout Vincentian history been the focal center for all rural settlements, and a single day's walk brought rural foods to the town market from the period of Carib dominance to the beginning of bus transportation. Travel from Windward Valley to Kingstown took about one hour by bus in 1972 and approximately half that time by the small vans that had come into use in the 1980s. The single town is still the source of many services used by rural people; for instance, all legal and banking services, the only hospital on the island, specialized training, and many types of commodities rural people have to purchase. Some commute daily to white-collar and service jobs. Others carry their produce by the sack to sell at the central marketing board. A dozen or more secondary school students take vans to town to attend the schools there. There are frequent visits between town and country to kin. The proximity of the village to the town allows town job holders of both low and high status to retain their rural residences. Poor rural relatives keep their contacts with urban middle-class kin and offer as much value in choice fruits and vegetables as they receive from their comfortably situated town kinsmen. The boundaries between town and village are continuously traversed in both directions; townspeople retain their rural sentiments, and villagers become knowledgeable about town life-styles. Although no village residents are members of the small island elite, black or white, sons and daughters of several village families have achieved money or professional status abroad or have married Vincentians of considerable achievement. These persons actively maintain their rural family ties, and some of them also participate in national politics, health care, and musical arts. They represent a link between the village and the black elite. The rural origin of many persons of high national status contributes to a sense of common culture, even where there are large differences in life-style. Because the village was always my place of residence and subject of study, my knowledge of town life is less than desirable. But the many rural and urban interchanges suggest that the middle- and lower-class town and village lifeways may be similar and mutually familiar. Thus the rural model of shared culture between the middle and lower classes may apply to the town and the nation, and the village may be considered representative in some degree of the nation.

Our class model of close relationships between strata contrasts with

Austin's analysis in Jamaica (1984). She builds her analysis of class differences on two contrasting communities, working class and middle class, where life-style is relatively uniform within each community and vastly different between the two. The class-segregated communities that serve Austin's point of strict class cleavage are a recent social type and are suburban. In St. Vincent communities that include both lower- and middle-class persons are traditional as well as rural. In the stratified villages, of which Windward Valley is one, residents have witnessed class mobility, and social distinctions are regularly demonstrated. At the same time, common factors are also visible. These villagers' knowledge of class is probably more precise than it would be if they lived in communities composed of only one class, owing to the experience in personal relations across classes and the presence of a wider segment of the class hierarchy. Knowledgeability of class styles facilitates the model of class mobility evident in Windward Valley. In Austin's model of upward mobility, the attributes of lower-class culture are left behind in the achievement of middle-class status. I suggest that although there are signifiers of middle-class culture achieved in upward mobility, attributes of lower-class status are retained in the process of acquiring these new characteristics. My view is based on the familiarity among members of the two classes in this village, the similarity of domestic organization of families of both classes, and the common participation in schools and churches. Where the upwardly mobile have remained in the village of their lower-class past, their sharing of class attributes is more to be expected than in single-class neighborhoods or situations in which persons leave the village. The small size of Vincentian society, as well as the greater restriction in middle-class wealth compared to Jamaica, may contribute to lesser cultural opposition between classes. Few middle- and high-status employment opportunities are available, and a modest salary level restricts consumption differences except among small numbers of elite families in the Kingstown suburbs. Austin's argument is that ideological and institutional domination of the Jamaican working class by the middle class and political brokerage regulate contrasting class interests. Although I do not disagree with her conclusion, I do not think this domination need result in a rigid division into class cultures such as she poses.[3] One reason the middle class remains culturally connected with its lower-class roots is the richness of lower-class culture. It encompasses broad values and broad interpersonal relationships. Austin described wine shop gatherings and fundamentalist religion as providing lower-class persons' self-definition. Also part of lower-class attributes are the claim to genuineness evidenced by the use of the creole language, the styles of manipulating different emblems of value, the traditional rituals of resolution of low- and high-status values, the training and context for practicing independence and a strong sense of self, the lesser domination of women by men, and a more emotionally expressive dramatic style, all attributes that will be described below. Much of lower-class culture may not easily or willingly be shed by upwardly moving people.

WORKING AND CONSUMING

In some parts of the Caribbean a decline in small farming has been attributed to the effects of migration, including not only loss of a labor supply, rejection of farm work, and removal of small land holdings from cultivation, but also the use of remittances from émigrés for imported foods and other commodities. In the growing inquiry into the effects of Caribbean migration on the sending societies, more questions have been raised than answered and more variation than uniformity has been found (see esp. Philpott 1973; Rubenstein 1977, 1982, 1983; Stinner 1982; Georges 1990:241–44). A different recent emphasis on a high valuation of land as a symbol of kinship pointed up the continued importance of land holding in many parts of the Caribbean (Besson 1987). The symposium papers brought together by Besson and Momsen (1987) described effective practices and traditions in small farming and in the transmission of land use and ownership, affirming the persistence and readaptation of the traditional cultures. This work contrasts to the emphasis, found in many migration inquiries, on the undermining of local culture by world capitalist systems (Rubenstein 1983; Trouillot 1988). Rubenstein's (1982, 1987b) discussions from both points of view, using both local particulars and global theory, showed that these forces act in a dynamic tension. Trouillot also integrated the two perspectives in his study of peasant farming in Dominica, and he saw an erosion of traditional rural social relationships resulting from the adaptation of peasant banana production to the demands of the European market. In my observations in Windward Valley, I am impressed by the effective, tradition-based work patterns in small farming and suggest that associated social relationships are retained.

Windward Valley people pursue a number of kinds of work. Small holdings and rented plots are cultivated for sale and subsistence. Estate employment is available on one small nearby estate in copra production, and two other more distant estates employ wage workers, but the four- or five-mile walk from Windward Valley makes most estate labor a difficult option. Wage labor on road maintenance crews for both sexes, in trucking agricultural produce for men and in banana packing for women, is available. Until 1979 the arrowroot factory was operated by the national Arrowroot Association and employed approximately twenty men and women for half of the year. After it closed a banana packing station was built in the village by the Banana Association, and it provides employment for ten or more persons one day each week all year. Arrowroot has to be taken by growers to a factory several miles distant. Crops other than bananas are taken by sacks on the public trucks to the Kingstown wholesale market. Several traffickers buy in the village and transport small amounts of produce by boat to Trinidad and sell at the market there.

Bananas are marketed through the Banana Association and sold to the Geetz Company, which buys in the Windward Islands and ships to England. In the 1980s banana collection improved in Windward Valley over 1972 methods. A boxing plant was built so that local growers could carry their stems directly to it each week, and methods that allowed growers to box the fruit in the grove where it was cut were developed, thus there was less chance of bruising in the handling and fewer fruits were rejected. Truck roads extended further into the growing areas and the field-packed boxes could be picked up at places easier for the grower to reach. In 1972 the association bought from the producers at collecting points and then trucked the fruit to a boxing station on a large estate. Collection hours were not always met as scheduled, and the extra transport and transfers resulted in loss of sales and lower quality. Medium and large growers usually transport their stems from the groves to the banana station in a car or truck. Small growers' stems are head-carried or carried on narrow wheelbarrows to the boxing plant. Medium and large growers hire helpers to cut and field-pack their bananas, and they sell more often than the one day a week served by the boxing plant because they can truck their fruit to other stations. The building of a local plant thus represents an important improvement for the small growers, and moving it from the estate location to a village where most growers are small and medium producers represents a significant transfer from serving an estate to serving small producers.

Family labor accomplishes all of the production processes for small growers. One family's harvesting methods on one day illustrate how they combine diverse labor resources and coordinate the schedules of family members who hold salaried jobs. Early one morning three brothers and their stepfather went to the mountain grove where they cut the ripe stems, removed the bunches of bananas and sealed the cut edges with paper, and cut beds of tree fronds to lay them on under the banana plants. One son then returned to the village to take a van to his job as schoolteacher. At eight o'clock their mother and grandmother reached the grove. The grandmother set up the cardboard boxes that were stored in a shed and distributed them through the grove while the mother packed the bunches of fruit in the boxes with sheets of plastic padding. The oldest son arrived, and he, the younger sons, and the grandmother head-carried the boxes as they were ready to the shed. The stepfather tended the patches of sweet potatoes and other vegetables interplanted with the bananas. The grandmother picked the ripe mangoes and inspected the pods of cacao beans on the trees. Only the two schoolgirls were excused from work and were sent off to school. An older daughter should have helped, her mother complained, and should have brought her two young children up the mountain, but she stayed home with them. The family worked with great zest in the cool, damp grove. The sons and stepfather wheeled the boxes on a narrow cart down the steep paths to the boxing plant where the husband and wife waited to have their boxes inspected and weighted. It was 4:00 P.M. by the time the mother reached home, seeming refreshed and relaxed by the long day's work and their earnings. She set about cooking a big dinner, and soon the oldest son set off for his night-shift guard job in Kingstown. The relaxation and good spirits of the day's work, the one day that week when the family could earn money from their land, were the regular accompaniment of hard work. Depression, ennui, and quarrels often accompanied idleness. The local wisdom is that people are lazy, especially young men, and exhortations in sermons, speeches, and newspaper columns are to work and not be idle. Lack of enough work, enforced idleness, appears to be more the problem than avoidance of work.

This family, and its one work day, is not entirely typical, as no single family and no single occasion is; however, this illustration contains certain typical elements of the work process, and what is more, these elements differ from the labor process described for a closely related island, Dominica, by Trouillot (1988:198ff.). Significant aspects of the interpretation of the West Indian family derive from the labor process in both Trouillot's account and mine, lending importance to these differences. Trouillot sees a trend in small-farm banana production toward male control of the labor process and earnings. He argues that this industry has augmented female subordination by driving out the older, more diverse rural economy where women could earn and control cash through the cultivation and sale of various crops and through estate labor. Their labor in banana cultivation is subsumed under the sale of the produce by the male head of house, who is also the "principal laborer." In the Dominican village of Wesley, women work as part of male-dominated households. With the earlier type of crop production by women disappearing, Wesley's female-headed households are reduced to insecurity and instability. The long-standing view in West Indian analysis of female-headed households is that they are extremely disadvantaged; I defend the contrary view, seeing these households as functioning similarly to male-headed households. Part of this argument lies in women's access to wage work and the earnings from the sale of crops, including bananas. Other factors of independence, choice, the effects of changes over the life cycle, and women's receipt of support from sons, are equally important. Between the Wesley account and the Windward Valley account, there are factual differences in women's access to earnings, and there are interpretive differences in the place of the female-headed household among all family types and thus in the culture of interpersonal relationships. The last two points of difference will be discussed in later chapters; here I am concerned with women's work and earnings in relation to those of the men in their households. This includes discussion of cooperative family labor and women's occupations.

The tasks of cultivation and harvesting are not always carried out by such a large family contingent. In the Windward Valley case, the oldest son was purchasing the three acres of mountain land where the family grew bananas. His mother had arranged the purchase from her brother, who, having no son or son-in-law in the village, agreed to favorable terms for the sake of transmitting part of his land to a "poor kinsman." The oldest son and the mother received the sale price for the bananas. The stepfather was more knowledgeable about cultivation than this young purchaser, who had not participated in cultivation when growing up because his household had neither owned nor rented land. His stepfather, a recent entrant to the household, worked neighboring land for the seller. The family acknowledged his skills and labor, but he was not a "principal laborer," as Trouillot characterizes the peasant form of labor (1988:210ff.). Some men and women worked alone and some worked with a son. Husband and wife often worked together, sharing many aspects of labor. The husband-and-wife teams who cultivated bananas appeared together at the boxing plant in their pickup truck or walked there together, both unloading and both present as the grader examined their stems. Traditional crops were often tended by women alone, but also by husband and wife. Children often brought their parents lunch and water in the fields. Most days an elderly couple worked together in scattered rented fields growing ground nuts, corn, and sweet potatoes for sale. Equality of these couples in labor and companionship was evident and suggested equal voices in the use of their earnings.

Thus in Windward Valley traditional patterns of cooperative labor are still practiced, whereas Trouillot observed the banana industry introducing a trend toward male control of production and profits. This trend may be present in Windward Valley, but it is not as pronounced as in Wesley. Partial compensation for it in the Windward Valley banana industry is provided by the employment of more women than men in the boxing operations. A division of jobs at Wesley is not indicated, but in Windward Valley three men are employed, one as a grader and two as truck drivers. A recorder may be a man or a woman. Six or seven women at a time wash and pack the fruit. Because packing is women's work at the plant, it has remained their job when it is done in the grove, and experienced women not only pack their own fruit in the grove but also are hired for this work by other growers. The boxing plant continues a division of labor similar to that of the old arrowroot factory, now closed, which provided more jobs for women than men. In Wesley, Trouillot noted no other wage labor for women than estate work. In Windward Valley an additional form of wage labor for women is road maintenance. The lower wage for women than for men in road work as well as in estate and banana packing jobs has been much to their disadvantage, but they do not at present, nor have they in the past, labor primarily as part of a male-dominated household as they now do in Wesley. The availability of wage labor for women, scarce and low paid as it is, has helped support female-headed households.

Trouillot reported on a locale where peasant banana cultivation has been pursued to the exclusion of other crops because of its greater profitability. There may be a similar trend in St. Vincent, but it is not as marked as in Wesley, and social changes that Trouillot saw as associated with it would be hard to perceive in Windward Valley. The Wesley boxing plant is the largest among fifteen in the area and ships the greatest volume of any station on Dominica, and so Trouillot described an intensely developed case. The smaller boxing plant in Windward Valley poses less opportunity for the social distinctions that the Wesley plant generates.

Highly valued subsistence foods make up the greater part of local consumption, and much of the village clothing is also produced locally. Although many imported products are purchased, the use of locally produced foods and clothing indicates a degree of self-sufficiency. Local food crops are the staples of diets in all homes, both poor and well-off ones. Many families plant subsistence crops and perishable vegetables on their house lots, and many households have a "mountain piece" with fruit trees and cultivated vegetables. A household with adult male labor and many children usually cultivates a great variety of kitchen crops, at a minimum sweet potatoes and the tania root with its callilou greens; and many families plant lettuce, tomatoes, green onions, eggplant, edoes, and other vegetables. Most families have access to breadfruit and mango trees, and many cultivate several of the great variety of delicious and healthful fruits that grow well under local conditions. With hard work and varied strengths and skills, large families often grow most of their food. Local vegetables are not only the staples but are savored for their freshness and flavor. Some families make regular use of boiled green bananas, the free rejects from banana grading at the weekly sale for export. Boiled bananas win few enthusiasts, but a visitor soon learns to join in the appreciation of the subtle tastes of plain-boiled tubers, served in combination meal after meal. Breadfruit has come to be an epithet in local self criticism, as in "our breadfruit mentality," and its nutritional value is low, but the starchy fruit is a favorite food. Cash crops also are used in the household kitchen—ground nuts, cacao, breadnuts, and arrowroot starch. Rice is an imported food and appears seldom in the local diet.

A few people prepare cassava meal from the bitter manioc root, a food product introduced by the Carib Indians and still popular, although the skills for its preparation are not widely practiced and the price of finished cassava meal is relatively high. Because it takes several days of work to produce the small quantities, it is mainly a home luxury. Its Carib origin adds to its current appeal, and some young men have learned how to make it from elderly persons. A cassava factory in the village is used by those who want to prepare the refined meal. The large manioc tubers are grated on a nail-punched metal sheet held over a wooden tray.[4] A hand-operated wheel press extracts the bitter juice from the grated roots, and a five-foot-wide cooper basin is used for roasting the grated and leeched pulp. This copper pan is a relic of the old cane boiling equipment from the local estate. It rests on stone piles and is heated by a small fire built under it. The pulp is gradually added to a warm pan and the whole quantity is pushed back and forth with long-handled wooden implements as it slowly dries to a coarse meal. The preparer has to judge the proper temperature of the fire and keep the fire steady and the meal moving. The factory owner, in whose yard the equipment is set up and covered by a tin roof, posts a list of rules and the proportion of the batch of meal to "pay the pan," and he judges when the batch is dry. Before roasting, the cassava roots have been reserved from a grower, dug, transported, washed, peeled, grated, and put in the press. The day after the roasting and after the portions have been paid to the grower and the factory owner, the processor often uses the pan again to make sweet farina by roasting the meal with coconut milk, brown sugar and grated nutmeg. The plain meal is made into wafers and baked on an open pan. The open-sided factory near the center of the village becomes, in this long, slow refining process, a conversation nucleus with several pushers and a fire tender, the owner and passersby. The owner is one of the good village storytellers, and the young men bakers, doing this minor work only as assistants to their grandmother, practice the art of telling miraculous tales here during the long day of work and rests.

Local fishing has declined since 1972 when four to six dories launched from the shipping bay most fair days, each carrying a crew of one or two men. They were Windward Valley men and their boats were made locally, powered by an outboard motor and some powered also by sail. They fished by hooks and lines in the open sea along the coast. Launching and landing were difficult in the rough surf. A wave washing over the boat in landing could wash out the whole catch lying open in the bottom of the boat. Women and men who had come to buy for their own kitchens and for peddling in the village waited to help beach the boats. The best fish were tossed aside for the captain and the crew; the buyers clamored for second best. The fishermen sold at regulated prices and weighed the fish in a scale. The villagers bought all that was brought in. Some buyers salted some of their purchase and dried it in the sun. Only one man and his son fished in 1984, and no one fished in 1986. Fish sellers from the leeward side drove to the windward villages at both periods, more regularly in the eighties, and sold the fish taken by net in the quiet leeward waters.

Fish consumption is not high and meat is eaten even less. A weekly or bimonthly market for beef and the butchering of one animal usually serves the demand. Dividing a whole carcass with a cutlass into the one- or two-pound pieces most housewives buy keeps the butcher stall open all day—a place to show one's metal with quips, rejoinders, and a monitoring of the fairness of the service. The children sent with a bowl and the household order become familiar with the displays of self and verbal skills. The pace is too brisk for storytelling, the gathering too diverse for gossip, and the open exposure is met with displays of strong personality to guard against the always expected hostility. Other meats, such as pork and goat, are offered privately and usually without a market, and home-raised small stock is usually not eaten at home but is sold. Small flocks of various fowls are kept for producing eggs. In 1972 two bakers with large wood-fired ovens sold baked goods, and housewives took them their pans of batter for baking bread and cakes. By the 1980s there was only one such baker. The bakery in Kingstown sold bread and rolls from a van during both periods. Breads are a small extravagance, and most families have bread less often than the starchy vegetables. Home ovens are made of oil drums and fired with charcoal, and it is a special occasion and a devoted cook who finds time for this labor.

The variety and abundance of locally grown food allows good nutrition, but many conditions have to be favorable, such as the ownership of at least a small plot of land; an adult man, either a husband or grown son, in the household to cultivate the ground; and a woman sufficiently unburdened by other responsibilities to prepare a variety of foods to assure balanced nutrition. For poor families the village is a safer locale nutritionally than the town, for there are usually surplus vegetables and people willing to give them to needy persons who associate themselves with well-supplied families and give occasional aid in return. Even in the village the margin of sufficiency is narrow. Families on small, steeply graded lots, or lots with two houses and many children or lacking adequate labor resources, don't have enough food. Some household members visit relatives where a milk cow is kept or fruit trees grow in the yard, and housewives who cook for a large family sometimes regularly feed a relative. Some voice recollections of childhood hunger. People express contentment in terms of having enough to eat, and no longer having to "fight" for food, as young women in the early childbearing period are often characterized as doing. Enthusiasm for traditional local foods runs high and is an important element in local zest. These foods figure importantly in folk songs, the village queen contestants' songs, and prayers that with lyrical phrases praise the scenic beauty, the bounty of the trees, and the soil.

Most clothing needs are served by seamstresses and tailors working in their homes. Seamstresses make all children's and women's dresses, pants, and shirts as well as all school uniforms and some men's and boy's work clothes. One tailoring shop makes men's clothes, their daily wear and their black funeral suits. Four to six women in the central village, and others in the outlying settlements, spend much of their working time making clothes for their clients. They all take apprentices. Fabrics are imported and most are purchased in Kingstown and brought to a seamstress, who suggests designs pictured in her American dress pattern book. School uniforms are required for all children from the lowest to highest grades, and the need for them is constant. Contrasted with 1972, the 1980s showed a large increase in fashionable clothing worn by women and men. Work clothes for everyone were not quite as ragged as in 1972. The seamstresses' and tailors' prices were only slightly higher, and they still produced almost all clothing. Imported ready-made clothing, such as shoes and other small items, are purchased in Kingstown. Local garment sewing is one craft industry that remains adequate to island needs and beneficial in keeping down imports.

In water resources, local technology is not in control, and the Water Authority's arbitrary actions show bureaucratic disregard for the populace. Water is pumped from a mountain reservoir to public taps on the main road. In 1972 several families had piped water from the public line to their houses, and in the 1980 census 47 percent of the houses in the village had running water. The high mountains in the island interior provide a plentiful supply of pure water, but it appears that the pipe system has become overtaxed. Periodic closing of sections of the supply lines is not an announced policy, but this is what happens. Often the water authorities turn off sections of supply lines, for reasons seldom explained and at times unpredictable, so that many people have to draw their water from the main hydrants, most of which are in the center of the village, and carry it long distances up the steep hillsides. For weeks at a time water runs in some sections only in the middle of the night, but so far as the public knows there is no water shortage or inadequacy in the supply lines. With more people having invested in water pipes to their houses, many wait for it throughout a long hot day, no dishes washed, flush toilets (installed in 23 percent of the houses) not used, the laundry carried to the river. Morale sinks until water in the pipes brings everyone alive—water is splashed all around, and hydrants are allowed to run continuously. The Water Authority's refusal to accommodate the residents by explaining policy and announcing schedules reflects the bureaucracy's inattention to public service. The residents do not expect any more rational treatment.

INTERRACIAL UNIONS

Family histories that include interracial unions illustrate the social relationships and values associated with race. Several village families demonstrated descent from white Scottish and English ancestors in their genealogies. These family histories provide insight into the meaning of color and status, revealing the personal level of race and value creolization. The life histories of interracial unions and their progeny are prevailing topics of interest in the village. Descent itself, apart from race mixture, is of great interest, and the knowledge of descent is complex because most descent lines are intricately interwoven by sequential unions. The stability of the population allows widespread knowledge of fellow villagers' personal histories.

Miscegenation was linked by law and ideology with status in New World societies. Throughout Afro-America the social hierarchy of class and race was expressed in the mating patterns of high-status white men and low-status black women in nonlegal unions. The legal restrictions and social ideology that upheld this practice, in one of its many variations, are demonstrated in Martinez-Alier's (1974) study of court cases in nineteenth-century Cuba in which interracial couples petitioned for legal marriage. The requests were opposed by family members and by the state doctrine of the obligation of "lineage purity," and they seldom were granted (1974:15). When the petitions were granted, the grounds were those of the church in support of the recognition and legalization of families and faithful unions (1974:42). Martinez-Alier's purpose was to elucidate the social hierarchy of race and class. Additional questions that her material raises concern the effect on the society of the desire for legal interracial marital status and the example of stable interracial families based on concubinage. These questions can be posed through the family histories of interracial unions in Windward Valley. They give insight into local procedures toward creolization. The interracial unions that were stable and respected, as they appear to have been, exemplified new creolized identities and thus furthered processes of social change. The offspring of interracial unions who were recognized and helped by a high-status parent represent an intermediate status between the plantocracy and the working class, a position that in some areas opened the rigid racial and social structure of Caribbean societies to greater continuity of social relations. This significant process, much studied in New World societies, has been generally considered different in the Iberian and the North European colonized areas, with the Iberian colonies developing an early and extensive free, racially intermediate group, which had a dynamic role in the emergence of creole cultures, and the North European colonies usually denying acknowledgement and freedom to interracial offspring and thus maintaining stronger racial status polarization.

Hoetink's comparisons of different "socioracial structures" developing under the colonization of different European cultures and under different economic and demographic conditions demonstrate great variation and show that the relations of the free intermediate group with the white elite varied more widely than in a simple dichotomy between Iberian and North European colonies, and that even between the two Dutch colonies of

Surinam and Curaçao, the presence and roles of these groups were markedly different (Hoetink 1973:6ff.). Following this model of variation, the Vincentian family histories likewise show that interracial unions were proceeding along lines usually overlooked in the existing analytic models. In these examples, coresidence of the interracial couple was usual, wealth was transmitted, and unions of respected statuses were lifelong. One Windward Valley case calls attention to the effects of low-status white male parentage on racially mixed descendants. The presumption that the social advantages of such unions would ordinarily have been slight brought little attention to unions of this type, but this case will show that the descendants did have advantages. Another case shows white and racially mixed women marrying below their racial status yet maintaining relatively high status in these marriages. In Windward Valley more typical cases of high-status men mating with women of lower color status, in coresidence and extraresidentially, had both typical and atypical social outcomes. Also of interest in these cases is the apparent amicability of the Windward Valley interracial unions, especially as power and prejudice is so much a part of this subject. Cooperative relationships would have furthered creole identities more than relationships seen as antagonistic or exploitative by the social group.

Two lines descend from a white Scottish *bond slave*—the term the descendants used. The Scottish bondsman fathered a daughter and a son in Windward Valley by two black women. His daughter had her mother's surname, as is usual when there is no marriage, but he gave his surname to his son, a not uncommon practice for either daughters or sons. Both his daughter and son had died before I began my fieldwork. Four persons in the third generation of this genealogy were informants, and three unrelated informants confirmed the race and nationality of Grandfather W, as we will call this man, and gave other information about the family. His daughter's 1871 date of birth was established through her age at death, ninety-six, in 1967. The reasonableness of her living to this age is supported by her son's recent death at age ninety-eight and the fact that all her children who lived beyond childhood, eleven in all, have lived to advanced ages. From her 1871 birth date, the arrival of Grandfather W in Windward Valley is estimated as about 1865. This date is near the end of the period of importation of contract labor, which began in 1846. Small numbers of indentured laborers were obtained from Great Britain during this period. These circumstances lend credibility to the family traditions of Scottish ancestry, allowing time for the bondsman to work out his contract and arrive in Windward Valley.

His daughter's children and grandchildren spoke frequently of her:

"She taught us the rough and the fine." Her children had more village schooling than many people of their generation and could read and write unusually well. An unrelated informant described her as "a very nice lady" and "a big Methodist," and said her skin color was light and her hair wavy. Tending to confirm the race of Grandfather W was the information that his son owned five house lots on the edge of the Old Village and his daughter owned three lots contiguous to her brother's property. Few blacks owned land in the old plantation village in that period. Permission to squat and build a house there had to be obtained from the plantation manager. That inheritance and boundaries came to be acknowledged among the residents is indicated in the squatters' later engagement of attorneys to establish legal claims, a procedure that was necessary because the estate survey conducted for division and sale in 1931 did not include the Old Village. Grandfather W's eight lots, which were left for his children's use, were on the western face of the valley wall where it curves out into the path of the winds from the ocean, exposed to hurricanes and treeless, less desirable land than the central slopes where houses and trees were protected from winds. When Grandfather W came to the village, the weather-beaten cliff would likely have been unclaimed, considering the low village population of that period. The white bondsman appears to have been a squatter there on the fringe of the black settlement. He was still there when his daughter had her first child at age twenty in 1891, and "he did not like that black child," one granddaughter said. All her subsequent children are said to have been by another black man. They were said to be lawful children, but the fact that they all have their mother's surname indicates that the term *lawful* is used figuratively, as is sometimes done in reference to the children of long-term common-law unions. Grandfather W left Windward Valley some time after the birth of this first grandchild. "He all about," one of his granddaughters had been told by her mother. A granddaughter born after 1910 does not remember him. He left his daughter three house lots and his son five, and hers were the highest and most windswept. This "inheritance," for the claim was only squatter's rights, was relatively large, for most families had only a house spot or two, and some a garden plot.

Aside from the small benefit of these lots to the two family lines, other slight economic and status advantages of mixed parentage are discernable. Grandfather W's son was a minor shop keeper. His ownership of five lots was remembered as impressive to a man of his children's generation. His daughters said he strictly ruled the family. He enjoyed music and he sent to Scotland for a book of vocal and organ music. His father may have provided directly or indirectly the inspiration for reaching out to the white homeland, or the church hymnal title page may have reverberated with a desire to connect with his father's country. He was among the few who kept a cow, and milk is often a relished memory of some childhoods. His daughters had only one child each, and in their old age having never entered a common-law or marital union, they tended to put on the fluttery air of higher-status women. They lived on the family house lot, building two relatively ornate cement-block houses before 1972. Their brother had emigrated within the West Indies, and with his earnings he had purchased the only fine house in the village, a house built for the concubine of an estate owner who is a figure in a family history discussed below. When Grandfather W's grandson purchased the house, it had fallen into disrepair and soon afterward it collapsed. Among the children of Grandfather W's daughter, all emigrated except two daughters. Several of them lived in Trinidad, and one son returned with earnings enough to buy land. He had done farm labor in Trinidad, Cuba, and the United States and was an early land purchaser when the local estates were divided. Also owner of a shop that his wife managed, he had become by his old age in 1972 an owner of approximately twenty-five acres. His two sisters who remained in the village had supported themselves by wage labor. They had no legal or common-law mates and continued to live in the maternal house. The six unrecognized children of one had grown up and helped her, whereas the other sister's only child, born when she was past thirty, emigrated to England and sent her money occasionally. Lacking land and labor resources to produce cash crops, however, they were subject to the scarcity of employment and low wages affecting all the island, especially scarce and low for women. By the time the Scotsman's great grandchildren needed house lots, the extra lots were important assets. Aside from the daughter's house, which was home for the two granddaughters, the other two inherited lots were left to her favorite grandson. One was used as collateral for a loan to send a great granddaughter to England. The payments on the loan were made by this son's mother and sister from intermittent heavy labor, thus giving them eventual ownership, and this sister was allowed to build a house there in 1979. The son built on his remaining lot in 1986. By that time the growth of the village population, and the increase in the cost of land, meant that the house lots provided an important margin of security for these descendants. The land history is an element in the account that helps to confirm the race of Grandfather W. The slight information about him falls into a consistent pattern in which the information that he was white is reasonable. Claims of white ancestry in the West Indies are said to have mythic aspects, but the consistency of information helps to establish a genealogy as historical rather than mythic. A fifth-generation descendent of Grandfather W migrated to New York and cited his genealogy in a verbal clash with a New Yorker. Saying the racism there was a shock to him and a brand of prejudice he had not met in St. Vincent, he told also of being called an "African." "I say to him, 'My great grandmother was a white woman and my great great grandfather was a white man. So how you say I am African?'" The descendants of the white indentured laborer claimed to be better because of their white ancestry and claimed it loudly in each generation. With no material advantage other than several barren house lots, the poorest descendants acted out shreds of higher-class behavior. They strove for accomplishment while constantly limited by the constraints of severe poverty, being considered low status by other villagers, and having no opportunities. They strove by many means: through pressure on the children to achieve at school, through a cooperative family economy, and through fundamentalist religion. Pride, haughty manners, ready self-defense in arguments, and a sense of self-worth were the main achievements of the members of this family. Vigor and pride are widespread and important. Other families acquire these qualities from whatever they can summon up. This family attached their pride to their ancestry and to their barely visible phenotypic features. Race and parentage and the status they imply are among the counters that can be used as personal resources. In a society that conceives of the social field as dynamic, as Vincentians tend to do, any status signifiers take on social importance. Statuses are judgments of many parts, and manipulation of reputation has been described with some frequency in Caribbean societies.

In the second genealogy the white English father was an overseer for the valley estate. He lived in the local estate house with his white wife and children in the late 1920s and early 1930s. He had a son by a dark village woman, recognized him, gave him his name and helped him financially. At each period of fieldwork, his half-sister by the same mother and a black father told the well-known village story, perhaps first repeated by a servant, that the overseer's wife objected to his recognition of his son, saying, "You put me down," and that he replied, "I not put you down, they respectable people." The mulatto son cared well for his mother. He married a widowed village shopkeeper who had returned home from Trinidad with her first husband to open a shop. The shop thrived, and with his father's help the mulatto son acquired a moderate acreage of land, and from their businesses they and their four children were able to emigrate to Brooklyn in the mid-1970s, leaving their lands in the care of a manager.

The third genealogy is that of a white English estate owner and his concubine. An ornate house with balconies and fretwork was built on the main road of the village by an elderly local white estate owner for his young mate, a daughter of a black village woman and a mulatto overseer. Behind the fine house, her mother built her wattle-and-daub house and bore her other children by black men. The two houses formed a cooperative kinship unit. During this time the young woman bore a black child. Her bold adultery did not bring an end to the concubinage, and it lasted until the planter's death. The child was sent to the care of an unrelated village woman and died within a year, the cause of death identified by village women as marasmus. The baby's death was a distressing village memory, and the only case of marasmus identified in a village in which medical terms for illness are seldom heard. It was told as a tragedy rather than an occurrence for which the mother was to blame, for her actions were to be expected under her circumstances. The sad acknowledgment that she had to let her black child die expressed the tragic dimension of the racial status system, which they all understood. The estate owner and his concubine had no children. In addition to the Windward Valley house, he built her a fine house in Kingstown and they traveled widely in the West Indies. After his death she married the mulatto overseer of his brother's estate several miles up the coast, and she moved to a more modest house there. She inherited both houses from her white keeper and sold them both. Her mother and a black half-sister continued to keep close ties with her, and her sister would walk with fresh fish from the beach to her house and took her laundry home. Employment as a laundress—work advantageous for women because it can be done while tending one's children—was hard to come by in the village. The black mother and sister continued to benefit from her rise in status.

The fourth genealogy illustrates the reverse of these cases of female hypergamy. In two succeeding generations, women of high-status families married dark, lower-status men. In the small population of whites and even smaller population of high-status whites, there may have come about attitudes of acceptance concerning women's marriage "down" the racial scale. The Windward Valley descendent who was the main informant is called Mrs. H. Her maternal grandmother was a white Scottish woman married in Scotland to her white husband before the couple emigrated to St. Vincent and bought a small estate (probably about 1860). Of their two daughters and one son, all born in St. Vincent, one daughter married a Vincentian-born white estate owner and one, born about 1885, married a "dark" man who practiced the relatively well-paying trade of carpentry. They lived on a large estate where he was employed. Their three sons grew up to be managers of the same estate, and their daughters were trained to tasks of the estate house. Two of their daughters emigrated to New York and later moved to Trinidad, living in comfortable circumstances. Another daughter, Mrs. H, was born in 1908 and married at age twenty-nine in 1937 a "dark" carpenter, age thirty-three, from Windward Valley who met her while he was employed on the estate where her father was also a carpenter. Her age at marriage and her virtue, demonstrated in having no children before marriage, suggest that advantageous marriage prospects for a mulatto woman, even one growing up in an estate house, were not numerous at that time. This may be related to the depressed economic conditions during the 1920s and 1930s and to the relatively small number of people in the planter group. White landowners' desertion of the colony may have reduced the chances of hypergamy for white and racially mixed women and initiated pressures for their marriage to darker partners. The owner of the estate where Mrs. H grew up gave her a dowry of house furnishings. Did he make this unusual gift in lieu of being able to arrange a marriage of higher racial status? Greater acceptance of racial integration may have become customary if social conditions caused similar alliances.

Mrs. H brought her furniture to Windward Valley to the newly constructed room attached to her husband's family house on a small plot of former squatter's land near the beach, recently deeded legally. Her husband's sister and she did not get along, and so her husband moved their room to a lot he had purchased in the 1931 estate division and later built a cement-block house there. Her husband had previously worked in Trinidad and for periods after their marriage continued to work there. He died working on a carpentry job in St. Vincent in 1958. Mrs. H always spoke of him with devotion, and clearly the marriage had been happy. By the time of my 1972 fieldwork, two of their sons had emigrated to the United States and were both well employed there. Their four daughters lived in Windward Valley, one married to a U.S.-trained civil service employee of medium rank, two at home in the type of relationship called *visiting*, and the youngest engaged to be married to a highly respected young civil servant. Among the fathers of the two unmarried daughters' children were men of achievement who lived outside the village. The oldest granddaughter from these unions, who had been recognized and helped by her light father, was the common-law wife of a well-to-do black marine engineer. This young woman used the term *elite* for herself and her husband, and they lived in an expensive house in a highly prestigious area. Mrs. H was treated with much respect, and her sons' achievement, one as a physician and the other as an accountant, was the reason most often given for the respect accorded her.

Not a person to easily allow closeness or interrogation, especially as I had sought informants among those who were below her in status, it was only on a return trip that I was able to establish a more trusting relationship with her and her daughters. At this time she invited me inside to talk and wanted me to hear the family history.

Mrs. H clearly was middle class in the village context. Her house was situated "on the flat," the level central part of the village with other middle-class families. Her modest house was similar to neighboring middle-class houses. Unlike some of the families she employed no servant, possibly because a granddaughter, whose mild spastic condition had prompted the family to keep her out of school, enjoyed caring for the house. Mrs. H herself did all the cooking for the large family, which at different times contained one or both of her unmarried daughters and their eight children. Her two sons' achievements abroad afforded not only great pride but also regular financial help and a trip to the United States for her and her unmarried daughters. In the years after her husband's death she had not fared as well, but at that time her sons and daughters were local primary school-teachers and helped out. Her husband had bought estate land and planted it with fruit trees, and she continued to manage these farmlands. One son won the island scholarship to the University of the West Indies, and when his medical training there gained him entrance to the United States for further training, all of this land had to be sold to pay for it. In Mrs. H's family line her racial status was effectively maintained even with a marriage to a man of lower racial status, her racial type conferring a kind of absolute status. One of her daughters said, "We so dark because of our father." They all acted the role of high-status women, which in the village context is middle class, and all chose their mates from higher-status men. Their participation in visiting marital unions did not lower their status. They and the other villagers made it clear that they were far above ordinary people. One of them was called "Mrs." and the surname of a previous high-status mate. *Mrs.* is an honorific; *Mistress* is used to address a legally married woman. Thus the status acquired from a well-born mulatto mother, a status not too much diminished by a respected black craftsman father and bolstered by becoming schoolteachers and by high achieving brothers, maintained these women's positions. Visiting unions are not more associated with the lower class than the middle class, and it is a regularized practice with proper forms. Although not favored, the example of this family well attests to the social acceptance of this form of marital relationship.

The histories of these families affirm in some respects that the hierarchical system of race and class found throughout Afro-America determines the codes of interracial mating. It is striking, however, that these histories contain much information contrary to the prescriptions of this hierarchy. For a white woman to marry out of her race was proscribed, but here a white estate owner's daughter and her black husband were employed on another white-owned estate and raised six children there. In the next generation of this family, their mulatto daughter married a black man and maintained a high-status rural family. Equally abhorrent to the racial hierarchy was the adultery of a white man's black concubine with a black man. In this case the woman acquiesced in the abandonment and death of her child from this adultery, but she did not lose her status or her inheritance as would be expected according to prevalent racial views. These cases do not suggest that present formulations of the hierarchical relations of race and class are wrong, but, rather, they remind one that actions contrary to social systems often occur. These countercultural interracial events must have been influential. As reversals of colonial-imposed values, these local dramas represented the social viability of interracial families. Epitomizing creolization, they symbolized the transformations taking place in the social order. As forces for creolization, they not only produced legitimate, middle-class, and racially intermediate families, but also furthered the growth of local identity by successfully violating the colonial race system.

PARENTAL TIES

Although the organization of creole families has received major analytic attention, the meanings associated with this system have been studied less. The main contributions and debates of the 1960s and early 1970s concerned the systemic characteristics of mating and the family. For this question the taxonomic method of Michael G. Smith was well suited to sorting out types of mating and variations in systemic characteristics (M. G. Smith 1962). At that time the explanation of meanings invested in these systems, which was put forward by Rodman, achieved some concurrence (Rodman 1971). He proposed that lower-class persons only partially comply with the values they accept. Although not practicing legal marriage and legal parentage, they nevertheless value these legal statuses. They accomplish this through what Rodman called *value stretch,* whereby attitudes of *personalism* and *permissiveness* allow the nonobservance of codes they believe are correct. This interpretation is Rodman's; he did not arrive at it through his informants' explanations. It assumes European and American meanings of marriage and legitimacy, and whether these were West Indian mean-

ings as well was not asked. In his interpretation domestic morality is inde-
terminate, and self-justification substitutes for conviction about propriety,
and thus the existence of culture is negated. The study of meaning and ideology of the family has had a new start in the ethnohistorical research of
Martinez-Alier (1974) and R. T. Smith (1977, 1987, 1988). They have documented Caribbean reinterpretations of European family concepts during
the colonial period. Their studies of transformations in European family
ideas and practices among all races and classes make essential the ethnographic study of local meanings and contexts of family forms. Impetus
to these inquiries has come also from increased interest in ideological and
symbolic aspects of culture. Part of this new anthropology, Besson's studies
of Jamaican peasant culture, show that legal and nonlegal forms of mating
are all valued in terms of the purposes associated with each, and both female and male headship of families have value. She notes that the practices
have strong moral force, and finds them to be part of a culture of resistance
to colonial elites' domination (Besson 1988). Thus she describes the meaning of the system to the members of the culture. The meaning of the domestic system also has been the focus of research with middle-class Jamaicans.
Jack Alexander (1976, 1978, 1984) was able to elicit and record detailed
discussions of the meanings and interpretations of domestic practices. His
rapport and methods achieved rich and discursive responses. My own attempts to understand my informants' constructions of meaning and value
do not have as expressive a textual basis, but use a broader cultural context.
My lower-class informants did not engage in introspection in interviews, as
the Jamaican middle-class informants did, and they withdrew in response
to my introduction of a tape recorder by saying, for instance, "I don't look
back, I had it so hard." I thus made use of casual encounters to introduce
my questions and had to remember the responses for later notation. Just as
important as their responses in conversation with me were their conversations with others in my presence, as well as their invitations to accompany
them on visits with significant persons. These visits and exchanges often
seemed intentionally explanatory in the choice of person to visit and the
message I was to overhear. This intentionality, as well as many impromptu
verbal explanations, made it clear that my informants expressed regularized ideas about familial practices. The rural middle-class families I
worked with also did not engage in introspection. A large part of their reticence with me was due to my extensive association with lower-class informants, which to those in the middle class showed my lack of proper status
discrimination.

I will describe the meanings I found in the familial practices as I proceed. My analysis owes much to studies of the structures, systems, and origins of these practices in the Caribbean. I was able to start with definitions and orderings of systemic factors, finding them applicable in my field site, and to pursue what the system means to people and how its meaning varies over the life cycle. It was clear that the family practices had great import in personal lives and self-concepts. My objective was to find a cultural level of the local institutions.

Family relationships are the central feature of village society. Strong attachments between mothers and children and marked social emphasis on obligations between fathers and children represent much of the emotion and force of village life. Considerable complexity in the matter of nuclear family membership contributes to the high level of social attention and social action surrounding family relationships. Obligations and sentiments between other close kinspeople may also be important, but they take second place to parental ties. The complexity in family relationships arises from the different mating arrangements found here and in most West Indian societies. These mating arrangements differ most importantly according to whether the couple takes up a common residence, and according to the legalization or nonlegalization of the union. Marriage is legalized and the couple has a common residence; common-law unions are not legalized but the couple resides together; and in visiting unions the man visits the woman in her house, which is usually her parent's house. All mating forms are socially recognized, and customs are associated with each type of union. Marriages probably endure longest, but they are easily broken by separation or divorce. Common-law unions appear to last as long as marriages but their dissolution involves no legal complications or sense of lowered status for the woman, as follows a dissolved marriage. Visiting unions may endure a brief time or for years. Women ordinarily are involved in only one such union at a time, whereas men sometimes have more than one visiting mate.[5] Marriage carries with it legal rights and responsibilities and legal birth status for the children. Couples living in common-law status have no legal rights or responsibilities, except as courts sometimes award them, and their children have to be legally recognized by the father to be his heirs. Children of visiting unions are seldom legally recognized either at birth or later, but it is possible to establish the legal paternity of such children. Social acknowledgment of paternity is usual. Support of children is less frequent, although women devote much attention to the recognized social fact of paternal obligations to their children. This way of structuring the interests and attachments among parents and children leaves an open field for promotion of those interests and attachments in culturally regular ways.

Also of central importance is the effect of the union forms on household composition and organization. Moreover, moral values are associated with these union forms, affecting churches' judgments of couples and affecting persons' self-concepts. There is much talk and thought about these intricately varied forms, especially in relation to the self.

Recent research on the kinship resulting from nonlegal unions and on some of the social characteristics of the union forms has brought much clarity to the subject. That kinship through nonlegal unions is as much recognized as legal kinship has long been stressed by Raymond T. Smith. He has recently confirmed this through his study of historical materials and genealogies from different socioeconomic strata in Guyana and Jamaica. Concerning the structure of genealogies, he concluded that "the focus here on differences between classes has shown them to be few . . . The most significant finding is that non-legal unions generate extensive and enduring kinship ties; . . . Equally important is the finding that men are important links in the chain of kinship in all groups, contradicting the idea that unstable conjugal unions expunge males from kinships networks and genealogies" (R. T. Smith 1988:79).

Several significant findings on the social characteristics of women in different mating forms have also contributed to clarification in these matters. In Roberts's research on fertility and associated practices in four West Indian societies, including St. Vincent, one finding that is most relevant to these interests concerns the social status of women in visiting unions. The women's level of education ranked midway between the lower school level of women in common-law unions and the higher level of women in marriages (Roberts 1975:203). Based on the 1960 census, this finding suggests tradition more than change. Was the visiting union, which had often been represented as little removed from promiscuity, sometimes as close to prostitution, higher in status than the common-law union that often had been prefaced with the adjectives "stable" and "faithful"? The same ranking relationship was found by Betley in the Vincentian town of Barouille. Terming the three conjugal relationships *keeping* (comparable to my use of *common law*), *visiting,* and *marriage,* he found that keeping was held in the lowest esteem because it demonstrated the desire to be a couple but the rejection of the obligations of marriage. Visiting was ranked higher because it was the testing of a relationship that might become marriage or keeping, but did not yet convey rejection of marriage. Almost equal numbers of household heads were in each of the three types of conjugal union (Betley 1976:112). In further research on Jamaican women's mating behavior, Roberts and Sinclair (1978:284–89) wrote:

Popular views that the visiting union exposes the woman to hardships and that she faces particular difficulty in virtue of the absence of the male from the household do not find much confirmation from the present findings. Careful consideration of views of respondents points definitely to their position that this form of family accords them a degree of freedom and independence which they hold to be greatly to their advantage. Even from the standpoint of the support of their children and the family as a whole, they maintain that the absence of the partner is by no means a disaster. . . . In so far as the children play a role here, a factor to be reckoned with is that women may prefer a visiting or common-law union as these ensure fuller control, and even complete custody, of their children, which may be lost in formal marriage.

Sutton and Makiesky-Barrow's discussion of family and gender relationships centers on their premise that sex roles in Afro-Caribbean societies do not represent the authority-subordination axis found in European societies, and they describe the different, more equal gender relations in a Barbadian community. This is a particularly important issue because much attention is being focused on the nonequality of women in public sectors such as trade-union membership, political office, and employment (see especially Clarke 1986). Although women are disadvantaged in these arenas, they maintain a strong traditional social position and a tradition of female autonomy and authority. Sutton and Makiesky-Barrow (1977:322) sum up: "We have found that women's independent income-producing activities, combined with their positions within the kinship system, provide a basis for their autonomy and self esteem and for maintaining a relatively equal balance of power between the sexes. Moreover, they operate with a cultural ideology that attributes to women and men a similar set of positive valued characteristics and abilities and that identifies parenthood and sex as two highly valued experiences."

Discussing the peasant women of Martha Brae, Jamaica, and critiquing Wilson's (1973) dichotomy of European-derived female "respectability" and indigenous male "reputation," Besson (1988:12) writes, "I have argued that their respectability, focused on the house and yard, Baptist Church, and family system, is not a mirror image of Eurocentric values but an aspect of the Afro-Caribbean peasant culture of resistance." Her portrayal of women's community authority and organizational dominance and their experience of sexual freedom greatly enlarges the scope of ethnography, which for long has dwelled on male sexual superiority and rejection of family responsibility.

My own view of the domestic culture of Windward Valley sees it as a well-articulated system. The absence of a common residence for the parents and children of visiting unions, the first child-bearing unions of most women and men in Windward Valley, accounts for some of the associated characteristics. Although the fathers are outside the household, their attachment to the mother and child is considered strong and valuable, and much attention is devoted to demonstrating links to fathers outside households. In this village visiting unions most commonly endure for the birth of two children and then either dissolve or change into a marriage or common-law arrangement. Families tend to have a schematic form in which sequential sets of full siblings, or sequential single children, are linked by attachment and responsibility to different fathers outside the household. When a woman enters a coresidential union, as a majority do later in life, her husband may be the father of only her youngest children, or even none of them. Her older children are expected to be cared for by their own fathers until adolescence, and thereafter the father-child tie is expected to continue as a sentiment. Because the household contains several sets of siblings, differentiated by paternity yet unified in their maternal kinship, patrilateral obligations toward the children in the house come, or should come, from several external sources. Paternal ties from a man's point of view are described as "he have children all about": his children by several women are living in different households. From a woman's point of view, her children are usually collected in her household while their fathers are "all about." Children generally go to the father or paternal relatives to ask for regular allowances of money for support and special needs, expressing the household's multiple sets of siblings and lines of obligations. One effect of the several lines of paternity among siblings is that the children in most households are more differentiated than children in coresidential nuclear families. This differentiation is one factor leading to individuated interpersonal relationships as a fundamental orientation of Windward Valley culture. This schematic plan is varied in practice, and nuclear family households are an ideal and often occur. However, the absent yet caring father/husband and the matricentered household depict the village's primary experience of the nature of families.

Although extraresidential mating, termed *friending* in the village and *visiting* in most analyses, is more informal than marriage and common-law unions, it has formal elements, and these formalities are kept in the public attention by the close kinspeople of the woman participating in this type of union. The couple's meetings ordinarily take place in the woman's house, and her mother or parents take on a cordial, or at least a facilitating, relationship with the daughter's friend. Paternity in these arrangements is known by the family and neighbors, and ordinarily the friend promises the woman's parents that he will recognize and care for their child. When the couples meet some place other than the girls' homes, their parents and neighbors usually know about the relationships and thus paternity is known, but promises of responsibility for children may not be made to the parents.

If a couple stays together for the birth of a third child, they customarily set up a household together, and many women who bear many children under the visiting practices eventually reside with a husband. Most middle-aged men and women are head couples in households. Women who never marry or have a common-law husband raise their children with or without help from childrens' fathers, through their own hard work, living in their family house, sharing in the family plot, with aid from their mothers, and, eventually, aid from their sons and daughters.

The web of relationships that results from sequential extraresidential mating makes kinship identification complex. Multiple paternal lines among siblings make the knowledge of kinship important. A person cannot be called a child of a family—both parents have to be identified. Whole and half-siblingship is usually specified, and whether half-siblings have a common mother or a common father. Many descriptive terms are used; for instance, terms for siblings include *same mother same father, same mother's children,* and *same father's children.* Descriptive terminology is extended to cousins, using the terms *two brothers' children, two sisters' children,* and *brother and sister's children.* Linkages to more distant relatives are familiar knowledge and readily described by adults and children. Conversations identifying kinsmen are commonly heard. Children, as they gather for an evening of talk, with or without adults, enumerate the persons "who call me Uncle" or "who call me Aunt" and name the child's half-siblings through his or her father or half-siblings through the mother, who may not live in the child's household. In conversations villagers identify the legality or illegality of their own births and those of family members and other villagers. Who raised an individual is equally well known and referred to in identifying persons. Fixing in mind scattered kinsmen and claiming the status of having kinsmen are accomplished in these conversations, and they convey also the pervasive individuated characteristic of personal relations, a concept with important ramifications.

That the paternal relationship establishes an obligation to support the child is a matter of central importance in Vincentian social thought. Carrying through the paternal relationship and the financial support that goes with it is an explicit value. The paternal obligation is independent of sexual relations with the child's mother, and because she is expected to be faithful to her current mate, the paternal obligation to her children is not related to her sexual services but to their child's right to paternal recognition.[6] Cultural norms are not always followed, and paternal support is often sidestepped in St. Vincent, as it is in the United States, but the rule is important in Windward Valley and men and women refer to it frequently.

Child-support payments are small and specifically for support of the child, not the household, but this does not differ from household income in general, which is made up of many small contributions.[7] A young village woman compiled a list of forty-seven children of extraresidential mating who ranged in age from infancy to seven years. The fathers of twenty-five of these children supported them, and two others were supported by their paternal grandmothers, a total of 57 percent of the children. In only two cases was the informant uncertain about whether the child had paternal support. Approximately the same proportion of emigrated men as men who remained in the village supported their children. Eleven of the children's fathers had left St. Vincent and thirty-six had remained, and 54 percent of the men who emigrated and 58 percent of the men who remained supported their child. The émigrés had larger earnings than the village men, but they were more out of reach of village pressures to support children. In an interview study of 1,359 Jamaican women, Stycos and Back reported that "the most frequent source of outside support (43 percent) is a previous mate who fathered one or more of the respondent's children" (1964:334). Roberts and Sinclair found that in Jamaican visiting unions, 34 percent of children under age fifteen were supported solely by their fathers, and those children supported by both parents brought the total who received paternal support to 58 percent (1978: table 9.6). Recognition of an outside child goes beyond money payments and is similar to full parental support. It includes the father's obligation to help the child until the child can contribute to his or her own support, through, for instance, paying for school costs, arranging an apprenticeship for a son, and giving clothing to both sons and daughters. The relationship should be personal and reciprocal, with the child owing services and affection in exchange for support. Fathers living away from their children were summoned by the mothers to discipline children, even in some cases to punish an adolescent daughter for disapproved meetings with men. Adults frequently reflect on their relationship with an outside father, recalling his gifts and regard for them and comparing legitimate siblings' inheritance rights with their own lack of rights.

Although the outside-father relationship is highly variable, there are regularities in it. The outside father is thought of as a potential resource for special requests, in case of unusual hardship, or for the favors he may be in a position to grant. The distance itself, the intermittent nature of relations with him, may be used to advantage. Although we do not have adequate data on this type of relationship, the following case will illustrate its complexities. Shortly before the birth of his first outside child, a man received a one-year jail sentence for stealing a shirt. When he entered jail, his pregnant friend from town was invited to visit his mother's house in Windward Valley—a gesture of recognition—but when the baby was born, the paternal grandmother did not "mind" it, having little income herself, indeed, having suffered the loss of aid from her jailed son. Her son could not support the child, a girl, and he did not recognize her legally and seldom saw her. She was raised by her mother and maternal grandmother, persons said to be more poor than the father and paternal grandmother. Some years later the father saw his daughter with a group of young children and learned that she had been left behind her age level in school. He felt ashamed, according to his niece who later told the latter part of the story, and asked his sister, a woman with unrecognized children and no resident husband, to raise his child. The child's mother "gave her" to her father, and he supported her in his sister's house. This case indicates that becoming a father in an extraresidential relationship has important effects on the father and his close kin. Ethnographies have been little concerned with the paternal aspects of visiting relationships, being primarily attentive to how the system legitimizes sexual freedom for men.

These parental obligations interlace the village as networks of aid or potential aid. The obligations may acquire more sentiment with age or more estrangement, they may become more valuable if the father prospers, or they may never be strengthened with gifts, but everyone is much aware of them. On several occasions informants purposefully took me to chat with persons related in this way, as though displaying their contact with me and informing me of their networks. A middle-aged woman took me to visit her father's sister in a distant village. Her relative's living situation was a little more comfortable than hers, and the visit was formal and congenial, lasting close to two hours. The caller used the "Tante" form of address, though her father had been a visiting mate and had fathered her alone of her mother's children. She had carefully arranged her news and planned her comments. Concerning her father she said, "He used to call me to come to he, say 'I love to see you because you remind me of Mommy, you have the look of Mommy.' But he never give me a thing." Commonly women keep ties with the female kin of the father of their child and with their own father, whether he recognizes them or not. Old visiting mates can be heard greeting one another in a jocular tone. A young woman's comment about a friend of her mother's who is not her father but a step-sibling's father, "He always says he will help me when I need it," indicates that the aid in this case may extend to a step-sibling of the man's child. Some of these ties have never produced help and are only bitterly noted. Along other ties obligations are met, or have been completed and continue to be ties of good will and potential aid. In the migrant communities abroad, where more job opportunities can be ferreted out than in St. Vincent, the network of male kin through nonlegal unions is surprisingly extensive, including paternal uncles, in one case even the husband of a paternal great aunt.

The demonstration of paternity concerns more than child support. It concerns the morality of the parent's relationship and the code of morality of visiting unions. This matter is of more concern to women than men because their reputations are closely bound with sexual morality. Men can be admired for having many women, but women are vulnerable to negative community judgments even when they observe moderation and faithfulness in visiting unions. Young women appear to be very much concerned with reputation; as they get older their concern often increases because of both pride in their standing in the community and religious scruples. Neighbors usually take no notice of an obvious visiting union, but if it becomes noticed, the comments are derogatory. Although privacy is sought within the hedged and walled boundaries of the yard and house, privacy is impossible in a village where most residents have lived all their lives. "People here does know and sees everything. They do know all about you," a villager said. Where moral judgments against the normal mating forms are felt on all sides, women summon up their public defenses. They stage their public acts of self-assertion at gatherings in the road, showing a strong presence and a clever wit. They identify their children's fathers and attempt to get recognition and minding. They keep up friendships and visits with the paternal kin. In these ways they confront a public morality that is judgmental against the actual informal norms. The practices of visiting unions find their public statement and justification in traditional songs, dance styles, funeral rituals, and popular songs. That the practices are not only the informal norms but also are functional in terms of economic and social organization is investigated in the next section.

HOUSEHOLD ORGANIZATION

Taking the problem of variation and commonality in domestic practices, I compared several aspects of household composition and economy in households with different headships and different socioeconomic levels.

Questions of which members contributed money to the household, which members had acquired the house, which contributors lived in the house, and whether dependent children were supported by residents or nonresidents were compared in a sample of sixty-five households as they existed in 1972. My purpose in these comparisons was to see what was common and what was different in these domestic practices across various headship types and social classes. Data were compiled from my interview records, the households were not chosen by sampling techniques, and a questionnaire was not used.

I had attempted to make a survey of households after having lived in the village five months, thinking I had come to be accepted and could expect accurate responses about who lived in a house and who contributed to its support. I began one morning carrying a pad and pencil and going to houses where I had not been before. I had not used any means of keeping records in public before, concentrating instead on accurately remembering conversations and events until returning home to write them down. My survey method caused open expressions of uncertainty and resentment. A group of workmen, some of whom were well acquainted with me, observed my work and reproached me. They were concerned about the way they would be described to the outside world. One man explained that he knew in England West Indians were represented as impoverished, an image he did not like. I had found also that people would not allow themselves to be photographed in work clothes or while carrying items on their head. I became more aware of the antagonisms and mere toleration toward my study among many villagers, and I discontinued the open survey. The widespread wariness did not disrupt good relations with many persons, and many open conversations continued. It was at this time that I first came to understand the strong individuality, the lack of a community consensus, the contrast between protective public postures and expressive emotional selves. I later found that my general interview records contained the information that had been sought for sixty-five households, with the exceptions indicated.

There is extensive variation in household headship and membership. My categories are not inherent and my criteria for placing households in certain categories are constructed. The term *female-headed* means that a woman without a resident spouse is head of the household. The term *couple-headed* means that a sexually united couple lives together in a house and the couple are the head male and head female. This category includes married couples and couples living together in a common-law union. I did not differentiate marital-union types in the couple-headed households because this factor appeared related primarily to prestige. In the internal functioning of the households, the presence of an adult male head was a more differentiating factor than the legal status of the union. In addition to nuclear families, the term couple-headed includes households in which the male head is not the father or grandfather of the dependent children and includes households without children. These two terms signify the absence or presence of a husband to the head woman. Both headship types include households with adult sons and daughters, some of whom may have visiting relationships.

Although most of the households easily fell into these two categories, some presented difficulties of classification. I followed census practice in classifying widow-headed households as female-headed, although I was aware that the economic resources of some widows were similar to those of couple-headed households, owing to inheritance of a house or savings from the husband. There are other anomalies of classification with a husband who has emigrated. In two cases prolonged separation of the couple and cessation of economic support from the husband led to classification of the two households as female-headed. In three households the émigré husband continued to visit and contribute to the family, placing the household in the coupled-headed category. Several households could not be included in either category; two households headed by a man without a resident mate, for instance, fell outside my classes, as did houses inherited and occupied by a brother and sister, although two houses each inherited and occupied by two sisters were categorized as female-headed. Because my interest is in households as integrative units, I omitted single-person households as a third category, which would have unduly complicated the tabular presentation of data without adding to the analysis. Single-person households in this village were comprised only of men, and widows or childless women with a house of their own had taken in a child or other companion to live with them. Some of the men who lived alone appear in the sample population as nonresident contributors to the sample households, although most of the nonresident contributors lived outside the village or abroad.

These problems of classification serve to call attention to the fact that single criteria are used to construct the categories of a household sample, and the categories necessarily include highly varied households. Categories similar to female-headed and couple-headed have been used in all household censuses in the West Indies, but with different criteria for categories in each sample and different analytic purposes (Betley 1976; Clarke 1957; Gonzales 1969; Horowitz 1967; Price 1988; Rubenstein 1987a; M.

G. Smith 1962; R. T. Smith 1956; Trouillot 1988). My topology differs from previous ones in several respects. It does not include all types of households nor all households in the community and includes only households that fit the characteristics of two types, female-headed and couple-headed. It divides households into two socioeconomic strata and compares variables on that dimension. Although social class has not been a variable in the other household topologies, except Betley's, most interpretations have explained family organization in terms of socioeconomic factors. By incorporating class in this comparison I intend a more precise consideration of this factor in rural society than previous household topologies have allowed.

My sample consists of sixty-five households, all in Windward Valley during my 1972 fieldwork. It includes 154 adults and 223 children residing in the households, and an additional 48 nonresidents who contributed to the households. The total of 377 residents represents approximately 35 percent of the 1970 village population of more than 1,200. I classified forty-five households, or 69 percent of the sample, as lower class and twenty households, or 31 percent of the sample, as middle class. The ratio of households of each class in the sample does not represent the class ratios of households or population in the village; I did not include all village households in the census. The 31 percent of the sample households that are middle class undoubtedly overrepresents that class. Fraser estimated that the middle class comprised 15 to 20 percent of the island's population (1975:199). The twenty middle-class households were all included to give the largest possible base; the sample is used to determine characteristics of households, not proportions of households in social classes. Household size ranged from two to fifteen persons. The mean size of households were: female-headed lower class, five persons; female-headed middle class, four persons; couple-headed lower class, seven persons; couple-headed middle class, four persons. I estimated the ages of household heads because age was not asked in interviews and adults in St. Vincent are as reticent about telling their age as they are in the United States. Age categories were: under thirty-five, thirty-five to fifty-five, and over fifty-five. Where the female and male heads of house appeared to be in a different age group, the female head's age was used as the category of the household. The households are in line with the usual West Indian late household formation, with 9 percent of heads under thirty-five; 54 percent of heads from thirty-five to fifty-five; and 37 percent of heads over fifty-five. A higher percentage of female-headed households had heads over fifty-five than did couple-headed households in both classes, but this was more prominently so in the lower class (heads over fifty-five: female-headed lower class, 52 percent; female-headed middle class, 45 percent; couple-headed lower class, 21 percent; couple-headed middle class, 36 percent). In the St. Vincent and Grenadines population there are more women than men in all adult age categories. The overall sex ratio for 1970 was 78:100. Men also have a lower life expectancy than women. I assume that the earlier death of male household heads would remove households from the category of aged couple-headed and add them to the aged female-headed category.

Comparison of household headship in Windward Valley and in the island of St. Vincent is shown in Table 2. The national census does not classify female-headed, male-headed or couple-headed households. In my Table 2 the numbers of Vincentian households are derived from an enumeration of females between the ages of fifteen and forty-four in which women are classed as "head," "spouse/partner of head," and other relationships to the head. In the census table, women over forty-four are not included, among whom a larger percentage would be "head" than "spouse/partner of head" because of the age structure of the population, thus undercounting female heads of house. The incidence of female headship in Windward Valley households is similar to islandwide female headship. In the Windward Valley group, 46 percent of the households were female-headed and 54 percent were couple-headed, whereas in the island of St. Vincent 43 percent of all households were female-headed and 57 percent were couple-headed.[8]

Tables 2 and 3 suggest two respects in which the two types of households are alike. The proportion of lower-class and middle-class households in each headship type is almost identical. Or stated as a comparison of class groups, as in Table 2, in both classes slightly less than half the households are female-headed and slightly more than half are couple-headed. Female-headed households are sometimes said to be commoner in the lower class than the middle class, although there has been contrary data from early studies. Edith Clarke's study of three Jamaican villages of different socio-economic characteristics found that the most prosperous and traditional village, Orange Grove, had the highest incidence of female-headed households: 24 percent in Orange Grove, 18 percent in Mocca, and 12 percent in Sugartown. Clarke included households of single women and single men, and thus only the relation among percentages, and not the percentage values, are comparable to those in the Windward Valley sample. Clarke notes that the female-headed households in Orange Grove all lived on family lands and were adequately provided for (Clarke 1957:149, app. 9). Table 3 suggests that female heads of both couple-headed and female-headed

Table 2. Windward Valley and St. Vincent Household Headship

Households	Windward Valley			St. Vincent[a]
	Lower Class	Middle Class	Total	
Female-headed				
Female head organized household	15	6	21	
Female head succeeded deceased husband	4	3	7	
Two sisters succeeded deceased parent	2	0	2	
Total Female-headed	21 47%	9 45%	30 46%	3,198 43%
Couple-headed				
Couple present	22	10	32	
Wife present, husband emigrated	2	1	3	
Total Couple-headed	24 53%	11 55%	35 54%	4,174 57%
Total	45 100%	20 100%	65 100%	7,372 100%

Source: Virginia H. Young, "Household and Structure in a West Indian Society," *Social and Economic Studies* 39, no. 3 (1990).

[a]Population Census of the Commonwealth Caribbean, 1970, vol. 8, pt. 2, table 9, p. 210. This source ennumerates "Women Aged 15–44 Not Attending School by Relationship to Head and Union Status," and places the women in the following categories: head, spouse/partner, child of head/spouse, other relative, boarder/relative, and domestic employee/relative. We count a "head" as a female-headed household, and a "spouse/partner" as a couple-headed household, and include the total women of all union types.

Table 3. Employment of Female Heads of House[a]

	Female-headed Households				Couple-headed Households			
	Lower Class		Middle Class		Lower Class		Middle Class	
Engaged in remunerative work	13	58%	5	56%	13	55%	5	46%
Not engaged in remunerative work	9	38%	4	44%	9	37%	6	54%
Status unknown	1	4%	0	0%	2	8%	0	0%
Total	23[b]	100%	9	100%	24	100%	11	100%

Source: Virginia H. Young, "Household and Structure in a West Indian Society," *Social and Economic Studies* 39, no. 3 (1990).

[a]The forms of remunerative work include: school teacher, mid-wife, wage labor, domestic, sale of crops, and sale of home craft products including confections, clothing and basketry.

[b]There are two more female heads than female-headed households because two households are headed by two sisters.

households are engaged in remunerative work with similar frequency. Women's ability to earn money has a negative relation to household headship and class. It is a matter of chance and primarily reflects limited opportunity.

Table 4 indicates that almost two-thirds of the households receive support from adult sons and daughters, resident or nonresident. These contributions more commonly go to female-headed households than to couple-headed households. Dependence of female-headed households on adult offspring is common in the West Indies. Support for couple-headed households, however, is usually considered to come primarily from the male head or the head couple. It is therefore unexpected to find that from one-third to one-half of Windward Valley couple-headed households receive supplementary support from sons and daughters.

Female-headed households often have been described as those containing a mother, daughter, and daughter's children, but in this sample, the daughters' residence, contributions, and their children's residence are not only associated with female headship but also occur with similar frequency in lower-class, couple-headed households, as suggested in Table 5. In this respect the two types of households are again similar, except as middle-class, couple-headed households differ slightly from the shared pattern; and a characteristic often attributed only to female headship describes couple headship as well. The sons' residence confirms the similarity between couple-headed and female-headed households. Resident sons lived in all types of households. Nonresident sons contributed to all types of households except couple-headed middle class ones. Table 5 shows the residence of daughters' children. Almost as many couple-headed households as female-headed households have daughters' children residing in them, again showing that a feature often associated with female-headed families is here found commonly in both major types of families, and again pointing to similarity of the households.

Table 6 shows the incidence of house ownership. Individual ownership was the rule; no couple responded that they owned a home jointly. Of particular interest is the high incidence of house ownership by the female in couple-headed households. Both classes display this pattern equally. The female of the couple usually owns the house because of the husband's late entry to a previously female-headed household. None of the male heads lived in houses they inherited, and, when they owned their house, they had built or purchased it. Throughout the village there was only one case of a parental house owned by a male heir, and it was purchased from the other

Table 4. Household Contributors and Residents

	Female-headed Households		Couple-headed Households		Total	
	Lower Class	Middle Class	Lower Class	Middle Class		
Households with resident and/or nonresident contributing sons and/or daughters	18 86%	7 77%	12 50%	4 36%	41	63%
Households without contributors other than head(s):						
with dependent children	3 14%	2 22%	9 38%	3 27%	17	26%
without dependent children	0 0%	0 0%	3 13%	4 36%	7	11%
Total	21 100%	9 100%	24 100%	11 100%	65	100%

Source: Virginia H. Young, "Household and Structure in a West Indian Society," *Social and Economic Studies* 39, no. 3 (1990).

Table 5. Households with Resident and Nonresident Daughters

	Female-headed		Couple-headed	
	Lower Class N = 21	Middle Class N = 9	Lower Class N = 24	Middle Class N = 11
With resident daughter(s)				
With her children	2 10%	4 44%	4 17%	1 9%
Without her children	5 24%	2 22%	1 4%	1 9%
With nonresident daughter(s)				
With her children	7 33%	0 0%	6 25%	1 9%
Without her children	2 10%	0 0%	4 17%	0 0%

Source: Virginia H. Young, "Household and Structure in a West Indian Society," *Social and Economic Studies* 39, no. 3 (1990).

Table 6. House Ownership

	Female-headed Households			Couple-headed Households		
	Lower Class	Middle Class	Total	Lower Class	Middle Class	Total
Owned by female head:						
Inherited from parents	8	2	10	4	2	6
Built by owner	3	3	6	2	1	3
Inherited from husband	2	3	5	0	0	0
Total owned by female head	13 62%	8 88%	21 70%	6 25%	3 29%	9 26%
Built by male head	0 0%	0 0%	0 0%	11 46%	8 73%	19 54%
Built by son/daughter	6 28%	1 11%	7 23%	2 8%	0 0%	2 6%
Ownership unknown	2 10%	0 0%	2 7%	5 21%	0 0%	5 14%
Total	21 100%	9 100%	30 100%	24 100%	11 100%	35 100%

Source: Virginia H. Young, "Household and Structure in a West Indian Society," *Social and Economic Studies* 39, no. 3 (1990).

heirs. Most of the women living in inherited houses had cared for the house owner in his or her last illness. There were no known quarrels over house inheritance such as occurred with some land disputes in the Jamaican villages studied by Edith Clarke (1957:55). In Windward Valley women's services to their parents appear to be compensated by inheritance of the house. Although men can more easily pay for building houses than women, women can acquire a house through the obligations owed her by her children or siblings.

These findings indicate that differences between female-headed and couple-headed households in membership and means of support are not sharply drawn, and, in fact, the two kinds of households are quite similar in these respects. There appear to be common practices central to the maintenance of households, participated in to different degrees but nevertheless a shared system. The households of both headship types rely to a large extent on several contributors; there is no single breadwinner. This is one factor that reduces the importance of a resident conjugal partner. Adult sons and daughters are found in more female-headed than couple-headed households and more lower-class than middle-class households, but all types of households contain these members or receive support from them with considerable frequency. Also indicative of similarity between the two types of households is the frequent house ownership by the female heads. This pattern of household organization is exemplified in most respects in three of the categories, female-headed households of both classes and couple-headed households of lower-class status. Middle-class, couple-headed households differ most from the other three categories, reflecting an ability to participate in more elite norms and values.

The idea of a common domestic system has not had wide currency in West Indian studies, with the main exception Raymond T. Smith's work on the family and kinship (1970, 1973, 1977). Similarity among diversely composed households has been overlooked because interest lay in categorizing types and explaining differences.[9] The interest in types coincided with the overt folk-value differences among the many varied domestic arrangements. Faced with much variability in this area, both the members of the culture and outside observers have augmented the differences and not noted the similarities. That female heads and couples maintain households similarly shows a broadly inclusive household system and is in agreement with Roberts and Sinclair's (1978:248–49) conclusion that women think the mother-and-child family is not necessarily disadvantageous economically.

STRUCTURE OF DOMESTIC GROUPS

Factors in the structure of households are indicated by considering the head woman's position and role. In most households the female head is the only person with whom all other members have reciprocal relations. The husband, if present, is the father of only some or none of the children in the household and usually has children in several other houses. The husband is obligated only to the wife and his own children. The children are differentiated by different fathers, each child or set of children linked with a father who is usually outside the household. The set of children is related to half-siblings in other households through their father, a full recognized relationship no one else has. The adult sons and daughters are obligated primarily to their mother, and personal feelings determine their relations with their full siblings or half-siblings. The mother is thus the only member of the household who has an obligatory relationship to all members. The head woman is the hub of the dyadic relationships within and without the household. Thus the household itself can be described as an ego-centered network. The fact that households are enduring residential units and kin groups means that in addition to the dyadic ties centered on the female head, there are interlocking diffuse sentiments; that is, siblingship and father-child bonds also unite the households. The household is thus both ego-centered and a diffusely linked group, but the fact that the mother is central and forceful and the father's position is not central and is not consistent gives preeminence to the household's matricentered aspect.[10] The model of an ego-centered network also refers to the nonboundedness of the household. It is not a bounded unit in terms of parental obligations in that each member may be connected to a single supporter outside the household. Nonboundedness is also characteristic of the sexual practices of sons and daughters who have mating relationships outside the residence.

The network of dyadic relationships has been identified as characteristic of Afro-Caribbean societies. In noting the "Westernization" of Caribbean societies, Mintz has stressed extensive individualization of peoples. Referring to a comparative lack of "community based institutional nexes . . . and kinship-group nexes," he observed that "probably the main basis of social interaction among rural lower-class people—who make up the bulk of the population in Caribbean societies—is to be found in their ability to establish short- or long-term dyadic social relationships with those around them, either along lines of common interest, or to satisfy particular individual needs" (Mintz 1971:40). Citing the Puerto Rican custom of selecting godparents for one's children, Mintz noted:

But this network or web does not, in fact, create a social group in which each participant is actively related to every other. Rather, a father who chooses consecutive sets of compadres for his children stands at the center of a radial system, maintaining individual dyadic relationships with each compadre. Again, the market women of Haiti enter into personalized economic relationships with series of clients . . . and the system is different, consists of a different "group" for each participant in it. Hence the distinctive quality of Caribbean rural social structure may be its heavy emphasis on individual dyadic ties, as opposed to membership in social groups having some corporate institutional or kin basis. (Mintz 1971:40)

Other uses of a network model of dyadic relationships have been in labor recruitment and labor exchange, small-scale enterprise, emigration aid extended among kin, and generalized kinship aid (Whitten 1965; Dirks 1972; Rubenstein 1987a; Stack 1974). Finding this type of organizational unit in the household suggests that the behavioral basis of it is transmitted through experience in the home. If the home is a key in the complex of network behavior and thought, there is all the more reason to see a systematic domestic culture as real, clear, and class spanning.

The household system has other general cultural characteristics in addition to the matricentered structural pattern. Households also have a high content of volitional activity and positions in contrast to ascriptive activity and positions. This is illustrated by all household roles. The head female must make choices about the composition of households, replacing lost sources of support, and deciding who can occupy the house's limited space. Persons are sought and selected from among the potential contributors and their dependents. Purposefully composing a household stems from the nature of parental obligations, from the fact that they are not generalized to the nuclear family unit but are the obligations of each parent separately. The composition of households thus rests less on ascription than on will. Household membership is less standardized by kinship than in many cultures, less ascribed and more deliberately composed. Persons are kept and excluded, seek entry to a household, and are sought. A unit composed from diverse potential kin is a different unit from a kin-ascribed household. These households are not reinforced by larger kinship units, marital property, or marital exchanges. Lacking reinforcement from other structural units, the heads of house are free to compose their household. The household stays together because of the active leader and the members' will to stay. The construction of households out of various prospective members is illustrated, for instance, by the head females pressuring their daughters to leave the household because they have too many children and an old female head of house naming one son among many whom "this house is for."

Lower mean household size in female-headed households is contrary to the image of female-headed households as tending to become larger through the inclusion of daughters and their children and suggests that the female head, as sole head, composes her household more stringently than when a resident husband influences household composition. Contention over rights to stay in a house plagued a house inherited jointly by two sisters. Aside from the two sisters, the house was occupied by the first sister's daughter and her seven children as well as the first sister's son. The second sister had no offspring in the house, and she resented the overcrowding and tried for years to force her niece to leave, but because the first sister was co-head of the house, she protected her daughter's and grandchildren's rights to residence there. This quarrel illustrates the unusually small role of ascription in household membership. Where children are to live is also a volitional matter, and there are ordinarily different options. Ascribed residence on a kinship basis seems to be quite easily altered, and volitional arrangements are common.

Jack Alexander (1976:36) described a volitional element in kin relations in his work on the meaning of kinship among middle-class Jamaicans: "The area marked off as 'relatives' is experienced as an area of action; whether informants' behavior is in accord with the norm of enduring, diffuse, solidarity or not, it is experienced as an action, not a reflex. It is this experience of action that demands, so to speak, a subjective aspect in the collective representation of 'relative.' " Writing of rural St. Vincent, Rubenstein (1980:336) found a low degree of ascription in parental roles, which he says are achieved rather than prescribed. The closely related characteristics of volition, nonascription, and action seem logically associated with the high variability of West Indian domestic arrangements.

In summary, overtly dissimilar domestic practices in St. Vincent have several common aspects and effects. In actual organization and means of support most households are similar. The rules of paternity and practices of child support are similar for low- and high-status unions. There is a consistent internal structure in households of all types: an ego-centered network, the same form of small-scale organization that has been noted in other areas in Afro-American societies. Finding the same model of organization in domestic units as in other small-scale organizations illustrates quite extensive cultural patterning. Further, volition and nonascription in family and kinship relations appear to be partially responsible for the wide variation in the composition of households; that is, a cultural factor accounts for some of the variability in domestic forms, whereas variability has been previously explained primarily by socioeconomic and historical factors. Cultural processes are clearly present in domestic practices. Ideas and codes make extraresidential fatherhood part of the shared and conventionalized domestic practices; that is, the adaptive low-valued form of parentage is made part of the domestic system by some of the same ideas and codes as support the high-valued form of cohabitational paternity. The common domestic system and the ideas and codes defining the rightness of adaptive practices provide a degree of social integration among persons of low- and middle-class status and among persons practicing high-valued and low-valued domestic forms.

Trouillot's account of family organization in the Dominican village of Wesley is quite different from this account. His typology of households carries out his emphasis on the male "principal laborer" in the peasant family, and in doing so it obscures the nature of female-headed households. The typology does not sort out actual households but is instead a set of conceptual categories. It constructs a young male-headed "Type One," and a middle-aged, male-headed "Type Three," separated in time by a "transitional" and "fluctuating" "Type Two." Female-headed households can only occur in Type Two, but the type is not exclusively female-headed and has no shared characteristics. This typology's inattention to female-headed households is not because they do not occur. The census of a sample of Wesley households shows 35 percent of households are female-headed. Information in the census is restricted to headship and size of household and does not include the age of the head or the relationship of household members to one another, which would have allowed better characterization of both male- and female-headed houses.

The distinguishing feature of family structure is that both mating practices and households take several forms. These several forms are ideologically tolerated and can provide economic security. Each form is morally constructed and each also is familiar to the cross section of classes, and the codes of proper conduct and proper feeling for each are conventionalized. That West Indian mating roles have long been perceived as a sign of disorder and absence of morality is partly ethnocentric and partly a preference for simple analytic systems. In analyzing cultures generally, propriety in mating has been seen as having one form, and couples and households that differed were seen as aberrant. With close analysis, variations have come to be perceived.

The experience in the anthropology of China provides a lesson for West Indian studies. In the study of Chinese culture, a single rule of marriage, defined in traditional law and custom, was long described as the representative form, and poverty was thought to be the only source of variation. Study eventually revealed that there were variant forms of marriage with variant rules, and the variations achieved the central values of the higher status and legally codified forms. China, the supposed bastion of family law, the society that depicted familism as an archetype, actually practiced marriage to an adopted sister, delayed transfer of the bride, transfer of a husband instead of a bride, and brides' residence in sworn spinsterhoods—as much variation in mating as in West Indian societies (Topley 1975; Huang and Wolf 1980). The difference between Vincentian and Chinese systems is that the Vincentian mating forms rest not on arrangement by a parent or parent surrogate as the Chinese system does, but on free entry into all types of union. The similarity in the two societies is the regularization of multiple forms. The assumption that cultures produce one conventional form underlay the study of both systems, and the perceived variation was accounted for by lapse of convention. The discovery was that values could be carried out by several organizational forms, and values were more monolithic and more pervasive than the forms serving them.[11]

It may be that values are too embedded to be achievable only by the segments that can practice the dominant convention, and societies develop several forms of convention to carry out values. The West Indian domestic system is a set of related alternative forms sharing and achieving the same familial values apart from variable social prestige. It achieves the important general social purpose of organizing differences into a coherent system. Some members of the society could pursue an economically efficient and idealized male-headed form of family. Women who did not enter this kind of arrangement, for whatever reasons, could achieve household security and respect. The alternative household forms compensated for gender inequality by allowing women freedom from the personal domination of a mate and an acceptable way of eliminating a mate's authority in her household. As the female-headed household matures, the head female increasingly plays a respected role. Because there is little discrimination against bastardy, except in laws of inheritance, and children are judged in the community for their own comportment and ability, a single woman's children are a demonstration of her worth. If female-headed households and visiting mating are seen as unrealized forms of male-headed households and coresidential mating, and if we note that in Dominica and in St. Vincent, respectively, one-third to one-half of households represent these practices, the society cannot be thought to have any encompassing stability. Seeing these practices, however, as enduring sets of customs suggests their functionality and their inclusion in the prevailing morality. Below I describe the maturing household as well as women's opinions about their different options, but before going on with this phase of household organization, certain aspects of childhood learning should be taken into account.

CHILDHOOD AND SCHOOLS

The interaction of parents and children is a useful vantage point for seeing the regularized handling of emotionality and conventionalized status relationships. Both adults and children are proceeding through a life cycle with regular cultural and social limitations as well as possibilities contingent on personal qualities and personal situations. The regularities in the life cycle are not only the ethnographer's distillate but also social facts perceived by individuals and against which they gauge their personal qualities and situations.

One theme of interpersonal relationships in families is the interplay of overt, pleasurable excitement with external controls on emotional expression. Pleasurable emotion and attachment are stimulated and gratified in depth. In the ordinary experience the chances of emotional isolation and libidinal inhibition are slight. Inhibition of love or withholding gratification of attachment needs seldom occurs. The children are among the most openly expressive persons, and babies are the favored recipients of loving gestures from most household members. Whenever one visits a house where there is a baby, an adult or child will be holding and fondling it, and loving attention, very fully expressed, is synonymous with the presence of a young child. The mother herself may be the least demonstrative of all the household members. Women are often occupied with many household tasks and may play with the baby only when she has finished a long day of washing, cooking, garden work, and, often, carrying water. If she is busy, it is the other children—the sons of all ages in the house, the young women who still do not have their own child, the father, often the grandparents—who surround the baby or young child with affection and laughter. The father, like the mother, is the busy distant boss, sometimes genial, sometimes strict, often absent in the daytime or entirely absent from the home. It is common for young parents to be preoccupied with responsibilities and problems. The house is emotionally balanced between exuberant juniors and potentially stern seniors. But when the seniors relax at the end of their day's work, they take the baby for their own pleasure and fondle and kiss it as the other children look on. The young women's laughter and delight in kissing the baby and the young men's quiet, passionate cradling and facial nuzzling seem erotic. Young children learn libidinal stimulation, and children and adolescents freely express the erotic emotion they have learned. Thoughts about laughter and race came out one day in a comparison a Windward Valley woman made between Queen Elizabeth and Princess Margaret. When the Queen visited St. Vincent she attended the Sunday service in the Anglican church in Kingstown. The woman, an Anglican, obtained an aisle seat. "She a nice, nice lady. But she white! She white! Margaret brown. Margaret joke with everybody. She laugh, she laugh, she brown." The women of Windward Valley have a great talent for joking and laughing. Laughter in women often permeates their bodies, weakens their limbs, and sends them into sweeping contractions at midbody. Men laugh heartily with postures similar but less deeply collapsed. Laughter is a household and friendship bond.[12]

Whereas the adolescents and young adults seem to communicate eroticism to the baby, the mother communicates security, care, and control. When babies are taken away from home—to church, to the medical clinic, on a visit, or on a bus trip—their contentment and placidity are extraordinary. The caretakers, usually the mother or grandmother, are quietly attentive and indulgent, with food and drink, breast or bottle, and gentle codling and pacifiers keep infants and young children sleeping or quiet for long periods. If a baby becomes agitated, it is usually handed to an older child to be taken for some type of care, then returned to the mother in the church pew or the clinic line or carnival grandstand.

It is rare to see or hear a baby or young child cry. In five weeks in Windward Valley in 1984, for instance, the only crying I saw was two babies taken to an elementary school show, where the high-decibel level of the microphone converted the music, stories and laughter into shrill noise. The babies screamed unremittingly in response; the children tending them endured a long time, then took the babies to their mothers, who were outside waiting out a downpour and watching the show. Indulgent and constant care ordinarily forestall crying, and in this incident one of the mothers brought her baby back to watch the show and successfully coddled it into quiescence.

Children cry from whipping, which is both severe and infrequent, threats serving well to keep most children and teenagers obedient. Tantrums are also seldom seen. Following punishment children often sulk and keep a close watch on their mother. Children may persist in attempting a forbidden action and their mother persist in threats. These contests of will may be quiet or loud. An annoyed mother sits as two children enact an imaginary situation in whispers nearby, with any louder action bringing the mother's murmur, "I lash you." A father overhearing children's quiet conversation warns, "I hear you." The mother is obliged to "break" the child. Children are "stubborn." Mothers administer severe lashings to adolescent boys and girls, and even a large fourteen-year-old boy can be seen crying and cowering and trying to fend off his mother's whipping. The other children and adults are seen smiling approval when a child is punished. Deprivation of food or confinement are not used as punishments. Children of all ages are expected to remain in the yard unless they have permission to leave. Many "slip off" and risk a lashing. Children also are "tongue lashed," and their explanations of their behavior are not called "talking back" but are listened to and usually end the reprimand. It is right to explain oneself. The lash is a form of external control. Even an automobile dent is said to be from a lash in children's conversations. Severe punishment does not seem to erode children's pride and self-assertiveness. The disciplinarian mother is foremost the succoring mother, also the organizer of the household, and children show an early awareness that their security in the house depends largely on the management of the female head.

Emotiveness and control are also the theme of other key childhood experiences. The issue between child and adult of leaving the yard is a focal matter, and teaching performance ability is another central experience. In both areas emotional expressiveness and individuality are allowed and are countered with control and authority. Although expected to stay in the yard under the mother's direction, boys "slip off," as their mothers say, and play in remote areas of the village, sometimes stealing and roasting a breadfruit to eat or riding the scooters that they make themselves. Girls are given permission to leave the yard in groups, usually with young children to tend, and they run into the hills, "up on top where you see all around," in exuberant and imaginative play. "We did meet a sleeping bush and we did bow our heads down," some girls reported. This play is mildly disapproved, but rather than a cause of punishment for disobedience, it is ignored by parents, and for children it is an exuberant release from control. Boys are allowed more freedom to leave the yard than girls, but when girls do leave, the tone of their play is of secret exhilaration. The stricter control of girls is seen in their tasks of washing dishes, laundry, and sweeping the inside of the house, whereas boys sweep the yard and take the goats to pasture. Girls tend babies, whereas a boy is given a hen to start his own brood or a goat to start his own herd. When girls care for animals it is usually to help their brother. Adolescent boys go to the beach to swim with others their own age despite the danger of the surf, whereas girls go only with groups of young children supervised by a young woman. The boys' greater freedom presages their freedom in sexual liaisons and in their extra-household relation to their children. The girls' strong connection to household matters later includes visits from a mate. It is accepted that a man who visits her at home acknowledges the prospect of pregnancy. The inside/outside meaning for boys and girls is established early.

Self-assertion is encouraged in many ways (cf. Wedenoja 1989:92), and among them is teaching performance style. When adults relax, especially after supper, children participate with adults in conversation and they tell amusing stories, sing, imitate a radio or television voice, and recite their school or church memorization. Children are encouraged to exhibit style and humor, and most are so ready and proficient in doing so that they are frequently reprimanded or slapped for overassertiveness, until they can exhibit an admired combination of decorum, provocativeness, and good speaking style. From early childhood, "friendliness" has been commended and shyness, called "selfishness," has been reprimanded. Girls as well as boys are taught public presentation. At these times nothing competes with the personal interchanges, and even the constant radio or television background of news, reggae, and calypso is turned off. This is a society where entertainment is in the family and among persons. Television sets were common by 1986, but the conversations on the porch took up many more hours than the television screen in the living room. Storytelling ability and conversational style are part of learning a strong and graceful verbal presentation of the self.

Individual presentation is more important than conventions in encounters. Conventional greetings are not employed; greetings typically have much content, and are relevant to the immediate situation. Conventional exchange using polite forms and good manners expresses distance, impersonality, and often status. Here conventionality is a sign of dullness. A clear and content-specific verbal message is much preferred, and often the exchange is a clever challenge and witty response. Deference, for example, is not taught, and even polite address to adults is seldom taught. Children are not usually impolite, but politeness is not stressed. In a community that remembers its slave origin, deference is not a popular social form. Not polite deference but challenging quips between equals is the currency of social exchange. This is one of the points of the performances and stories in the evening family gatherings. Although many current-event topics, past memorable events, and ghost stories make up these evening talks, another common type of story is the *Anancy tale,* a type of animal tale in which the point is often the smart quips of the disadvantaged animal to the animal king. The clever answer is the response of equality and the strongly individuated self.

The exercise of the individual self in childhood may be quite strident, especially in late childhood and adolescence. A boy, for example, will address another boy his same size saying, "You small. You big as a worm. You a fowl. You a snake. You small." Girls playing palm hand, a jacks game, will readily accuse their partner of cheating. I often heard insulting names called out but did not see the use of physical force by boys or girls. Although parents say they punish their children for quarreling with friends, I did not see this, and, on the contrary, heard them approach the opponent's parent in forceful but reasonable defense of their child. Children seem to have a strong sense of self. For example, a bright ten-year-old girl said of a classmate, "She dull. She fail the last test. She fidget all the time. I come first or second in reading and spelling."

Commentaries on the personal sense of identity by Meyer Fortes and Anita Jacobson-Widding are relevant to this Vincentian practice of self-assertion. Fortes (1983:395) considered self-assertion a common human means of self-identity: "If you want to know who you are you have got to show it." You know yourself and show it in your work and your products—or by following a personal taboo, observing ritual rules, or wearing certain clothes and behaving in a certain way. Fortes remarked on the many differences the Tallensi of West Africa draw among themselves, and how they notice and talk about many minor differences of practice, thus emphasizing the identity of persons with particulars. Commenting on the symposium in which Fortes made this point, Jacobson-Widding drew a contrast between self- assertion and the defensive definition of the self through rules of avoidance and protection of the body and its products against persons who have structural power over the self-defender, which is a widely occurring manifestation of concern with self-identity. She went on to review the symposium discussions concerning difficulties in achieving a consistent sense of self that arise from ambiguous statuses and values incorporated in cultural institutions and concepts (Jacobson-Widding 1983:30). These discussions of identity illuminate relationships in St. Vincent, where one finds no village or kinship hierarchies specifying authority and subordination, and even authority of the husband/father is commonly kept at a distance. There one does not find the rules of avoidance that Jacobson-Widding interprets as protection of the identity against dominance; instead, the practice of self-assertion is the means of protecting the sense of identity. Vincentian identities founder on the third problem discussed, ambiguous statuses and values.

The erotic dancing style of young adults, of "shaking" the pelvis in syncopated rhythm, loosely extending the arms and bending the knees to one side as though the body is suspended, is performed by children as well as adults. Gestures from this dance style communicate exuberance in public interpersonal behavior and are frequently seen. The gestures may be encouraged, allowed, or restricted and are handled differently in childhood, adolescence, and adulthood. Somber two-year-old boys and girls urged to dance respond with a slight tilt of the hips and receive appreciative laughter. Young children may perform the movements briefly, but more often they dance only in response to prompting, seldom seeking attention in this way when not called on to perform. In staged performances, for example at school, the youngest girls are given dancing roles, but children are restrained and are likely to refuse to move. Girls of five or six were featured in several of the carnival bands on the large town stage, dancing along with the adults in the more reserved style of these performances, and they delighted the audience. But the restraint of young performers expresses their knowledge that the sensual dance is too adult an emotional expression for them. The pelvic dancing is practiced by older children guardedly, for they are both reprimanded for it and encouraged in it. In girls' ring dances during school recess, one sometimes sees the traditional children's dance with strutting and clapping followed by a female teacher joining the ring and leading the pelvic dance. The more formal movements of carnival dance style represent a newer style, less familiar in the village than the erotic shaking. Jacob Elder described children's performances in Trinidad and Tobago that were similar to those in St. Vincent:

> Parents present at a song-dance session have to bring pressure to bear upon their children to "show the motion." It is clear that this temporary approval of parents for children to perform what is usually regarded as an obscene act must be confusing to the youthful players, although they usually perform it readily in the absence of parents . . . I have seen parents administer violent flogging to a child who refuses to obey adults as well as the game leader to "hug and kiss you' partner." The parents take the view that the child is manifesting "vice" (precocity) as well as disobedience of parents in public, which is a much worse offence in the parent's estimation. (Elder 1964b)

Edler's point about mixed signals of encouragement and punishment in erotic dance expression is similar to my observations. I see these mixed signals as carrying the messages of an African-derived appreciation of sexuality on one hand and the social and moral difficulties of women with unrecognized children on the other. These aspects of child behavior stand out prominently and are clearly related to the main currents of adult social interchange. In this community erotic emotion is important in childhood and in adulthood. It is made part of social exchange in the treatment of children, is conventionalized in the traditional dance style, and it is allowed remarkably free and open expression. Escape from the strict household is also allowed, making clear the externalness of control. Punishment is severe and threats of physical punishment are adequate to maintain control of children. Thus expressiveness and self assertion are taught and regulated. Vincentian expressiveness extends to emotions such as anger, which is expressed more than harbored inwardly. Outbursts of anger in children and adults are expressed in invective speech rather than in uncontrolled anger. Explaining oneself is very common, and explanation in angry talk seems to effectively discharge anger. Shouts often are mixed with boisterous laughs, and these exchanges do not embarrass companions and are quite allowed. Adults who have a quarrel are likely to confront each other with explanations, self-defense, and clarifying actions and words. Explaining oneself brings an end to quarrels through open disagreement, a state of affairs that is acceptable. Everyone is expected to state their views and the facts as they know them, children as well as adults. The strong self is respected and disagreement is natural. Both sides support their position, and it is unlikely that either will say "we agree then" or "there is no problem."

Imposed on a cultivated erotic and emotional self, however, are high-status moral codes. Persons who learn conflicting codes can perhaps only be sustained by a strong sense of self. Because Vincentian families often lack the force of a closed group, and because the fathers are scattered, the need for protection against moralistic judgments may be keenly felt. Sentiments of family identification are strong, but when faced with the public morality, their kinship structure leaves persons exposed. Not part of a bounded group, not strengthened by a common kinship with siblings or reliable paternal identification, status and identity need reinforcement. This reinforcement comes through learning public comportment—displays that asserts that one is ready and able to protect oneself. The individuated person must show his or her strength and characteristics. Conventional, that is, unindividuated, actions such as proper manners and styles are not the most effective kind of interpersonal exchange, for significant groupings or categories of persons as reference points for such conventions do not exist. Personal strength rests on the individuated character taught to children.

The contrast between the lessons taught Windward Valley children and poor black children in the United States indicates a fundamental difference in their cultural situations (Young 1970, 1974). I have written about the teaching of a strong sense of self among the children in a southern town and in a Harlem community program, but among these groups strong self-assurance is needed in a bicultural situation—one in which both standard American culture and traditional black American cultures are learned in the course of growing up (Valentine 1972). The teaching of a strong sense of self may be a widespread feature of Afro-American cultures, appearing, as I think it does, in both U.S. and Vincentian societies, but basic differences in cultural context bring about different uses of a shared item of culture. American black children are introduced by their mother to the "contest" as a form of performance. She sets up the contest with herself in authority, and the child is urged to test her authority. U.S. children are taught to maintain self-direction in the face of authority (acted out by the mother), proceed with their own objectives, carefully observe the authority's mood, persist in the face of threats, but finally obey after a demonstration of purpose. Windward Valley children are taught a sense of self in order to display their ability to carry on admired forms of talk, to maintain "bright" but cautious relations with others, and to defend themselves verbally against neighbors' criticisms. The authorities with whom U.S. black children are being taught to deal will play a much larger role in their sphere of action and opportunities than most Windward Valley children will experience from national or local persons of authority. Blacks in the United States have had to maintain a sense of their personal integrity in the presence of authorities from the standard culture—schoolteachers, police, welfare agents, and others. The necessity of acting in two cultures and the relatively important level of rewards and discipline from authorities of one of the two cultures they have to master have made important the teaching of a strong sense of self.

St. Vincent does not have a bicultural situation such as the one American blacks learn to live in (cf. Rubenstein 1976). In general, it hierarchically arranges high and low reference points and persons, and the principles of their form of hierarchy are understood at all levels. Parents are models for authorities, and childrens' behavior toward their principal public authorities—their teachers—follows codes of behavior to parents. This is not the case for blacks in the United States. Also in contrast to the United States situation, Vincentian police are not of a different race. There is much less police surveillance for prevention of adolescent misdemeanors and less confrontation with them as authorities. Rural police act through parents, and the parents punish. In Kingstown, where there is more theft, the police directly handle adolescent crime in some cases, but nowhere is there the level of police surveillance that urban blacks in the United States see. In terms of rewards, American authorities are gatekeepers to school success, social services, and jobs, whereas Vincentian authorities have few rewards to dispense. Scores on Vincentian school examinations almost entirely determine school advancement. The grades of each child on the final primary and secondary school examinations are printed in the newspaper at the end of each school year, and the number of subject examinations passed gauges entry to secondary schools, qualification for jobs, training opportunities, and entrance into postsecondary education off the island. The point is not that examinations are objective instruments but that they remove from persons of authority the role of rewarder and punisher, and in this they illustrate for Vincentian children a different social context for teaching about the self and authorities.

Apart from achievement in schools, there is a culture of schools, and it is closely tied in with lower- and middle-class rural culture. Some investigators consider schools representative of metropole values and removed from lower class culture (see Wilson 1973:231), but I think this is the case in only a few Kingstown schools, and not entirely so there, and that the general run of schools represent respected values in lower- and middle-class terms, not in elite or metropole terms. Primary and secondary schools are channels between village culture and national identity. Apart from the teaching of literacy, skills, and exam preparation, schools impart values related to participation in a national identification. Primary school teachers come from among the late adolescents and young adults of the community who have completed primary school themselves. Termed *pupil teachers,* they can raise their employment grade by five stages by attending teachers' classes at the University of the West Indies Kingstown extension branch in the summers. Many do so and have become experienced teachers, but many lack training and secondary school education. Clearly there is a disadvantage in the low level of training, but there is an advantage in that the cultural and personal familiarity of the teachers eases the children's adjustment in school and cultural learning is continuous. Continuity represents another contrast with the U.S. black situation. There a mutual lack of a basis for communication has often characterized the interaction of black pupils and white teachers, and a discontinuity between home and school has created the necessity of defending the sense of self in the face of high-status codes from another culture. In the Vincentian context, the hierarchical structure is represented in the vertical relationship of parent and child and the more status-laden relationship of teacher and pupil. The teacher has high status and acts the role of aloof, impersonal, disdainful, strict authority. This role is played also in white-collar and professional jobs: shop clerk, bank teller, nurse, bureaucrat, and police officer. The low-status person also is aloof and disdainful in response but is not in authority. The primary school class is large and seldom has a room to itself and allows no indoor activities other than sitting densely packed around the group table with the teacher at the blackboard presenting a lesson. Periodically she will leave them with work and step aside while they quietly seethe with "group-ness," the connection around the circle transmitted in shoves, slaps, scowls, and pressed shoulders and legs. The teacher is a familiar village person. Both status differences and commonality are acted out through the teacher's disdainful authority and the pupils' suppression of boisterous-ness. Secondary school teachers in villages and rural towns are among the graduates of island secondary schools and most have no additional training. Only in Kingstown are there secondary schools staffed by better-educated teachers—whose achievements give them higher status—most other secondary school teachers are as close culturally to the students as the primary school teachers are. There have never been elite primary schools. The students in the top secondary schools come from primary schools that even in Kingstown are much like the rural ones.

Almost all children now go to school because school attendance is respected and enjoyed. Even low achievers ordinarily complete primary school, and many attend secondary schools, in part because employment for teenagers is scarce. Parents sacrifice to keep their children in school, buying the expensive books and uniforms, paying the bus fare if their child is able to attend a town school, laundering the uniforms so that school children look the part for a high-status institution. Many low-achieving teenagers hang on, scraping by, appreciating the prestige of school attendance. Failing and having to leave school are felt by both parents and child as the end of opportunity. In the 1980s the heightened national pride among teachers brought a new energy and purpose to the schools. They are motivated for national improvement; they value the Vincentian culture and Creole language; their sights are less on emigration than the teachers of 1972, because their new pride in their role is preferable to low status abroad. They promote greater equality between the sexes and responsibility for contraception and parenthood. Many of them have helped expand the use of folk themes and the vernacular in literary forms, which were introduced by earlier teachers.

Some Vincentians master the schools, and some win places in the better schools. Some of these students go on to the University of the West Indies, and a few go to English or Commonwealth universities, for which the entrance requirements, unlike American colleges, are based on a common examination system. These persons recognize the problems in literacy and education. The prime minister has said in several speeches that "the problem of this country is knowledge"—a statement of many meanings. In addition to the sorely needed technical knowledge of modern equipment and transactions and knowledge of their place in world history, he seems to mean knowledge of their society. Many members of government come from the intelligentsia, the class that helped create an ideological basis for nationalism. Anderson's inquiry into nationalism in postcolonial areas points out the colonial intelligentsia's participation in the nationalism of the colonial power, through school systems brought from the mother country and through teaching the values and language of the rulers, and their parallel role in creating an anticolonial local nationalism (B. Anderson 1983:106ff.). In St. Vincent this double identity was experienced by the local intelligentsia, and Ebenezer Duncan's textbook exemplifies it well. Local aspirations gained more prominence than metropole values from two sources of support: the early strength of populist politics and the school system. The schools' interweaving of status displays with the interpersonal styles of lower-class culture starts the future intelligentsia on their way to a transformational role.

Child fostering, a widespread practice in the West Indies, and in Windward Valley called *loaning a child,* sets up interpersonal situations that illustrate these points. Mothers allow a child to do errands for a better-off household and often to live in the household and be fed and clothed there. Their foster home may be in their own village or in another place. Children's work is valuable to their own or their foster families. In addition to their house and yard work they are sent on errands, carry messages, and buy items at the store. They are sometimes enlisted on banana collection days, with boys and girls of eight to ten carrying a stem of bananas on their heads and strong teenage boys carrying two stems. Girls and boys of eleven and older carry a two-gallon pail of water on their heads, and their faces often express extreme strain under the heavy loads. Twelve-year-olds carry adult loads. To be fostered is thought to be an opportunity, however, because the foster family is better off than the child's family. The fosterer chooses the liveliest and seemingly most intelligent children, and the relationship is maternal and admiring. A generation ago these children were not sent to school by their mistress, and some adults recall resenting this deprivation much more than the hard work. Now children are sent to school, and they may be clothed better than they would be in their own families. Some children go from one mistress to another, occasionally taking the initiative themselves by, in some cases, finding a home they would prefer and ingratiating themselves there. Sometimes a mother will take her child back if she is disappointed in the child's care or opportunities. The mother also recognizes that her chosen child may be her brightest. A bright boy is brought back home more readily than a bright girl because he has better job prospects. The relationship of a child in a foster household illustrates the combination of emotional closeness, independence, and inequity characteristic of hierarchical relationships in this society (Sanford 1974; Soto 1987).

In one case observed, a girl was being raised by her father's sister. This girl joined the family at age six and was a few years older than the youngest daughter in the family. Although she had as much freedom in social relations as the two daughters and five sons in the family, she had many more chores than the youngest daughter. The mother said, "There was a time when [the two girls] were the same. Now [the brother's child] not the same as [her child]," referring to insufficient money provided for the girl's clothes from her father and justifying buying more for the one than the other. The family was poor and no one received much. Still immature at thirteen, her foster mother warned her that she could not stay if she got pregnant. She was the child most often put down: "You think you white? You not white. You black." But among the brothers and sisters she could not be said to suffer any discrimination, and hard work was expected of all the older ones as well as the adults. By age fourteen she was said to have become too rude, and after severe treatment she ran away. The girl's own father and mother took no responsibility for her in this case because she had been placed under the authority of her father's sister. The sons said their mother had been too harsh with the girl, although they would not criticize their mother on other matters. They do not know where the girl went to live, but they think she found another servant position through the secondary school she had been attending in another village and where she continued to go to school.

I observed another fostered child who lived with an old couple. According to her new mistress, she had been in a foster family where she was treated "just like a servant." She began stopping by her new mistress' house and ingratiating herself, and was soon asked to live there. Her work could not be called heavy, except for carrying water, and the elderly mistress carried as much as she asked the girl to carry, both obviously straining under their loads. They were equally strong minded and were empathetic. The girl quietly waited out occasional tirades, which usually were directed at her for spending too much time out hearing gossip while she went for water or to the shop, but she knew she was appreciated for the rumors she brought back. She showed great empathy when the mistress was sick. She occasionally went to visit her own family, and her older brothers sometimes stopped by at her foster home with a dollar for her. She probably derived more self-esteem from her good food and clothes and her very free role in this middle-class house than she would have had in her mother's impoverished and overcrowded house. She returned from her home visits exhausted and depressed, telling of making fudge and wearing a long dress, but without any pleasure showing through her deep sadness. Her father had promised her money for shoes, but "he lying there drunk." She had tried to rouse him in the evening and the next morning and could not.

These children have cultivated the talents of independence even more than children raised by their mothers. Their adeptness in this valued characteristic is probably more important to them than excess tasks or unequal status. They have been chosen and given opportunity and they are not dependent. They move on and they try to benefit where they can. In a society of many grades of status and no expectation of equality, they probably do not suffer psychologically for their second-class status. The particular version of hierarchy in Vincentian culture contains a striking amount of contact and sense of closeness between bottom and middle levels.

GENERATIONS AND GENDERS

Although an adult daughter commonly raises her first children in her mother's house, and often raises all her children there, the beginning of a new generation within a household is not harmonious. Pregnancy in a visiting relationship signals a drop in status, and women try through punishments and tongue-lashings to prevent their daughters from following this course. Well before puberty mothers become anxious about their daughters' approaching fertility. Girls of eleven receive warnings in the company of the family that "she can't stay here if she gets anything." Here the word *anything* means a child, as in "she didn't leave me with anything," commending a girl who emigrated before bearing a child. The use of *thing* for *person* connotes the derogation of illegitimate birth and the threatened rejection of the infant, and by implication rejection of those behavior patterns that are lifelong and ubiquitous. The mother invokes a standard that is unlikely to be upheld for long, which she herself, along with most women, did not observe. The woman knows that her daughter's childbearing not only enlarges her own responsibility and the claims on her resources because the daughter and her child will remain at home, but also reflects on her reputation through lowering the girl's reputation.

The breech between mothers and daughters is eventually healed, but the mother's adoption of the public view of illegitimate childbearing is a difficult situation for young women; that the mother, the most loved and protective person in the girl's world turns against her daughter for the eroticism learned from infancy onward is a harsh reality. The mother's suspiciousness and threats, and her knowledge that sooner or later the daughter will probably fulfill her worry, bring to an end the pleasurable and playful relationship typical of Vincentian childhood. The emotional conflict suffered by girls must be bewildering and saddening, for later in life, when the mother finally relents, a close relationship between mother and daughter is typically renewed, showing that the daughter's attachment had not been broken. That this breech may precipitate teenage pregnancy by withdrawing the girl's main source of security and love is possible. A similar view is presented in a study of Vincentian teenage pregnancy conducted by a Vincentian woman, Valerie Beach Murphy (1982). She thought that lack of close companionship with teenage brothers and sisters exposed a girl more to seeking emotional companionship in a sexual relationship. She included in her questionnaire to pregnant and nonpregnant teenage girls a question about the presence of agemates in the girls' households and found that a much larger percentage of pregnant girls than nonpregnant girls lived in households with no other adolescents. She interpreted this finding as an indication that teenage companionship at home could forestall girls' sexual involvement, and it seems likely that preservation of the mothers' closeness also might delay her acceptance of courting.

The strong sense of self taught in childhood is particularly important for a young woman. She needs a strong ego to face her premarital pregnancy. She is required to leave school entirely and to stop attending church while pregnant. She continues to spend her leisure time with friends. She may continue a compatible relationship with the suitor, which constitutes acknowledgment of paternity, and the propriety of a visiting union. It is common, however, for the first union to dissolve. After the birth, the girl's situation is more pleasant because her mother and family members enjoy the baby and cooperate in its care. She goes to public gathering places with her baby and with her friends, who share in the child tending. A woman will say her daughter must breast feed her baby because the baby's father does not bring money for milk; however, breast feeding is the general practice and is ordinarily defended as more economical. The young mother continues to live at home and remains under the authority of her mother or parents. For an unwed woman to accept the low status of living in the friend's family house, where she is said to be "just used" by him and his family, is rare.

Both the girl and her mother come to see her as engaged in the usual course of the life cycle; repeated childbearing before a mate will provide her with a house and support. Her mother's attempts to control her give way to a cooperative alignment of mother and daughter sharing the support and burdens of the house. If a daughter brings in too many unsupported children, the house becomes overcrowded with dependents. If her children receive support from their fathers, their maternal grandmother usually is satisfied, and if they do not receive support, the young woman usually contributes money to the household by the heavy, underpaid labor available for women. Often the grandmother is engaged in the same kind of work. Loyalty and cooperation is restored, but usually after years of quarreling. Thus the mother's opposition demonstrates both the daughter's disgrace and her own upholding of morality and proves the girl's dependence on the mother for shelter and assistance. In this way, and in many other ways, an unmarried mother becomes, in a brief generation, a moral arbitrator and a provider. By the time a single woman's children are young adults, she has usually augmented her resources by contributions from her children's fathers and the earnings of her eldest sons. Although the antagonism between mother and daughter is genuine, it is also a symbolic playing out of the codes of propriety. The mother establishes her own respectability before her children, her church, and her community. Through the exercise of maternal authority and becoming the head of house, as she usually is by the time her oldest children are adults, she achieves a respected status. Women whose children have been born in visiting relationships experience a transformation in status, judged by conventional standards. The proper conduct of her children, and especially the labor resources of her sons, add to her image as head of a family. When she gets her own house—often built by herself and her sons over a long period of time, carrying beach sand for cement blocks, molding the blocks, then constructing the house, buying scraps of linoleum for the floors, and buying a bed at least for herself—she achieves great pride as head of a house. One woman who had acquired a house in this way said, "They did get a different view of me then. They did not know my thinking was so broad. Those guys said anyone who come in with me will be a success." Indeed this is for many women the time when her visiting mate joins her household, often entering legal marriage, often at the same time converting to a church. Even though achieving a respected status over time is usual, the position of a young girl bearing her first children in visiting unions and living under her mother's authority is difficult. This arrangement is considered the proper and safe one, however, and women warn their daughters about the dangers of coresidence with a man, particularly male violence.

Incidents of wife beating appear often in women's conversations. Some say men's violence is worse in marriage, because if you flee to the police, they say you must return to the husband. On the other hand, a woman's grandmother told her, "Never live with a man unless he marry you. When he has to pay the doctor to care for you he not so beat you, but when he not married to you he just beat you and leave you. Stay home and care for your children. Don't move in with any man." The granddaughter added, "So even though I have those children I not go to live with a man." Women may keep outbursts of male aggression, and a husband's authority, at a distance by remaining in visiting relationships and in the partial protection of their parents' or their own house. Common-law unions, however, are thought right. They make a woman head of her own house, afford a couple privacy, win independence from her mother, and also allow an easy dissolution if desired. Marriage is more valued, allowing women the title of mistress, celebrated by church ceremony and a reception, thereafter nostalgically recalled, and the status of marriage is always noted in telling family histories. Women say that the safety of marriage is uncertain and its durability unsure. Marriages and common-law unions usually dissolve if the couples are not compatible. One young woman whose legal husband had left her and their four children worked in road maintenance in the village, always cheerfully and assertively displaying to the village her ability to support her household by her own work. Her father and mother, who were seen daily working in their scattered small plots, had helped her build a pole, wattle-and-daub house on a lot on the main road belonging to her former husband—with his permission but not with his help. This visible location, added to her ditch clearing on main roads, advertised her competence and seemed intended to do so. After a few years she was married again to a husband who her mother said was very good to her, and they had moved to Trinidad. Women's safety and support may be attained in serial mating, foregoing only status. However, some women say they have hoped that each visiting mate would decide to stay and set up a household.

Women's relationship to their sons is quite different. There is no cause for a breech at adolescence, and women express love and approval of their sons even as they are rejecting and punishing toward their daughters (cf. Sargent and Harris 1992:524). Boys become sexually active later than girls, delayed probably by competition with men. Even after a young man becomes a father, his own mother's responsibility for the child is much less than for her daughter's child, because the infant's mother and maternal grandmother have the primary responsibility for its care. Only occasionally does a woman take her son's child to raise, and this occurs at the request of the child's mother. Sons' earning power is greater than daughters', and their labor is needed to bring the family garden plots into cultivation. So women's relationships with their sons are unencumbered. Their sons are welcome to remain living at home and their mothers try to retain their loyalty and their financial support, trying to delay not their sexual activity but their departure from the house.

The young men have a role to perform in the community and in relation to older men. Criticism of young men by older men is usually abundant: they do not want to work, they prefer to idle at the bridge, they steal from their father's garden and fruit trees. In fact young men experience high unemployment and low land ownership until they inherit the family plot. Many of the jobs open to them are part time, and their responsibilities on the family lands require only periodic labor. They spend much time outside of households and some live alone. They gather at the crossroads and on front porches, often playing dominoes and checkers, and they drink together in shops. The term *young man* is used regularly, with "he is a young man" made in explanation of sexual liaisons. A similar phrase explains the breakup of a youthful marriage: "He wanted to be a young man." Young men serve the community through singing for wakes and memorials for the dead, in which the songs are intended to keep mourners awake and in this way protect them from the ghost of the deceased. They sing all night in the houses of the mourners and in the morning gather at the crossroads continuing their songs. They are much admired by those listening from the windows of their houses. Although they are commended for their sexual exploits and ribaldry, they are equally commended for the role they take in church schools, which are often part of revivals. Young men attend revivals, and many lean in the church windows and show off their knowledge of Scriptures in the schoolroomlike format. Biblical knowledge promotes reputation as much as singing songs and telling tales. Young men are not conspicuous churchgoers, but they gather much familiarity with the Bible as children, and this is reinforced by listening at the edge of revivals and street meetings. Some men continue to manage the ghosts and assert license throughout their lives. Many others "come inside" a household and are churchmen in middle and old age. In both types of roles, old men walk with dignity and are granted high status, whereas young men play the lower-status roles of youth. The dignity of the elderly is notable. The old farmers ride their donkey to and from their gardens, resembling Bible illustrations of the father of Jesus. The high status of age should be demonstrated and acknowledged. The young men represent license, are allowed it and are admired for it. Kept in their age group by the older men's construction of them as propertyless and idle, their contribution to the community is to sing about license with the authority of folk tradition.

Abrahams and Wilson describe a dichotomy of values, male and female. Abrahams (1983:98ff.) depicts male roles as expressions of license associated with the performance styles of road marching in contrast to the propriety of women's realm in the home—"the road and the yard." In Wilson's (1973:122ff.) "reputation and respectability," men's activities are directed to enhancing their reputations in the company of other men, and women represent the respectability of kin relations and the home. For Abrahams the community positively asserts both male and female values in the tea meetings and other public performance arenas. Wilson is not concerned with the resolution of oppositions in values or roles, and instead sees "reputation" as authentically West Indian and "respectability" as representing British values and preventing with the realization of a true West Indian character (1973:230). To interpret the culture of women's domain as an intrusive element is improbable, and to see it as European-derived ignores even the early ethnography on women's actions. The newer research on Caribbean women and gender relations demonstrates the incongruity of Wilson's interpretations (Barrow 1986; Besson 1988; Gearing 1988).

In Windward Valley the gender dichotomy is matched in importance by another basic distinction, that between youth and middle age. Male and female roles and values progress in the same direction over time, uniting the genders and separating the generations. This progression reflects compatibility of objectives between men and women at each stage of life. At similar points in their lives, both men and women become concerned with time, death, the disturbing messages of local religion, and resolving the conflicting impulses that dominate mens' and womens' youth. The values, motivations, and roles that both genders play out in time show the closeness of men and women in culturally defined emotions. In contemplating the accuracy of gender dichotomies as an analytic tool, one must confront the character of gender relations in Afro-American societies. Ethnographies have generally depicted much comparability of gender roles and much acceptance of heterosexual compatibility. They also tend to agree that in youth both genders are sexually indulgent and wary of binding sexual commitments. In middle age both genders are likely to seek domestic unions. The similarity in the values men and women display indicates that oppositional gender categories may obscure as much as they reveal, and that they have to be joined to another analytic framework, the life-cycle sequences.

St. Vincent retains its traditional family system, and the family influences are strong. The problem of youthful pregnancy inherent in traditional Vincentian society has become much greater in a society in the process of modernizing. The population increases overtax island resources and facilities, and the cessation of education for young pregnant women becomes a societywide liability. The Ministry of Health is attempting to reduce youthful childbearing through public education and public health measures. Radio messages, newspaper cartoons, and articles, directed to men as well as women, educate the public on the modern view of teenage pregnancy. All clinics are equipped to distribute several types of contraceptives for women and inform women about them. Traditional attitudes, however, hamper the promotion of contraceptives. Clinic nurses, for instance, are directed to supply contraceptives to any girl or woman who asks for them and to advise them on birth control, but I was told by a local woman who has studied the situation that the traditional attitude, that it is not appropriate for schoolgirls to be sexually active, prompts the nurses either to refuse to give the girls contraceptives or to inform their mothers, or other persons, of their deception in seeking to be sexually active while in school.

Life histories, of course, differ. People act in terms of some part of the range of their culture's components or are able to avoid, by luck or by plan, the cultural bind. Unusual circumstances cause exceptions to the pattern; for example, a girl may avoid pregnancy because her family sent her abroad, or she may succeed in the school system and move into a clerical or professional position. But the great majority of Windward Valley women become sexually active while living at home. Information gathered on the marital statuses of deceased persons and on the birth statuses of adults and elderly persons suggest that there have been no fundamental differences in several generations in the childbearing cycle. In late 1990, however, a change in teenage pregnancies and the birth rate was reported by the Planned Parenthood Federation. A decade ago teenagers giving birth numbered 900 to 1,000 per year, but in recent years, 600 to 650 births to this age group have taken place per year. The average births per mother in 1990 stood at 2.7, compared to 7 in the 1960s. This organization finds that approximately three-quarters of women between the ages of fifteen and forty-five use family-planning methods (*Vincentian*, 11 February 1990). Another change I noted in the mid-1980s is interesting in view of these statistics. I think there had come to be more overt approval of extraresidential childbearing by many young women and men, and I think these converging trends are not contradictory. My impressions of young adults whom I know well suggest that they are both restraining sexuality and using contraceptives. Others seek religious identity to help forestall sexual relations. Most of them affirm the traditional validity of extramarital sexuality. This attitude is consciously associated with a desire to legitimize folkways and to reject the colonial-derived moral standards which condemn the folkways, an attitude explicitly promoted by some sectors of the nation's youth. Fathers of this persuasion acknowledge paternity and mothers are more defiant of public censure. Their perception of Vincentian folkways and their rejection of moral dilemmas is, in fact, well grounded. One of the traditional expressions of resolution of the double moral standard is in funeral practices. Public performance styles also express conflict and resolution, more so in the villages than in national performance styles. The next sections take up these points.

FUNERALS AND OPPOSITIONS

The many aspects of death are an important part of village rituals and peoples' voiced concerns. Funerals are the largest village gatherings, the main occasions outside church attendance that have specific dress codes—black suits and white shirts for men, and white, lavender, or black dresses for most women. Windward Valley people say some parts of their funeral ritual are distinctive of their village alone; they have a village cemetery, unlike many settlements where cemeteries are adjuncts of churches. The Windward Valley cemetery is located on a high bluff above the sea and can be seen from all over the village. The village history tells of the fight for the cemetery. There lie the remains of the grandparents and parents of the present-day elderly, and villagers look out at these relatives' graves and their own future grave sites daily. Some motion to the cemetery when speaking of a lost relative. The main road goes by the cemetery, and it is thought to be a likely roadway for ghosts at night. The sections of the funeral ceremony that villagers say are distinctive of Windward Valley are marked by two songs, "We Are Climbing Jacob's Ladder," sung while carrying the coffin up the hill to the cemetery, and "We Will Crown Him With Roses," sung after filling the grave and signalling the end of the ceremony. I did not find out how localities differ in funeral ceremonies, but I took the assertion of distinctiveness as an expression of pride. In the procedure for funerals, the family prepares the corpse at their house, places it in the coffin, and leaves it open for viewing the dead until the march to the cemetery.

The mourners gather early in the day to make flower wreaths. When four o'clock approaches, they form a procession behind the coffin bearers and the family, and all march in line, carrying the wreaths. They march to the church, if the deceased was a member, and then after a brief service to the cemetery, or with the death of a non–church member, they march directly to meet the minister in the cemetery. The gravediggers have been working, dancing, and singing in the cemetery since midmorning. Fortified with rum, which is all or part of their payment, they sing in syncopated rhythm "I'll Meet You in glory" and dance in the swinging style. Joined by as many as eighteen men, silhouetted on the high bluff, their loud mockery of sacred hymns is carried by the sea breeze down into the village. Many people go directly to the grave site, where they may talk with the waiting gravediggers before the procession arrives, and jokes are made, looking down into the deep-cut earth, about the sexual exploits happening even then in the old coffins of adjoining graves. The gravediggers' dirt-stained clothes, their drunkenness, the yawning window into the nether region of ghosts, the curiosity of those not bothering to make the respectful gesture of marching with the coffin, all express the violation of codes, disdain of piety, and defiance of otherworldly danger to the soul of the deceased. The gravediggers personify and exaggerate these elements. They are all village men. In all funerals I observed, even fourteen years apart, they were some of the same men, specialists in their role, and in each case of a funeral for a man were said to be friends of the deceased. Some say it is cheaper to pay them in money than rum. As they are digging the grave they measure it with a rope, then walk to the house of the deceased where the mourners are gathered and measure the coffin with the rope, a calculation repeated on several trips. Mingling with the family and mourners, they in their work clothes, the others in funeral dress, the diggers drunken, casting jokes to the mourners, the opposition of emotions is already in play. The gravediggers have a more prominent role in the total ritual than the preacher, who first appears at the church or meets the marchers at the cemetery to lead them to the grave site.

In the cemetery the diggers deftly suspend the coffin over the grave and stand at the foot. The preacher stands at the head, the family members stand on either side outside the mounds of earth, and other mourners gather in a dense group all around. The minister and gravediggers have opposite locations, different responsibilities, and as paired specialists they handle their two spheres of action, equally on scene, each giving cues to the other to begin their alternating parts. In the five funerals I observed, the two officiating roles were cast in the same way, the preacher representing church authority, the gravediggers comic and defiant of church morality. Each plays their role a little differently, depending on the sex and sanctity of the deceased. In one funeral for a man who had refused the church, the gravediggers mocked the motions of the preacher as he read the burial text. In funerals for women and church members they are equally prominent, but are more restrained, showing efficiency and skill and maintaining a brisk manner. At the same time, it is essential "to be read over" by a minister of the church, and even those who remain outside the church expect this ceremony and are granted it by church law.

The preacher reads the appropriate text and sings the opening note of the hymns. The gathered mourners sing, women's resonant voices leading, the men seeming to follow the women's more certain melodic line and knowledge of verses. Even nonchurchgoers know the hymns from school, street meetings, and revivals. When the readings are finished, the preacher signals the gravediggers to lower the coffin on its ropes. He then signals a hymn and leaves. The gravediggers move to all sides, lower the coffin, then begin hoeing the heaped-up earth into the grave, using the same implement as in farm cultivation and working with speed, flourish, and increasing comedy. The group continues to sing hymns, now started by anyone present. As the grave is filled, the family is sometimes seen to become impatient with the prolonged buffoonery of the gravediggers. A son of the deceased at one funeral urged them to be finished, and a gravedigger replied, "I will do it my way." When the grave is mounded up to their satisfaction, the gravediggers signal a syncopated swaying, a waving of wreaths, and a singing of "We Will Crown Him with Roses." The change in rhythm from hymns to syncopation, from propriety to jubilant dancing, is led by the gravediggers, who have the central position in the circle. This hymn concluded all funerals I observed. While some mourners are deeply grieved, others carry the ceremony to its closing expressions of relief at the completion of burial, and after all the verses, the people turn away and stroll through the cemetery and down the hill to their houses, or to the waiting buses that occasionally bring mourners from other places.

On the night of the funeral and for three nights after, a group of young men sings for the family and guests, keeping the family awake so that they will be on guard when the ghost of the deceased comes to visit them. They sing through the night again after the ceremonies for the dead on the ninth and fortieth day after death and one year after death, keeping the family awake so they will not be frightened by the ghost. An alternative ceremony many families choose is conducted by a group of Spiritual Baptists in the family house or yard. The members of this cult have participated in ritual spirit journeys called *mourning*, and their familiarity with the spiritual plane makes it appropriate that they meet the ghost, who is expected to visit the family at these times. Their syncretistic rituals incorporating Christian beliefs and symbols make them protectors, both of and against the dead. Many families prefer to be kept awake by the jaunty songs of the young men, and they enjoy the entertainment, making light of belief in ghosts and napping while the men sing. Encounters with ghosts, the men say, often take place on remote paths. If you meet a ghost, make a sign of the cross or strike a match and wave it as a cross: "They do fear the cross." Women and children meet ghosts on the road, especially at twilight and dawn, and also in their houses. The ghosts encountered are not a particular person, and only in a dream may a ghost be identified. A message may be given in a dream, but when awake, ghosts apparently do not speak but may impede your way or hold you down in bed. They may be seen sitting in the room and frighten a person getting up at night. There is much joking about ghosts. "I hear America too lighted to see the ghosts," one woman said. One can not guard against ghosts all the time, but on occasions when their presence is a certainty, the band of male singers or the cult group serves to manage them.

The men who dig the grave and the men who sing at the wake perform non-Christian tasks and represent defiance of church values and beliefs. The joking at the grave and the gravediggers' profane role is an affirmation of carnal pleasures that is decried in Christian teaching. In the humor and buffoonery and in the syncopated finale, the non-Christian side of their lives is asserted. At the same time, the preacher's role is essential. The two opposed views of the body and soul, and the affirmation of both views, represent a final coming together of the African and European contradictions in the culture. It is a comprehensive summing up at the end, a statement about the wide scope of values that have been played out throughout Vincentian history. Pride in the traditional funeral ritual of the village, the broad participation in it, and even the visual prominence of the cemetery contribute to rootedness. As the last event in the life cycle, death is bound with social reality more than ideals. Loss binds the mourners to acknowledge the real course of life. It is not a time for abstract moralism. The confident Christian promises, which are important in the religious quests of many villagers, have been read from Scriptures, and the hymns have comforted the mourners, just as they have expressed the shared values of many assemblies of religious and secular groups. Whatever the hopes for the Christian soul, the ghost continues to represent an earthly presence, a subject for jokes and tales.

In bringing together the contrasting positive values expressed in the funeral, there is a process of syncretism similar to the interplay of speech symbols described by Reisman (1970) in his seminal study of the ambiguity of values in Antigua. He demonstrated the play on statuses represented in uses of standard English and Creole, when each language asserts in alternating references the values of low-status genuineness associated with Creole and high-status knowledge associated with standard English. He took the diachronic process of syncretism in religions, which Herskovits had employed for Afro-American religions, and demonstrated it as a synchronic and personal process of bringing divergent values into relationship. The high-status and low-status forms could be asserted in usage and verbal plays on words. Divergent values could be integrated by the individual through demonstrating versatility in each mode of expression, asserting simultaneous adherence to different qualities through plays on oppositions. Combinations of high-status language and the language of ordinary persons demonstrated adherence to both elite values and the realities of lower-class life. It gave the person a means of relating antagonistic values in her or his own mind and in presentation of self. Plays on opposites became a demonstration of mastery of a culture of different statuses and values. The Windward Valley funerals, as statements of the different values that have governed the villager's life course, demonstrate this synchronic syncretism, or personal resolution of ambiguities. In Reisman's words, "This may be used to build ambiguous patterns into village life . . . The remodeling of symbols and the maintenance of a dual value system are thus intertwined" (1970:134–35). In West Indian lower-class culture there are formats and a ritual for expressing the often antagonistic values that are taught and must be encompassed in the mind and in the life course. The oppositions of respectability and nonrespectability discussed by Wilson are a similar play on statuses and values. Another example is in Bryce-Laporte's discussion of a middle-class family's use of Obeah to demonstrate strength and efficacy needed in a community contest, even though the lower-class connotations of that practice ordinarily require distance from it. The rich possibilities of plays on opposite values are employed in traditional public performance style, as Abrahams (1983) has described, and as modern carnivals could well be portrayed. As personal means of resolving difficult, often guilt arousing, contradictions in cultural directions, these styles of speech, these assertions of the rightness of oppositions, this ritual statement of opposite qualities made at the end of the life cycle, allow individuals to put ambivalence to good use and to relate themselves to the entirety of their complex culture.

The heritage of contradictory value codes sets up the conditions in which persons act using the range of options and symbols in the value continuum available to the rural, lower, and middle classes. Out of their pursuit of both high- and low-status behavior, and their fluency in status expression, persons encompass many of the divergent elements of their society. This way of life rests on strong self-consciousness and is accompanied by careful attention to both social ties and social distance.

SPIRITUALITY AND PUBLIC IDEOLOGY

There are numerous churches and sects in Windward Valley—Methodist, Anglican, the West Indian Mission, Seventh-Day Adventist, the New Testament Church of God—all with church buildings. Many other groups meet in the lower-story rooms of large houses where two of the groups that now have church buildings began meeting ten and fifteen years ago. A Spiritual Baptist praise house is in the village, and nearby settlements have their praise houses. All the churches and sects are attended by the poor and the well off. There is no Catholic church nearer than Kingstown to serve the Catholic Portuguese. The Methodist and Anglican churches are old and established, backed up by the large church bodies in Kingstown, and usually served by a seminary-trained pastor, some English and some West Indian. The fundamentalist churches stress conversion and Bible study. The Seventh-Day Adventists stress lay leadership and social issues. The Spiritual Baptists offer possession experience and brings their rituals into the paths and yards, employing symbolism of the rural landscape and subsistence gardens. It is close to the spiritual qualities of the villagers and is popular as a "supplement" to the other faiths. The fundamentalist sects, more than others in Windward Valley, emphasize preaching about the marital relationship and help both women and men observe marital fidelity by their emphasis on conversion and their promotion of fear of hell. There has been a trend toward fundamentalism for several decades. As the new, more vigorously proselytizing churches, they attract persons in crisis from the Anglican and Methodist faiths. Some fundamentalist churches use the imagery of purity and dirt, the clean and the garbage, for believers and nonbelievers. For villagers struggling with a dual-value system, this message may appear true—that immoral dirt and social garbage are inherent in visiting unions and out-of-wedlock childbearing. In devoting much of their preaching to the celebration of marriage and couples' faithfulness, these churches offer forgiveness for past sins and support the faithful unions into which middle-aged couples commonly have settled. Status achievement through moral restriction has been described in Jamaican and Trinidadian religious sects (Fischer 1974; Holland and Crane).

The churches and sects are also important in offering inner spiritual experiences in communication with a spirit world. Strongly spiritual prayer expresses a conviction of otherworldliness and a communion with spirit persons. Communication with the spirit world is achieved in group prayer occasionally in the conventional churches and commonly in the Spiritual Baptist sect. The valued and sought-after inner experiences of prayer and communication with a spirit world lead many people to participation in this sect, known also on this island as Shakers. The sect has no connection with the U.S. Shaker religion, although both derive from early Methodism. The two Shakerisms have different rituals and social practices, and the Vincentian sect incorporates elements of African derivation. The name Spiritual Baptist is now preferred by the sect's leaders. The Methodist Order of Worship and the Bible are its texts. It also employs symbolic emblems of water and cornmeal, a bell, white flowers and candles, titles of office, and insignia of dress.

A law against its practice (Ordinance No. 13 of 1912 To Render Illegal the Practice of Shakerism as indulged in the Colony of St. Vincent) was imposed in 1912:

> Whereas there has grown up a custom amongst a certain ignorant section of the inhabitants of the Colony of St. Vincent of attending or frequenting meetings from time to time at houses and places where practices are indulged in which tend to exercise a pernicious and demoralizing effect upon the island inhabitants, and which practices are commonly known as "Shakerism";
>
> And whereas it is expedient in the best interests of the said Colony of St. Vincent and its inhabitants that such meetings and practices should not be permitted.
>
> It shall be an offense against this ordinance for any person to hold or to take part in or attend any Shakers meeting or for any Shakers meeting to be held indoors or in the open air at any time of night and day. Owners and managers of estates must notify the Chief Of Police of any meetings of Shakers, building of Shaker houses, or be guilty of offense against this ordinance.
>
> Police have the power of entry without warrant. All persons must give their names and addresses to the Police or be liable to arrest and detainment.
>
> Any person guilty of an offense against the ordinance shall be liable, on conviction, to a fine not exceeding 50 pounds and in default of payment thereof to imprisonment with or without hard labor for a term not exceeding 6 months.

A motion to repeal this law and legalize Shakerism was made in the Governor's Council in 1939 by the progressive leader George McIntosh but was defeated in the conservative-dominated body (Kenneth John, *Vincentian,* 11 November 1988). The language derogatory of the common people, the infringement of freedom, and the force legislated express well the attitudes of the colonial government. Repeal of the law was achieved in 1965 because the chief minister, Ebenezer Joshua, practiced this religion and the Spiritual Baptists were strong supporters of his People's Political party and had raised the funds that kept it going in its early years (Kenneth John, *Vincentian,* 28 August 1992). In 1972 many rural and urban people continued to express disapproval of the sect. In the 1980s the sect was less ridiculed and often commended for its devoutness. Spiritual Baptists are now raising money to build a new church, and, with the main preachers educated, one of them lace robed, and one of them a convert from the Anglican priesthood, they are seeking more respect.

The leading Spiritual Baptist preachers are not unlike fundamentalists in differentiating "onlookers" and "Christians" in their open-air meetings and in stressing the Second Coming, when Christ will gather up the Christians and there will be no time to convert. Stress on doctrine and evocation of fear are still absent from the rural services and appear to express only a few preachers' views. Spiritual Baptist congregations and services remain much the same as they were when described by Henney (1974). Praise houses then and now are constructed of pole and wattle and located in the yard of a member. Conversion is prompted in dreams but is resisted because the prolonged baptismal procedures are considered an ordeal. Genuineness is "proved" through randomly opening the Bible with the positions of the thumbs pointing to verses deemed as messages to the holder. In services the Shakers commonly go into states of dissociation, which are interpreted as possession by the Holy Spirit. One can achieve several status levels with titles and rights through undergoing mourning rituals, but the male leader is sometimes said to interpret what privileges have been achieved and may refuse to grant statuses. In the mourning, days of confinement to the praise house and hours of lying immobile, attended by the faithful, bring a spirit journey with visions and sacred messages, which are likened to school learning. Schooling was a rare achievement in the recent past for the lower-class people who make up most of the Converted (Henney 1974:54–57).

Aside from the services in praise houses, local congregations of Spiritual Baptists hold street meetings, setting up a small table and benches and using a white tablecloth, white flower and candles in a glass of water, a Bible and a bell on the table, and protective cornmeal on the ground at the corners of a defined space. The services consist of Methodist invocations and hymns, Bible readings, prayers, and intervals for solemnly shaking hands with everyone present. A crowd gathers around the group of sect members, men more numerous than women, reversing the proportions in the congregations in most church services. The onlookers join in the hymns, everyone reverent, and often some of the gathered group would be, as they say, "seized by the Holy Spirit," and begin "jumping," a rigid, rhythmic knee flexing while standing in place with eyes closed, the body sometimes twitching—a light but true trance from which the man or woman would recover an ordinary facial expression and posture, still standing in place, after a period of a quarter of an hour or more. Seizure by the Holy Spirit occurs at other revival services and occasionally happens in churches, both fundamentalist and Methodist, and other sects, but seems not to occur in the village Anglican church, where the ecumenical assurance of the rituals, as well as the high-class status of the ordained missionary priests, seem not to encourage intense personal experience in the congregation. Some Anglican women are also full members of the Spiritual Baptist church, and wear the white kerchief obtained in conversion. Many members of the established churches say that they "like the jumping." Many wakes and memorials for the dead were conducted by Spiritual Baptist groups in the family yard of members of the established churches.

For the Spiritual Baptists, and sometimes for others, contact with the ghost of the deceased is sought. A wake for a deceased man as observed in 1984 began after nightfall in the house of the deceased with a gathering of approximately a dozen people. The next of kin, the deceased man's niece, who had cared for him while ill, and her adult daughters, were Spiritual Baptists. The small main room of the house was nearly filled by the small table in the center, and those attending sat on benches and chairs against the outer walls and in the adjoining small kitchen. The leader recited Bible verses, the doxology, passages of Anglican and Methodist ritual, and prayed aloud. The "mother," who in this case was the leader's wife, placed the flowers and candles in water, lighted the candles, waived them to the four directions and rang the bell to the directions, at points in the service. Small piles of cornmeal were placed in each of the four corners of the room. In his prayer, the leader journeyed to the spirit world and called, "Hello, Holy People" as he encountered one after another. They are the dead but are not named. His manner was intense, his eyes tightly closed, and he sweated profusely, but the ease of his return to a normal presence appeared to indicate he was not in a trance state. The next of kin prayed, also kneeling with eyes closed, but unlike the leader, they addressed God in conventional Christian form, giving thanks and asking blessings. Their words were embellished with the imagery of nature: paths through mountains and valleys, the beauty and sanctity. The ghost of the deceased was present but gave no message. Surrounded by sacred cornmeal and in the presence of the sacred objects, it was not feared. His niece said later that the deceased man had not been a member of any church or sect. The Anglican priest had read his grave service as a favor to his sister, a member of that church. Her daughter, a Spiritual Baptist who had cared for him and would inherit his house lot by his will, had no doubt that he had a Christian blessing, which came in his dream before death. When he was gathering up his sheep in his yard one night, he dreamed, one sheep was lost, but then he found it and brought it into the house with the others. "He had the blessing at last," she said, confidant that the dream had more truth than his rejection of church membership.

One member explained the sect in this way: "If you want to be a Spiritual Baptist you have to mourn. I mourn two times. You get your uniform, white kerchief and white all the way down [dress]. Not just the pastor, you yourself." This participatory characteristic—"Not just the pastor, you yourself"—is an important attraction of this sect. Although articulate sect members have described titles of office and authority vested in leaders, incorporating the West Indian love of hierarchy into a sect that is relatively unformalized, the role of the leaders appears to be mainly one of heightening the participation of all in the group. Unlike the Methodist and Anglican model of an invested preacher leading a congregation, a shepherd's flock, the rural pastor appears primarily to be a person who easily transposes himself to the spiritual plane. His spirit journey opens the way for the others present, who also easily move into an imaginary realm of holy people and sacred natural scenes. When the pastor leads the service, each part follows without a pause, moving from his recitation of creed to Bible reading, prayer, and hymns, with shifts of rhythm and dramatic emphasis but no division into parts, no interruptions, and no endings. The continuity of the recitations and synchronism of group and leader helps maintain a sense of otherworldliness. It is the sense of being as a group together on an imaginary plane that must have led the informant to say, "Not just the pastor, you yourself." In Windward Valley, these practices represent less a separate cult than a locus of the particular spirituality of the people. Its presence is not signaled in a central congregation or a building, in regular meetings or in an authoritative leader—although leaders attempt to make it a "church" and may succeed in adding these institutional dimensions to the widely diffused spiritual presence that characterizes the religion. The actual mental mingling of ghosts and Christian spiritual symbols is ritualized only in their practices, and for this reason the religion supplements all the other religious practices. For some people these are not important matters, and some prefer the conventional religion of the churches, but the sect's practices are elfin in their pervasiveness and frequent emergence from scattered bush households into the regularly occurring rites of passage from the pragmatic world to the world of spirits. In its reticent diffuseness, these practices replicate the interpenetration of parts in the rural culture, the linkages of kin between class strata, the mingling of statuses in the common forms of social and personal action, and the play on high- and low-status signifiers.[13]

Although inner spirituality is valued, the public aspects of religion have an important place, and these are served better in the churches than by the Spiritual Baptists. Some services are conducted as church schools, with emphasis on knowledge of the Bible, and these are popular with many people, especially young men, who enjoy the opportunity to display sharp minds and knowledge. Personal testimony of conversion is common and often given with oratorical flourishes valued on all public-speaking occasions. The officers of church societies give their reports with attention to speaking style. The formal presentation of the self, taught at home and perfected in school exhibitions, has frequent opportunity for display in churches.

Bible texts seemed to be, in 1972, the only literature in the village. People spoke of the mental stimulation of the pulpit: "I does like the learning," an uneducated woman said. Like the Spiritual Baptists using school as an analogy for the sacred messages they received on a spirit journey, she had a desire for mental exercise. People know the Bible stories in detail. Their rapid location of Bible texts was impressive, and most church members owned Bibles, carried them to church, and followed the Scripture readings. The Bible took the place of literature and was the only literature. By the 1980s there was a broader range of stories. Anancy tales had been introduced in the school texts and appeared commonly in storytelling, and there was an awareness of Caribbean literature. I heard ghost stories, told by both men and women. It was probably my better rapport with the villagers in the 1980s that allowed freer telling of ghost experiences. Expertise in Bible stories had certainly lost its premier place to the newly cultivated expressions of African-derived stories, as Anancy and ghost tales are recognized to be. Although there were in 1972 certain occasions, such as death, when explicitly anti-Christian themes had their place alongside Christian ones, the dominance of Christian ideas was clear. In the 1980s African-derived ideas, and particularly ideas associated with citizenship in an independent country, came to have an important place in ideology, not displacing Christianity but taking away some of its former pervasiveness.

The long-standing association of public expression and ideology with the churches suggests a continuity between the functions of religious institutions and the emergence of a nationalist ideology. In public discourse and ideological concerns the churches and the state occupy similar places. The new ideas of nationalism now supplement the principle unifying idea of the pre-independence era. Compared to 1972 political talk has a newly acquired expertise and relevance among ordinary villagers. Socially and personally political talk is effective in ways similar to religiosity. Politics is a suitable subject for the projection of moral principles beyond oneself to a public arena where others are judged and where one can be concerned with public issues instead of having oneself exposed to the community. People seeking self-respect in matters outside the constraints of their own social roles can talk politics rather than feel the guilt imposed by the moral codes and churches. They can express judgment, a far preferable self-image than that of a compromiser with conventional morality, which social custom almost forces them to be. On political issues they can agree with most of their fellow villagers, because districts tend to be dominated by one party. Far better to agree on public truths than to dwell on one's own almost inevitable moral transgressions. A national focus relieves both the narrowness of village life and the guilt from the contradictions inherent in the mating system. Concern with politics and nation can open up a focus outside the self and open social discourse. The churches also engage people in public rituals, wide organization, and compelling ideas. This function, now clearly shared by the stimulation of a sense of being a self-governing nation, gave the churches their importance.

4

Vincentians' Search for Their Culture

The post–World War II pan-Caribbean ferment of interest in local history and cultural identity was carried on in St. Vincent principally by the Kingstown Study Group. The participants' papers appear in *Flambeau*, a quarterly published from 1966 through 1969. Their motto was "Instead of cursing at the darkness, one lights a candle." Their writings are pervaded by pessimism, with the West Indian Federation dissolved to the great dismay of Caribbean intellectuals generally, and with local politics decried by purists for its populism and opportunism. The pessimism of *Flambeau* went beyond the local scene and referred to the island's dependence on world rivalries of the superpowers. It also reflected the extreme bitterness of victims of racism and resentment of economic domination by a few hundred wealthy island whites. These Vincentians had been influenced by the black Caribbean orators of the 1930s and postwar intellectuals and leaders Eric Williams and C. L. R. James. Their views were informed by Marxist analysis of class and history. What stands out in the brief period of *Flambeau*'s publication is their engagement with the problems of their society and their bitterness over racism and absence of opportunity.

The sudden proposal from Britain of independent statehood for St. Vincent and its implementation in 1969 changed the orientation of the Kingstown Study Group from protest to responsibility under independence. *Flambeau* ceased publication, and many of its contributors changed from critics of imperialism to policy formulators. The Educational Forum of the People appeared, a new name for much the same group. Through public meetings and published pamphlets its members identified and discussed many important issues in the organization and operation of Vincentian institutions—from schools, courts, and police to politics, economics, self-government, land reform, and rural development. They also were concerned with what bound them together and what gave them an identity, concerned with history, African origins, and Vincentian "culture," which they defined in anthropological terms: "The culture of a society can be looked upon as the collective personality of the people. It involves their way of life—their customs, songs, dances, food, dress, speech, writings, music, art and the rest. It is what makes them similar to some people and different from others" (Educational Forum 1972:45).

This group of Vincentian intellectuals advocated the recognition and promotion of Africanness in Vincentian music, religion, family life, and manners. They located one basic problem in the chasm between their society's European values and the people's inability to act and think as Europeans: "A hierarchy of Western social values has been superimposed on a people whose diverse backgrounds are not equipped to accommodate them. The society that results has a split personality and is monstrously artificial" (Educational Forum 1972:46). These intellectuals, who were more closely involved with European values than the general populace, who must have experienced more acutely than the common people the disparities and ambivalences between their Vincentian way of life and their elite educations, appear in hindsight extreme in their attribution of artificiality and personality conflict to their compatriots. Grass-roots culture has to be described to be recognized, and at that time the study of folktales, Africanism in religions, and customs and values of Afro-American societies was a nascent field and little progress had been made toward description of unified cultures. The educated men and women, most of whom had come from the common people, were either too close or too far to see themes of continuity and integrity.

The Educational Forum of the People embodied the creative spirit and dedication to national development that opened with the ending of colonialism. Vincentians were stimulated by their ideas and were impressed especially by the 1972 CARIFTA festival of dance and music that toured the islands and performed in towns and villages. Music and dance companies from the Caribbean, drawing on African-derived materials, became frequent visitors in the 1970s and in recent years have been formed by Vincentians. Folk dance has been revived and is a curiosity to audiences. The dances are European in form with African-like movements, as judged by choreometric standards, incorporated with the formal quadrille and maypole wrapping. Percussion, string, and wind instruments, constructed and played by a group of elderly male musicians, has also been brought before islandwide audiences as part of the new appreciation of traditional arts. Vincentian history has long been included in school curricula. Historical knowledge and interest now support the new sense of Vincentianness derived from tradition, although much of Vincentian history has yet to be written and much informative writing remains as fragments in periodic news columns. The view that St. Vincent has unique qualities that are a source of pride, distinctive characteristics as a nation, became prevalent in the mid-1980s, whereas it was a tentative idea at best among most Vincentians in 1972. The expression "our culture" is commonplace now, used by lower- and middle-class rural people, ministers of government, newspaper columnists, writers of letters to the editor, young teachers, and young artists. The new positive valuation of African-derived cultural elements in their society was well received by villagers, and they have added it to their many diverse values and opinions.

SPEAKING CREOLE

The Vincentian self-consciousness about culture includes a recent legitimation of the Creole language. Now young men and women use Creole in preference to standard English, the language of the media and most school instruction. Some schoolteachers defend this practice, pointing out that "it is their mother tongue" and standard English is a "foreign language." Only old people express disapproval of educated youths' use of Creole, the language an elderly village woman in 1972 had called "this broken language of ours." Schoolteachers use Creole among themselves. Some senior teachers, who have promoted the use of vernacular in school skits and songs about Vincentian life, are concerned about the interference speaking

Creole may have with learning standard English and stress the importance of using both. In the last few years, Creole phrases have occasionally been used for a desired effect in the press and in public speeches, appearing to be an entirely new style for those mediums. The best English usage has long been a point of pride, appreciated by the barely educated and practiced by the well schooled. Vernacular speeches, skits, poetry, and choral speaking are popular in schools. There has been some tradition in the recent past of writing in Creole, although it was reflected in *Flambeau* only in the use of aphorisms and in some of the poetry. An elderly Windward Valley farmer, quoted in Chapter 4, wrote poetry in dialect and standard English. He used standard English for moralisms and aphorisms and dialect for local history. A prominent rural school principal wrote much material for school performances in Creole and used folk customs among his themes. Several of his students who have become teachers carry on the art and their students sing songs that parody local life and local gossip themes, songs of advice to the young and songs of pride in the country, using both Creole and standard English. In 1986 a favorite song and skit (the song written by Beverly Regisford) was called "River Commess," meaning "river gossip":

> See Dora and Etelin to river they heading.
> One bundle wid dirty clothes de other wid bedding.
> Dora husband gane a town, Benji gane a boxing plant.
> They hoping to get home as quickly as they can.
> River comess oh! River comess
> River comess oh! River comess
> Dem grinding down dem clothes pan de river stone
> But dem mouth gwine like machine wid de river Commess

Dialogue follows, touching on young girls' pregnancies, a boundary fight between neighbors, a returnee from America making noise with his tape recorder, a woman of "too big fashion" stealing from a supermarket—"Lard wat a disgrace"—and a Rasta Boy jailed for stealing a ram goat and trying to escape in a fishing boat. Then the last verse:

> Poor Benji came home hungry lard nat a ting fu eat.
> Yo know when people hungry how dem does feel fu beat
> He pick up wan big stick and head towards river
> When Dora see he coming oh how she start shiver.

One of the songs of advice, again written by Beverly Regisford, went as follows:

These are not the days to sit down on vacation
Make your contribution to the nation.
Work in agriculture or as a mason,
And prevent starvation.

Other rural school groups do choral speaking of uplift themes with comic twists and perform English folk dances with precision and rhythmic gusto, intricate maneuvers requiring complex coordination of the dancers. Youth groups perform skits on themes of international and interpersonal violence and chaotic scenes of intoxication, drug abuse, and rape. They also present drumming, improvisational dance, and skits employing popular dance style. Choral speaking of a youth group in 1986 took the theme "We are free from slavery, and that is the irony." The school groups performed in the village carnival during the daytime children's event, and the older groups performed in the "cultural show." They also present their arts at other school and public festivities. These performances represent a popular art form with widespread participation and common occurrence, using themes drawn directly from local experience and thought, in which teachers, students, and audiences participate in the same thought, style, and enjoyment. The themes show a pattern of accurate social critique, recognition of the dangers of young adulthood, cynicism, and a sense of moral responsibility—not an organized sense of Vincentian cultural identity, but youth from both social classes searching, unsatisfied, employing both Creole and standard English for the expressiveness of each language, and dramatizing real Vincentian lifeways.

NATIONAL CARNIVAL

The widespread conviction that St. Vincent has a national culture has been linked in several public statements by political leaders to the annual carnival. A member of Parliament said in a broadcasted speech before that body in 1986 that "carnival is the only national event in which rich and poor, Black and White, all participate." A Carnival Development Committee member said before a rural audience, "Carnival gives us an opportunity to show all the world what we can do. This is your cultural heritage. It should interest you and show you who you are and where you are going. It shows the future of your country and where you want it to go." A newspaper columnist wrote: " 'Too much Carnival'—some complain—but the fact may be that Carnival is all the culture we have left" (Colin King, *Vincentian*, 14

October 1988). The certainty of those public figures that "we Vincie" share attributes, styles, and beliefs is a far cry from the idea of cultureless-ness of Caribbean societies long propounded by many commentators. Al-though culture is more pervasive than a single festival, carnival has symbol-ic meaning as an expression of the heritage and direction of the country.

A long history of carnival celebrations in St. Vincent can be inferred from observations in 1791 in William Young's diary: "December 26. This was a day of Christmas gambols. In the morning we rode out and in the town of Calliaqua saw many negroes attending high mass at the popish chapel. The town was like a very gay fair with booths, furnished with every-thing good to eat and fine to wear" (Young 1807, vol. 3:258). I have not found mention of observances at the end of Lent, but such a festive Catholic Christmas fair after mass suggests that Lent would not have gone uncele-brated. Parading, dancing, and music in African and English styles were performed by the slaves on William Young's estate at Christmas. Among the events were "Mumbo Jumbo and his suite. The Jumbo was on stilts, with a head mounted on the actor's head, which was concealed; the music was from two baskets, like strawberry baskets, with little bells within, shook in time. The swordsman danced with an air of menace, the musician was comical, and Jumbo assumed the 'antic terrible,' and was very active on his stilts (Young 1807, vol. 3:258). Stilts dancers, fantastic head masks, and swordsmen were later to be carnival features.

Historians of carnival see its early origin in the slaves' marches to the estate house at crop-over time, after six months of the year in demanding labor, a time of both relief and resentment. In Trinidad the anniversary of emancipation was celebrated with contests of rival masked kings and their bands in Cannes Brulé, named for the burning of the cut cane fields after crop-over. Elder and Hill emphasize the aggressiveness of the stick fighting in these contests. Black bands attempted to join the costumed Mardi Gras marches of the white upper class in Trinidad and were banned from them by law in 1859. Riots later arose from this exclusion, and police action was particularly strong in the early 1880s (Elder 1964a; Hill 1972:26–28). So far as is known, Vincentian marches at Mardi Gras were all-black events, but they also met with repression. An account of this history has been as-sembled by recent carnival organizers:

> The St. Vincent Carnival riots of February 11th 1879 actually preceded those of Trinidad which occurred in 1883.
>
> Our colonial masters, ever conscious of the force and power of a peo-ple's culture, had spared little effort to stamp out certain dominant forms. The drums which had conveyed news of the Haitian revolution to the slaves

were ruthlessly suppressed. So it was that in 1872 Carnival was banned. The Lieutenant-Governor in defending the move, stated that it was the custom of the "Lower order" of the people to dress in "fantastic attire" and wear masks, parading and dancing through the streets with sticks or whips "with which they struck at any persons passing by."

In 1879 however, the Vincentian people decided to revive their festivity at any cost. Revellers appeared on the streets on the evening of Saturday 8th February. Arrests were made on Carnival Monday and Tuesday. At about 7 p.m. on Tuesday evening the riots started, when people assembled between Pauls Gate and the Green. Police who had been summoned, had to beat a hasty retreat to the accompaniment of stones, sticks and bottles. The Lieutenant-governor himself was not spared, when Wednesday after an emergency meeting of the Executive Council, he was ferociously attacked by some three hundred to four hundred persons.

This then was the spirit in which Carnival was born; out of a struggle from which emerged a people's assertion of their identity. (Carnival Bands Association, *Vincentian*, 14 October 1988)

Themes of emancipation and the suppression of marches are illustrated by a 1983 song of Trinidad's Calypsonian, Mighty Sparrow (quoted in Segal 1988):

> Be prepared for bacchanal
> 100 years of Carnival
>
> . . . .
> Celebrate with me
> The 100th anniversary.
> It all began that blessed day
> When massa man took the chains away.
> Free at last from the plantation
> Lord, it was mas' all over the land.
> Beatin' box and dustbin,
> Dress up in Massa ole clothin'.

Slavery and emancipation represent the past; the themes of social commentary represent the culture of the present. C. L. R. James's early admiration of the Mighty Sparrow indicates the relevance to the Caribbean culture of the Trinidadian steel band and calypso styles, now adopted in much of the region:

> His talents were shaped by a West Indian medium; through this medium he expanded his capacities and the medium itself. He is financially maintained by the West Indian people who buy his records. The mass of people give him all the encouragement that an artist needs. Although the calypso is Trinidadian, Sparrow is hailed in all the islands and spontaneously acknowledged

as a representative West Indian. . . . For in most nations the popular music and the popular song come first, are usually centuries old, and the artists and intellectuals often build their national creations upon these age-old roots. I am sure that it is not all accidental that in the very same decade that West Indian artists are finding West Indianism, the native popular music and the native popular song find their most complete, their most vigorous expression and acceptance. (James 1977:191–99)

In the early twentieth century, the Vincentian colonial administrator presided over the Mardi Gras revelries and awarded an "administrator's scepter" to the best Calypsonian. In 1945 steel-band instruments and tuning equipment were brought from Trinidad by a Vincentian, Raphael Davison, who had grown up there and played for the first time in the Vincentian carnival. Even in Trinidad the pans were used only for percussion until a Trinidadian in 1948 developed a method of tuning them for a melody, and this use was introduced to St. Vincent the same year:

> "At that time we used to play mas' [marching in masquerade] and steel band together. My band had twelve people in it. . . . When I came here I did not see anything as in Trinidad. Not much people played mas'. And the type of mas' they had were made from cheap pieces of strings and matting. And on the Carnival morning people used to have to jig up to the administrator's house, jig up in front of him, and he will give the winning band five dollars and a pool of ribbons as prize." But he refused to "lick any colonialist boot" and took his twelve member band on the streets of Kingstown for the first Carnival street jump-up in this country's history, in 1945. (Anthony Williams, *Vincentian*, 26 October 1990)

In the period anticipating independence, carnival was supported by local businesses and planters, adding fine costumes and a Queen contest, bringing in Trinidadian steel bands, and elaborating the competition for Calypso King. Vincentian steel bands were performing by 1962, when the winning band was the local Police Steel Orchestra, a sponsorship that suggests a new compatibility of carnival and law enforcement. 1971 marked the change from Trinidadian to Vincentian Calypso singers and the local design and leadership of mas' bands, as well as establishment of a government committee to coordinate the festival. Carnival was moved to the summer season and is now promoted as a tourist attraction (Carnival Development Committee 1984).

Vincentians abroad increasingly visit for carnival, some performing as featured Calypsonians, others as mas'-band dancers, and Vincentian businesses in New York sponsor bands and contestants. Vincentians from abroad outnumber foreign tourists. Increasingly they schedule home visits at carnival time in addition to the traditional Christmas visiting season.

Émigrés maintain ties with home families and obligations are fulfilled as visitors enjoy the hospitality of their old homes, a vacation in the sun in scenic villages, a pleasurable change from inner-city life in New York, Toronto, or London. They bring metropolitan gifts and send larger remittances to repay the hospitality. The drain of capital and labor noted by critics of Caribbean migration (Chapter 3) could well be balanced with the closeness of interests among home and emigrated families, the periodic renewal of identity as Vincentians, and the enrichment of cultural and commodity exchange. The mixing of industrial-urban culture and island-rural culture is a well-established trend.

Inter-Caribbean competitions in carnivals contribute to recognition of shared characteristics and distinctive identities. Like the current movement toward political unity of the Eastern Caribbean states, promoted by several of the leaders now in office, the cultural exchanges through carnivals promote shared cultural expressions. There is widespread acknowledgment of carnivals as expressions of each country's best abilities, along with sports competitions, performing companies, and queen contests, which increasingly have both national and intra-Caribbean audiences. The government ministers' faith in carnival's symbolism of the unity of races and classes, and as a statement of tradition and future direction, expresses meanings and uses of the festival.

Currently there are more than one hundred Vincentian Calypsonians and many times that number of commentators on them. The following description concerns several styles and themes that seemed prominent in observations I made in 1984 and 1986, and perhaps stood out because they fit other points of ethnographic importance. As styles change, those I observed may move to the background.

As a medium for political and social critique, the Calypso song tradition augments the popular sense of involvement in government and politics. The traditional presentation of the administrator's scepter for the winning Calypso has been carried over in a sense of office as Calypso King. In 1985, shortly before the end of his year as reigning Calypsonian, the king introduced a new song called "How Can I Resign"? The song depicted his role as one of keeping public issues before his audience, issues of political, social, and economic problems in the island and worldwide. In recent years Calypsonians have sung about the dangers of monarchy, tyranny, corruption, despotism, and oppression. Political commentary is satirical, contentious, exaggerated, and often comic. Margaret Thatcher was included in a list of threats to the nation, because she wanted to run St. Vincent. Queen Elizabeth's 1984 visit to Kingstown and Bequia to commemorate fifteen

years of independence did not stir monarchical admiration in Calypsonians; on the contrary, one of them sang of the cost of carpets, the brevity of
her public appearance, and the Vincentian prime minister's failure to get
funds from "Queen Betty."

Vincentian political leaders are frequent subjects of Calypsos both
caustic and comic. The prime minister, James Mitchell, had been in office
for two years by the time of the 1986 Calypso contest. A member of a
wealthy family on the Grenadine island of Bequia, he had called himself a
fisherman. A song and skit depicted a "fisherman from Bequia" wedding
"Miss Vincie" and gave friendly advice. Another friendly critic sang, "Ease
up, fisherman. I feelin' the pressure." Another song likened Mitchell to the
African folk trickster Anancy. "He trick you, he trick me," went the popular lyrics. To be likened to the African folk hero enhanced his image much
more than the charge of trickery detracted from it. Mitchell commented on
the song in a radio speech: "Since the tune is good, the song is good. I
would never ban a Calypso"—making a bit of political capital at the expense of the prime minister of Barbados, Thom Adams, who had banned
the songs of a Calypsonian who had harassed him (Manning 1985). The
large number of Calypso songs concerning politicians reflects the popular
interest in public figures and government.

Another characteristic of Calypso style is its symbolization of the
power of mature men. The Calypso representation of mature male power is
conveyed directly in the age of the leading singers and is confirmed in the
style of dance accompanying the song. Most of the Calypsonians who
reach the town stage project an image of maturity and physical power in
marked contrast to a youthful style seen more commonly in smaller arenas,
a style that often adopts a Rasta Man image of matted hair. The mature
Calypsonians keep the beat with flexed knees and feet well apart, emphasizing strength, whereas the youthful singers portray lightness and agility,
sometimes with hopping and skipping. Young singers usually use a tenor
voice, in contrast to most mature Calypsonians' bass register and use of an
operatic bass laugh. Many singers have a supporting female dancer or a
backup group of female and male dancers. A mature singer is accompanied
by a mature woman whose dance style is a genteel and admired form of the
basic style, with small steps, bent arms, and knees close together, torso forward and hip movements subtly restrained. The same form can be seen in
mature village women, who may be the first to strike up a street dance on
special occasions. The mature dance styles are well marked and much admired. A frequent subject of Calypsos concerns prominent men of St. Vincent and their importance to the country. "When will we start to honor

Vincentians?" a singer asks as he recalls recent public figures and their roles. A singer tells of his grandmother's advice to him as a boy: "If you want to be a preacher you must . . . if you want to be a head teacher, . . . if you want to be a politician . . ." These songs have a serious tone. They indicate the Calypsonian orientation to mature male authority. The contrast between young and mature male roles in village society, with the older men's retention of land and authority and the expectation that young men are idlers and entertainers, is reflected in Calypso styles.

The themes and styles of mas' bands are high-minded and literary, and the dance style is reserved. The Carnival culminates in a daylong performance of eight to ten mas' bands of elaborately costumed dancers and musicians performing on a large outdoor stage and then parading through the streets of Kingstown. In an almost unvarying style of dancing and choreography, and in the steady beat of Calypso and reggae rhythms, band after band of dancers, each 50 to 150 men and women in tights, leotards, and emblematic accessories, many of the central dancers in huge gauze-covered wire wings and headdresses, presents a theme. The themes, announced and narrated by a commentator, are as varied as the performing style is repetitive. Themes are historical fantasies; abstract qualities such as heat, color, and beauty; or vital activities such as transportation, money, fishing, traveling, and hobbies. Titles of bands in 1986 were Beauty Is in the Eyes of the Beholder, Atlantis, Before the Conquest, Dilemma, Winter Wonderland, Mirage, Fantastique, and Perilous Journey. Perilous Journey's episodes were moral messages in a Pilgrim's Progress–like format: The Wizard (who takes the journey through the episodes), Black Hatred that Burns Like Fire, Jealousy and Envy, Unkind Words Stick on You Like Spears, Sweat and Tears, Better Do It the Honest Way, Spirit of Hope, Bad-Minded People Are the Forces of Evil, Rainbow, Light of Glory. Deriving from masquerade marches, the performers in each episode enter the outdoor stage, exhibit their costumes and leading figures in stationary marching movements, then march off and are followed by the next group. There is no dramatic action, the theme instead being depicted through the title, the costumes, and the narrator's commentary. All themes are danced in a similar style and form. Carib themes introduce the most exotic elements. A slower beat and a heavier dance style were adopted by one group representing Indians, but most Carib themes, such as sun worship, mourning paint, and stone worship—all received in uneasy silence in this totally Christian audience— were danced in the same style as purity, heat and color. Meaning is in the titles, the costumes, and the narration, not in the dancers' movements. The uniform dance style enables anyone to perform.

Preparation begins many months in advance, with band leaders choosing a theme and their group of artists making sketches and constructing the elaborate costumes and props. Outside their workshops they post the theme and episodes, the costume sketches and the cost of costumes to be paid by each performer. Groups of friends sign up as band members, and bands are sometimes sponsored by clubs, villages, and businesses. Although several thousand persons perform on the outdoor stage during the ten days of carnival, general participation occurs only in the street jam following the finale as the performers parade through the streets with the steel bands playing on floats and trucks. The townspeople dance and show their appreciation. The band dance style is not erotic, and the themes and narrations are both civic and high minded, seldom bawdy. The audiences are sedate viewers, and even the street jam dancing is relatively modest and orderly. Vincentian carnival is not orgiastic. It is a refined celebration, representing the ideals of decorum and the respect of "sweet" themes such as depicted in the traditional village tea meetings. Carnival is genuinely expressive of Vincentian social interests, and it's promotion as national culture is accurate.

CARNIVAL IN A VILLAGE

Village views of carnival express something of the relationship between nation and populace, town and county. In Windward Valley it is seen as a town event, drawing few viewers from this village even though bus and van transportation was convenient. It was ignored by the majority of villagers until the live television broadcasts began in 1986, when many viewed it for the first time. Young men, as well as a few matrons, might attend, but the bus fare and ticket price for mere entertainment was a consideration for many people. Fundamentalist churches condemned carnival as irreligious, and this view was held also outside the churches. Many people merely resented the crowds and disruption of town services. The Spiritual Baptists, among the poorest villagers, were not attracted to carnival, but they took a tolerant view and commented on the fundamentalists: "How can they forbid you?" Village autonomy in the face of political posturing takes a wait-and-see attitude and is more ready with criticism than with approval. Villagers' initiative and sense of their own worth run strong, and a group of young men from Windward Valley organized a rural carnival in 1985 and 1986. As background to this event the class diversity of Vincentian villages and their fully national view of themselves should again be pointed out.

The small size of the island, the single urban center served by adequate transportation in all directions, and the location in town of all specialized services have developed rural familiarity with town life. Emigration, direct between villages and abroad, has also spread a measure of cosmopolitanism and resources to the villages. Class diversity and mobility within rural society have made the village, to some extent, a cross section of the nation. With its close links to town, rural life is not specialized.

Four young men made up the carnival committee, all from the village of Windward Valley. They announced the coming event almost a year ahead, and the island newspaper carried a brief article about their plans. The carnival was named for the district, and many performing groups and a few of the audience came from villages all along the windward coast. I did not witness the 1985 event; this account depicts the 1986 Windward Valley carnival. In some respects the event closely followed the design of the national carnival, and in other respects it conveyed rural style and values. Following the town, but reduced in size and length, the week-long event included a queen contest, Calypso semifinals and finals, a "cultural show," a daytime school-age show and a final parade and "jump up" through the village. It took place the week before the town festival, when carnival fervor was running high. One mas' band was mounted. It took on the theme of racial injustice in South Africa, planned, costumed, danced, and narrated by village youths. When they were invited to bring their band to the town finale, they decided not to risk their complex costumes in a village performance. They followed town professionalism in setting up a headquarters, a "tent," in a large cement basement remaining from the demolished arrowroot factory near the center of the village, owned by the government and loaned to them by the Carnival Development Committee. The committee also loaned money, to be reimbursed from gate receipts, authorized several police officers on performance nights, arranged loans of sound equipment, and sent representatives to make opening speeches at the programs. The queen and Calypso winners entered the town competitions.

Major stylistic differences from the town carnival were evident in the Calypso themes, in skits which accompanied the singers and in cultural program skits. The rural Calypsonians used skits more than those in town, some singers adding drama to supplement, perhaps, the more amateurish quality of the lyrics. Of seventeen Calypsos, four were entirely devoted to the racial situation in South Africa, whereas in town only one in a program of equal length took that topic. The Windward mas' band took the same subject, enacting Prime Minister Botha and the imprisoned Nelson Mandela, calling it Azania on Fire, while the mas' bands in Kingstown used the subject in only one section of one band. The contrast is due to the emphasis on entertainment and the greater artistic sophistication in the national event, and suggests more outspokenness on race issues on the part of the rural performers. Among the rural Calypsos, four others took themes of sex, some comic and ribald and received with shouts and hoots, and others depicted violent and impersonal male control over women and were watched quietly and with discomfort. Town Calypsos were sometimes ribald, but none of the accompanying skits had the bawdiness of the rural ones, and the town mas' bands were entirely lacking in this kind of entertainment. Another four village songs concerned Vincentian political and social issues, themes closer to the town style but different in that two were more intellectual and idealistic and two represented more extreme and chaotic conditions than in town. A male schoolteacher with a blackboard and the flags of the United States, the Soviet Union, the United Nations, and St. Vincent acted out a lecture accompanying a serious Calypso about world problems. This staging of a classroom was respected in the village but would have been too stilted for town competitions. The other intellectual Calypso, sung by a woman and entitled "Nation Builders," construed the task of Vincentian leaders in terms of global relationships and sang in heroic cadences of an island nation worthy of the new stage it had entered. In a deliberate beat and standard English her song contrasted with the Creole and dialect that characterized the rural much more than the town songs. Lady Gypsy, as she was called, sang in the classical Calypso style used by most town performers. She was one of the village winners, appealing to young men and women but displeasing to many older men, who thought Calypso should remain a male style, and older women who disapproved of another cause she sang about that season, women's liberation. For the national competition the lyrics of her chorus were "I want to pop," expressing pride in winning, and the words, gestures, and costume conveyed double entendre worthy of traditional Calypso humor. Like some of the male singers, she used her appearance in the village as a stepping stone to a national role and did not sing there in a rural idiom.

Of the four rural Calypsos with political and social themes, two were more extreme in their depiction of social ills and were accompanied by skits portraying chaotic scenes. Town Calypsos took the theme "we on the wrong track" and sang of tyranny and corruption but did not approach the cynicism and disorder of two of the Windward Valley Calypsos, "Unfair Games Will Never End" and "Trouble in the Party." Of the seventeen Calypsos presented, they resembled three others that can only be classified as depicting chaos. They had chorus lines such as "we island dying slow" and

"St. Vincent on fire" and included skit episodes of transvestism, drugs, and police brutality. One, called "Welcome to the Gem of the Antilles," acted out tourists in drug stupors, intoxicated, violent, and confused. The traditional rural performance episode in which "rude boys" take over and bumbling chaos reigns has been adapted for themes of current disorder (Abrahams 1977). One Calypso was a good-natured, tuneful but vague political comment; another said "Leave Me Alone," but the singer's intentions were not clear. The committee chairman of the 1985 carnival said the theme that year was "We Kind of People" and that it had skits about "work gambling and love."

The tenor of the week's performances in part reflected a more open, or an increased, radicalism among some of the youth, among whom were the members of the village carnival committee. They were incensed by the racial situation in South Africa, which was particularly violent in the spring of 1986. The custom of speaking only in Creole had come into vogue, whereas two years before the same young men and women, although using Creole among villagers, had regularly used school English to high-status persons. They voiced outspoken defenses of unmarried youths' sexual encounters and childbearing. Rastafarianism, in a simpler form than in Jamaica, had been popular for some years but had become diluted, with almost any youth jovially called a *Rastaman,* and even radical youths sometimes using the term to mean thief. These styles and concerns of some of the youths, however, hardly account for the extreme themes of the songs and acts. The performers were numerous and diverse; some singers aimed at professionalism, schoolteachers acted along with laborers and farmers. Audiences laughed at the ribaldry, applauded the depictions of chaos, and showed reticence, perhaps fear, at the scenes of violence. Fundamentalist church members did not attend, but their children who were too young to have joined the church were allowed to go, and no criticism of irreligiousness was heard; in fact, there was no criticism of any kind, and many of the pillars of the village were in attendance. The themes and styles were familiar and popular. The more vivid content and depth of emotion compared with the national carnival suggest that the village show was more representative of popular culture and a more typical level of emotional and thematic expressiveness. The town might well see itself more openly expressed in the village. The traditional village tea meetings pitted the rude boys against the rule of decorum. The traditional rural Lenten carnival "brings the realities of life to the fore, emphasizing pleasure and freedom from social constraint and not only allowing license and highly aggressive behavior, but bringing it to high performance" (Abraham 1983:107).

The village carnival also had a ceremony for honoring two senior professional persons, a man who had been principal of the junior secondary school and a woman who had been the district nurse and midwife for many years. The gesture was original, not replicating any part of town carnival, and was placed prominently in the program. The young organizers seemed to want to dignify their show through expressing their respect for the woman who had delivered many of them as babies and the man who had helped many of them through the highest level of education in the village. The nurse had been made godmother of many children she delivered, and the principal had been one of the popularizers of Creole dialogue in tales and poems, which he wrote for school performances. These significant persons stood for the respect generally granted to older people. In the initial planning of the carnival, the organizers consulted several elderly villagers. They had learned from Fitzpatrick's local history that a carnival had been held in the village twenty years previously, and they went to the old men who had sponsored that festival to find out about it. They wanted to act in the tradition of the place and also celebrate the former achievements of their locale. In writing up their plans for the national newspaper, they stated that their carnival derived from former carnival traditions in two other rural centers as well. These other two rural carnivals had lapsed and no other village had since staged a full carnival with Calypso contests and cultural performances. In consulting the old men, they received a go-ahead, at least a reprieve from criticism.

Different as town and village carnivals are in message, the two genres have the same name, follow similar formats, and have a long common history. Their origins make clear the primacy of the folk tradition and the secondary development of the recent government-sponsored event. The origin of both is in the masquerading bands trooping through villages and towns and in front of the Governor's House, at one period rounded up in mass arrests, at another the band's leader acquiring a title of king and a scepter from the colonial government. As the modern festival in several Caribbean nations, it fuses all the celebrations of the people: the meanings of emancipation, colonial suppression, identity, fantasy, and license. The government has taken a folk tradition, but the folk performances have not waned. Even though carnival's full village form may lapse for years, its elements of performance are kept up by neighborhood musical clubs, Christmas marches, and wake singing, and full-scale performances can be remounted easily. At the time the full form is first known to have appeared in Windward Valley, it had benefitted from returnee villagers' observations of carnival in Trinidad, and twenty years later it had incorporated some of the elements of the national event. The national carnival does not seem to have drained or overawed the village productions. At the same time villagers are as concerned as the government about putting a national show before an international public. Villagers want to keep their émigré relatives from forgetting St. Vincent, knowing that most agricultural plots and most cement-block houses were acquired from earnings abroad. They also enjoy performing companies from other Caribbean nations and recognize the common genre of which their traditions are a part, and so they are proud of their nation's participation in the regional competitions.

Some of the different influences at work in the village and the town carnivals are easily apparent. The villages need not censure their productions to put their best face forward, as the town carnival is prompted to do to speak for the nation and address foreign audiences. The town musicians' more accomplished artistry allows them to dominate the stage, whereas the rural singers amplify their messages with skits that add content to their lyrics. Other differences between village and town represent cultural variation, some suggesting a far more explicit level of meanings in the village. The villagers are less adept at political commentary and satire, less concerned with being in politics, but they pay tribute to local leadership. The village is more outspoken about hard issues such as race and tourism, issues on which the government walks softly. The schoolteacher has a respected role in the village, and so he is in the skit with his blackboard and flags, speaking out on social issues. In politics there is "trouble in the party," and party men portrayed in mêlée look much like the grasping, posturing tourists. Cynicism about political leaders is not generally high, but Vincentians have a readiness to believe immorality of anyone, politicians included. The marginal attractiveness of the town versus the village performance is due to several stylistic and expressive differences. The romanticism of town costumes and the understatement of the mas'-band dancing are not attractive. The huge gauze moths borrowed from Trinidad and a hallmark of carnivals may be too unreal. The beauty of nature itself is much appreciated by villagers. The expense of the costumes keeps most villagers from joining a band, and the costumes are so fragile that they are used up in one wearing. The town dance style is dull compared to village dancing. It suggests the town night-spot dancing style of low-keyed eroticism. Social dances in the village community center have an exciting style, unlike the blasé town style. The village stage presents truly voluptuous female dancing, a version of the regular dance style, and it goes over well with all ages. The open social commentary and low restraint of the village skits show dancing couples verging into violence toward the women, and the audience sits silently. My impression is that the audience recognizes village carnival's authenticity. The village troupes put all the cards on the table. One aspect of the town mas' bands is strongly appreciated in the village and comes across clearly in radio and television: the high-toned moral messages of the scenarios and narration. The themes of rage and kindness, of suffering insult, and of hope are much like church sermons and are much admired in their secular form. If the costumes are too wasteful and the dancing falsely restrained, the moral statements are welcomed. Where emotion is not masked, the essential role of moral preachment is recognized. Embracing moral principles resolves the contradictions of the village life cycle. Thus the meaning of the performance is fully stated in the village. In combining traditional performance styles and newer national styles the village carnival preserves expression of rural peoples' concerns and keeps rural audiences abreast of national imagery. One might ask whether the clear-cut village culture remains fully conscious among the town middle class, the professionals and the visiting émigrés, so that they can continue to see the substratum of Vincentian experiences in the masked emotion of national style. Whether the town carnival conveys these lessons, while it enacts the modern-world attractions of fantastic costumes and blasé emotion, appears unlikely. The carnival is intended to both connect St. Vincent to other nations and be a statement of Vincentian identity. In the words of a Carnival Development Committee member, "It shows you who you are and where you are going." If it does this, both the rural and the town versions are needed.

For a decade, perhaps longer, small drama companies and dance companies have been organized, some of them started by Vincentians who participated in drama and dance in New York, others by local persons. They assemble and teach talented persons, write and choreograph their own works, and perform at local events such as the Windward Valley carnival and at commemorative occasions such as the anniversary of independence. They perform in the principal villages and in Kingstown. The government promotes them and sponsors a drama competition among secondary schools and among community groups, and conducts workshops in directing, acting, and writing for theater. Popular art in the genre of the Windward Valley carnival skits has appeared in these performances. A rural group announced that their theme would be incest; they were expected to expose and condemn it, but instead they produced a comedy on the subject, and the drama critic for the newspaper, a new post, decried it. Speech also becomes an issue: can Creole be projected clearly or is standard English necessary?

For government and the returned émigrés to go to the local communities for art is a measure of the confidence in their performance traditions and the desire to find and promote their own ideas and style and to overcome the increasing entrancement with styles of American television. The minister of culture said that "the dramatists who come out of this and future festivals should be seen in local sitcoms and other shows, which will gradually replace the foreign television programmes we keep complaining about" (*Vincentian*, 12 October 1990). In a recent address supporting Windward Island federation, the president of the Caribbean Development Bank expressed fears of the same foreign influences, as phrased by a news columnist: "Without a chastity belt provided by union, cultural penetration of the region could make a mess of our identity and pave the way for our virtual re-colonization" (Kenneth John, *Vincentian*, 24 July 1987). The objectives of the cultural policy are being backed up.

5

Discovering Culture and Seeking National Identity

This book has discussed the actuality of Vincentian culture, a culture with consistent meanings and systematic norms and values. The idea of a West Indian culture goes against both older ethnologies and many recent analyses. In them few unifying factors were found; few functional organizing systems and few replications of thought patterns were discerned. Other interpretations have concentrated on the divisiveness of the central formative factors of colonialism, class and race. I do not question the historical importance of these factors, but I have described forms of social and cultural integration that have nevertheless prevailed. A quarter century of political independence in this area may have made the difference in behavioral climate to give substance to the idea that societies tend to generate shared cultures. Political independence has nurtured the self-consciousness of unity and group identity. Thinking one's society has a culture is part of what culture is.

My initial field experience gave me the sense that I was observing self-conscious and systematic modes of actions and thought. My informants expressed rationales for behavior, and if I could piece together their words, I might see an underlying pattern in their overtly fragmented concerns and activities. The characteristics that might bring consistency to these activities were not readily apparent. Several potential windows onto a culture that anthropologists rely on were not initially useful. Kinship organization was minimally developed; organized groups were diffuse; social power came not from inside communities but from remote organizations; belief systems had the colonial stamp; rituals were few, and although their meanings appeared to be clear, I did not initially perceive patterning among different ceremonies. I considered and rejected the interpretation employed by some analysts that the poverty of the great majority explained their way of life in terms of situational responses for coping with material deprivation.

My first analytic procedure to define consistencies was the comparison of households having a head couple with those having only a female head. My two types of households represent the forms of visiting unions, consensual unions, and marriages that have been considered indicative of diversity in marital behavior associated with class statuses. I found that these different domestic forms had similar norms, organization, and moral principles and that rural middle- and lower-class families were similar. The households had matricentric characteristics, even those with a resident husband, and they tended to include adult sons and daughters and daughters' children. Most women had two or more children before entering a co-residential union, and her children usually remained with her when she moved to reside with a husband; thus it was likely that the husband would not be the biological father of the oldest children in the household. Men frequently delayed a coresidential husband role until well past young adulthood, and often they had children by a number of women and were obligated and related to several households. Where young men and women married, the husband had more authority than the wife, but these marriages frequently ended in divorce. Mens' diffuse parenting and sexual ties, and the growing productivity and family influence of the oldest children in the house, especially the oldest sons, combined to keep the husband more peripheral in the household he joined after a roving youth.

Once I was able to show a degree of consistency in the family and household, I looked to data on wider aspects of personal and domestic culture, specifically to customs related to the development of emotion and discipline. Typical indulgence in infancy and early childhood appears to encourage basic trust. The child is given considerable responsibility in the family and is taught kin relationships as well as the practices for eliciting fulfillment of patrilateral obligations. The boundedness of sets of full siblings within households and the degree of unboundedness of the whole household make both dyadic relationships and individuality important. A developed sense of individuality is expected, and the ways of asserting that one has a particular identity are taught to girls and boys and encouraged in confrontations with persons outside the household. Neither men nor women become immersed in a marital identity early, and they mature as self-reliant individuals. In cooperative relationships within households and among related households, as well as in client relationships, persons appear to retain strong individuality and to think in terms of an exchange of obligations. Although there are many cultural differences in gender, both women and men exercise near-equal independence in family, sexual, and marital roles.

After arriving at this formulation of a core of culture, I began noticing the newly emerged claims of "our culture" in the media and among my 1984 and 1986 informants. The carnivals of those years, the first I had seen, were manifestations of styles and themes that might be linked with traditions if I could further open up codes. Several prominent Vincentians described ways in which the carnivals represented aspects of the culture of the nation. In the village one heard messages not present in earlier fieldwork. Schoolteachers who had been taught the best standard English were defending the use of Creole, the formerly disparaged local vernacular, now referred to as the mother tongue. They were coaching their students in choral speaking of Creole verse. Moreover, informants' explanations of their actions and ideas often confirmed, in a startlingly clear way, the analyses I had earlier laboriously constructed from fragmentary data, and the rural carnival of 1986 was like an enactment of some of the principles I had deciphered in the systems of daily life. It projected emotional characteristics I had already seen in the life cycle and the household cycle. The village carnival had adapted the format of a sponsored national celebration to the styles of local expressive genres. The quality of genuineness had emerged in the rural complex, had culminated in this festival and had remained enacted daily in village forms and discourse.

Aware that my study of Windward Valley represented a more integrated and patterned culture than other ethnographies of West Indian rural societies had portrayed, I began rereading the meager historical literature on St. Vincent, seeking both comparison to other islands and early manifestations of a cultural disposition. The history I have written here draws on the extant works; I did not conduct research in primary sources where there is a need for extensive endeavors by historians. My historical sketch introduces the origin of Vincentian society, the characteristics of the colonial situation, the limitations of postemancipation change, and the early initiatives toward development. Some of my history is conjecture on subjects difficult to interpret. I have searched for the origins of two aspects of current Vincentian national identity, respect for government and the continued widespread practice of small farming. The attitudes toward government took me to the last quarter of the eighteenth century, when British power became secured. I see expression of identity in the slaves' failure to support the powerful Maroon-Indian assault on the British town and its fringe of unguarded plantations. I attempt to reconstruct the context of the period through identifying aspects of Maroon and plantation life that may have been widely congenial to the slaves, and those which may have been abhorrent to them, and from this portrayal I conclude that they were possibly aligning themselves with the planters and the government that stood above the plantations. Their descendants are not likely to ever know their views, and the slaves may only have been choosing the least dangerous course or may have been unable to engage themselves in the life-and-death struggle of the Maroons and the English. It is equally possible that they were choosing to protect the security they had in Vincentian society. Government may have been the distant symbol of legitimate authority, so that they saw themselves acting for the protection of society, not for the men who exercised power over them. That freed blacks sought help from the government is demonstrated in the experiences of Ashton Warner thirty-five years after this crucial war, when his freed mother applied to the governor to legitimize his free status and when Warner took the unsigned legal papers to a government clerk and was granted an exit from the island and from the estate that claimed to own him. An earlier generation of slaves may have perceived government as a means of redress worth protecting.

The planters surrendered their legislative roles in the 1860s, seeking through direct Crown colony rule protection from impoverished laborers' revolts. Sixty years later schoolteachers and professionals formed the Representative Government Association and stood up for local representation, winning a minority of the appointed seats for large property owners in each colony. The teacher-agitator in Windward Valley and the shopkeeper audaciously proposed to the colonial system that had extended no representation at all, representative district government. The idea of government as a focus of organization was unrivaled by structural groups or voluntary associations. When the colonial government imposed a tax on matches and beer, the listeners at the market square "people's parliament" attacked government itself, the place, the person, and the property. Not employers, who were the targets of most union organized actions in other West Indian colonies, but government was the target in these public declarations. Not all anticolonial movements in the British empire were directed initially and primarily to political authority. The rights for elections and political parties, once won, became the popular instruments for national participation. They drew on the popularity of traditional exhibitions of speaking. Attention to politics flourished as people deflected talk about local social relationships and substituted elevated extravillage political talk, thereby protecting self-esteem. The political culture and local culture are an interactive set, and the prenational culture fostered the political culture of the postcolonial self-governing state.

The historical background of the continued practice of small-scale farming has been looked into, and here I have questioned prevalent explanations. If St. Vincent were to be considered a place of preadaptation to peasantry through a high development of slaves' private productivity, attention is necessary to the intensive plantation production up to the end of slavery, evidenced in Higman's comparative demographic research, and also to the contemporary account of relatively severe slave practices by the slave Ashton Warner. If the mid-nineteenth century production by small farmers in arrowroot for export is to be seen as an accomplishment of a peasantry, it must be clear that the widespread inference that small land holding was extensive in this period appears to be unsupported, and small farming was carried out primarily on rented land. Following emancipation a diametric competition between plantations and small lease holders quickly emerged. The former slaves' arrowroot crop rivaled the estates' flagging sugar earnings. When estates changed from sugar to arrowroot, they glutted the market. Estates could play the market for the two export crops, keeping pace with European prices by idling either sugar or arrowroot, and often both crops. Sustainable by alternating export crops, estates were not divided for sale. A reverse trend was underway, the practice of buying up idle estates. Purchased by both local proprietors and London mercantile companies, estates not only remained undivided but were agglomerated under a handful of owners. Rental of land remained the principal option open to small cultivators. They themselves may have had more security in leasing than in purchasing land because of the wide fluctuations in the price for their main cash crop. With recruiters for temporary male emigration regularly on the scene, and individual emigration to nearby islands readily practiced, money for land purchases could be had, and the eventual offering of small plots, under the government's 1899 peasant land settlement program, sold out.

Only a strong sentiment for small farming could have maintained the skills, knowledge, customs, and ancillary values of the tradition over the many generations who accommodated to, and competed with, the various resident, absentee, and corporate landowners. When the estates sold out during the world depression of the 1930s, a Windward Valley farmer-poet celebrated the event with a recitation of local subsistence crops to which the land could finally be turned. Temporary emigration has helped to sustain peasant agriculture by securing the capital to purchase land.

In reviewing the few family lines descended from white and black parents in the village, I saw racial values in their experiential context. Black, racially mixed, and white are hierarchically ranked in the social order, but individuals in these categories, who make up families and live in the predominately black village are the immediate generators of local racial values. The strong emotions about racial appearances stem in part from personal knowledge of families, kinsmen, and neighbors of different colors. Racial values owe as much to the experience of mixed racial descent as to the statuses and privileges controlled by the racial components of the society. One family history reconstructed from its village members represented the mating of women "down" the racial scale in the late nineteenth and early twentieth century. These white and mulatto women were creolizing society through their legal marriages and stable families. Their marriages to local black men brought them into the plantation manager status and the rural middle class. Their history is the process of creolization, a process thought to have been rare in the British-colonized areas. Three women's histories do not indicate these unions were common, but their occurrence must have been influential.

Individualism is heightened by the multiplicity of social categories. The racially intermediate persons, the several types of marital union, and the gradations of status and means of status assertion or achievement heighten the concept of persons as individualistic. The emphasis on individuals and the practice of multiple social forms reduce the social value attached to the forms, and individuals transcend stigmas of low marital status by the attention to individual qualities. Values are felt and believed in, but they are also social emblems. As signs with fixed meanings, they differ from the mobile nature of individualism. Racially mixed unions were highly individual actions, in contrast to the mixing of cultural values.

A creole culture was gradually generated by the creole populations through the commitments they made to the island society, that is, in slaves' support of the power of the state even while they were almost powerless under it, in the tenacious pursuit of small farming, and in the investment of earnings and knowledge from emigration in the productive possibilities of home villages. Creole culture came to be codified in a local inclusive social morality that incorporated both high- and low-status directives and both respect and satirization of these elements. This system required a self-conscious playing of roles useful and appropriate to one's position as it changed through the life cycle and as it could be reinterpreted to one's advantage. Thus the locally generated social morality gives center place to a concept of person. It includes as well a variable system of family organization, with a progression of attributes associated with the stages of the life cycle. The behavior appropriate to personhood is displayed also in the values and styles of public performances. The latitude for personal role playing and the attention to the intrinsic qualities of individuals allowed persons of different shades of color and different ethnicities to make roles and statuses for themselves in communities and in the polity. In this system the individual has much responsibility for self-definition. There is security and reward in conscious and culturally fluent demonstrations of strong selves. To maintain personal equilibrium and social competence involved standardized ways of maneuvering between contradictory moral directives. Mastery of diverse cultural elements is demonstrated in references to different judgements of value, in changing positions and values in different parts of the life cycle, in demonstrative linguistic usages, and in regularized rituals. Polyglot traditions have been brought together in this way, and persons can win out over a history of treatment as nonpersons. National unifying factors reside in values and concepts of the nature of the person and in the meanings and morality of social structures.

A culture is not a sense of national identity, nor does national identity include the many facets always present in a culture. National identity must also be distinguished from nationalism. A culture is deeply embedded in the person and some of it has been learned in childhood, and this part of culture, as well as many later learning experiences, may be unconscious. In contrast a sense of national identity is conscious, learned mainly in adulthood, and may be only loosely connected with culture, even opposing culture. Persons may see the world through the lenses of the culture, or they may be more objective users of their culture. A sense of national identity implies no more than a sense of belonging to a nation. Some persons may live more in terms of culture than national identity, and others may think of themselves with the opposite references, that is, more in terms of the dimension of national identity than in the habits, assumptions, and custom-

ary reasonings of their local, embedded, and largely unconscious culture. I
have suggested that the oppositions characteristic of Vincentian culture, especially those embodying morality, can be transcended in part by casting
the self as a national person, and in that case the large-scale reference may
serve the individual better than the culture does. Vincentians see national
identity in terms of the governing structures. Power, which the government
is thought to have and to some degree has, creates resonant imagery in the
minds of persons who have grown up with personal power and status enactments and learned to play their parts in individual contests and cooperative groups. The assertive individuals maintain and defend their own
good reputations, win their own contests, and show their own authority.
The leaders' winning of elections and authority gains them legitimacy, not
just in terms of political democracy but in terms of the culture. The national
entity is a representative of the people not only in elective terms but also in
its representation of the principles of the culture.

This kind of national unity differs in some ways from recent anthropological formulations of cultures of nationalism. Fox's term *nationalist
ideologies*, referring to "the cultural production of public identity," is not
well suited to the Vincentian case (Fox 1990:4). That nation has no set of
ideas that could be called an ideology. Cultural ideas that are oppositional,
action-dependent, and variable do not appear to be materials for an ideology. Nationalist sentiment expresses itself in the connections of the populace, through local informal social codes, directly to national and political
issues. The process is to talk about government rather than to value a set of
ideas about ethnicity or nationhood. Another limitation I see in using Fox's
framework is in the nonspecificity of his presentation of the idea of public
identity. Culturally produced public identity serves his formulation as a
less rationalized element than ideology. However, the studies he has
brought together do not investigate the internalization of public identity.
Apparently in accord with his efforts to avoid the psychologizing that he
criticizes in the older national culture studies, Fox does not draw a relationship between public and personal identity. The national and ethnic ideologies discussed are not shown to be national and ethnic identities. In her
paper on Romanian ideology in Fox's volume, Verdery calls for a psycho-
anthropological explanation of the connection between public ideology
and personal identity, referring to "a subjectivity of a national kind that
responds emotionally when such symbols [as constructed heroes of Romanian history] are flourished" (Verdery 1990:91). This has been attempted
for St. Vincent. Unlike the Romanian experience, national concepts of and
for St. Vincent have not been constructed by elites. The sense of being a

national entity derives from sources and routes in the culture and society of the common people. Because of cultural factors, government is an important reference point in the process for maintaining personal identity. The relation between polity and person is not one of symbolic identification or belief in an ideology. In a more self-interested way, the person values government as process and as a symbol of nationhood and attaches the self to politics to enhance self-image. Vincentians are wary of hero making and respect authority only as it represents people like oneself. Their public identity is not an inner essence such as the Romanian elite have invented. It is a counter in interpersonal negotiations and a stabilizer of self-image.

The idea of culturally constructed personhood developing in anthropology and sociology has the possibility of being a discourse to substitute for concepts of personality when referring to cultural systems, and to avoid projecting personality onto culture (Jacobson-Widding 1983; Jackson and Karp 1990; Kondo 1990; Giddens 1991; Epstein 1992). In St. Vincent, where the self is minimally defined by social structure and individuality is encouraged to be strongly expressed, the concept of personhood is more easily accessible to analysis than it would be in some societies, and it may have greater significance in the total culture; however, this dimension would not be insignificant in any society.

Neither does Anderson's framework, in which "the nation is always conceived as a deep horizontal comradeship," apply well to the Vincentian case (B. Anderson 1983:16). His apt image for nascent nationalism, to imagine oneself part of a community, is described as persons thinking that the unseen members of the nation are doing what they themselves are doing. A sense of community is hardly to be found in Vincentian local organization. The culture posits not sameness of persons, actions, ideals, and values but diverse ways of serving broadly construed values, and it requires respect for both low-status and high-status ways of acting. Vincentians imagine a social entity that is continuous from low to high statuses, from poor villagers to ministers of government, a vertical image, not a horizontal one, one suitable to the usefulness, in village thought, of hierarchial relations. Far from embodiment in "community," Vincentian national identity is to be seen in the public contest.

Nor do Vincentians have a nationalism of being a chosen people, having a valued tradition, or having a national cause such as rivalry or fear of domination, causes that have fueled nationalism in other states. National self-importance, which can give impetus to a "sacralizing" of history and ceremony, such as described by Kapferer in Australian nationalism, is not characteristic of a society still resentful of its impotence under a racist colonialism and still overcoming the imputations of racial inferiority. The national cultural policy, quoted in the Introduction, states, "Colonial tutelage has alienated the majority of our people from a true sense of national pride and self confidence." No ideology of superiority, even pride, has been able to grow up here. Furthermore, sacredness rests on clear symbolism. Both Africanness and Britishness are part bad and part good, foiling symbolism and generating the play of oppositions characteristic of traditional performances. These complex communication forms thrive, and project the ambiguity of symbols, providing no materials for sacralization. The sacredness of Christianity is a shared value and is the only sacred tradition of the society. It unites Vincentians and West Indians, but, as Hobsbawm has suggested (1990:68), it is too universal to be a centerpiece of nationalism. Sacralized national ceremonialism has made no appearance. Independence Day is occasion for politically contentious speeches and a holiday, which in rural areas is taken to mean no government wage work and no mail delivery.

The government has not responded to proposals to name the death anniversary of Chatoyer and Ebenezer Joshua National Hero's Day. In the ceremonies that took place on this anniversary in 1992, the Carib chief Chatoyer, about whom history provides scant knowledge, evoked far more attention than the well-remembered and controversial Joshua. The complex role Joshua had to play at his stage of history and the cleavages he worked with and brought about resist myth making. Chatoyer's role, however, can not symbolize the long political struggle against colonialism, a struggle so complex that it compromised all the Vincentian leaders who fought in it. A nation of freed men who learned their only revered tradition, Christianity, from their colonial masters, Vincentians have nurtured no sacred symbols and no racial or cultural mission. Only government itself, however much criticized and opposed in its composition and policies, is the symbol of nationalism.

National identity thus is an easily accessible feeling. Another idea, however, competes with nationalism: identification as West Indian. West Indian leaders have long fostered this identity through maintaining a goal of a West Indian federation of independent nations. Many of the West Indian intellectuals considered the English-speaking region as much a natural entity as the demarcated colonies. The admirers of English government envisioned themselves following the British model as self-governing states in political union. The high value of government had generated strong interest in political procedures and formed an unused pool of political talent eager to exercise its political sense.

The region had long been connected in many ways, in the administration of the Windward Islands by a single British governor; in inter-Caribbean organizations of trade unions, teachers, and the Representative Government Association; and in internal trade. Laborers and peasants were familiar with many points on the West Indian circumference through the migration of family members and through the regular marketing of produce consigned by farmers to small sellers who carried sacks of fruit and vegetables by schooner to nearby islands. This wider circumference became increasingly envisionable with visiting steel bands, Calypsonians, and dance troupes, and with interisland cricket and netball matches. The best Vincentian students attend the University of the West Indies at its Jamaican, Barbadian, or Trinidadian branches. Some have felt shocked by the contrasts to home in these elite and "fast" places, and many have made lasting friendships. Oil workers' families returned from Curaçao and Aruba know a degree of urbanness far greater than found in Kingstown. Domestic employment with urban Caucasians in Port of Spain has exposed rural Vincentian women to more extreme racist attitudes than they had opportunity to encounter in St. Vincent with its few employment opportunities under whites, and some have chosen to return to farming at home, much broadened in knowledge of the area. Interisland marriages, especially with neighboring St. Lucians and Trinidadians, and marriages at places of migrant employment, are not at all uncommon at all class levels. Migration of trained personnel among the islands has long taken place. Many appointed positions go to non-Vincentian West Indians, with numerous judicial, business, technical, and church positions filled by persons from other English-speaking Caribbean nations. These experiences form a basis for West Indian identity at all levels of society. National identity and West Indian identity have coexisted, and the wider framework has moderated local nationalism. Joined to the modest sense of national importance, the other circles of identity have contributed to an international orientation.

A new proposal for federation, a political union built on the economic cooperation achieved in the Organization of Eastern Caribbean States and open to the seven member states and other West Indian nations, was made by Vincentian prime minister James Mitchell in 1986. After a deliberate and cautious period with careful attention to gaining engagement with the issue, the four Windward Islands are proceeding alone and have organized the Regional Constituent Assembly with broad representation to meet in each of the nations to draw up a proposal for federation to be presented for popular referendum. The assembly met in each of the Windward Islands between January 1991 and January 1992, hearing papers on proposed structures and speeches by incumbent leaders and by delegates. It soon became clear, however, that some parts of the population see their vital interests threatened. Bureaucrats and civil servants fear a shrinkage of posts with the consolidation of four nations into one, and they fear competition from job contenders from the other islands. The leaders of minority political parties are wary of federation and have enough popularity to defeat it. They are all poised to win leadership from the present generation of leaders who are past their prime of popularity and as incumbents are blamed for the problems of their societies. When the second convening of the Regional Constituent Assembly was about to take place in St. Lucia, the minority leader there declared his party's opposition to federation. However, in the next election his party failed to unseat the incumbent prime minister. In a four nation contest over one premiership, a minority leader of one constituency would not have a chance. A rising political claimant in St. Vincent supports the goal of unity but is concerned "whether there would be safeguards to ensure that opposition parties do not become marginalized and the incumbent governments do not use political unity as a means of entrenching themselves in power" (R. Gonzalves, *Vincentian*, 12 April 1991). Other Vincentian opinion leaders, the apparent majority, write of federation as an historic entry into the consciousness of other nations through quadrupled size and through demonstrating the ability to bring about political unity. Furthermore federation is destiny:

> But, on the question of unity, there is a certain mysterious something, a mystique, a nostalgia beating in the breast of every Caribbean person in the diaspora. . . . Hard nosed politicians trivialize the emotional appeal, as if man can live by bread alone. . . . the latest attempt follows a long tradition of earlier attempts, of undisputedly local impulse, to forge the islands into some form of political union. (Kenneth John, *Vincentian*, 19 April 1991)

Kenneth John cites the history of recent statements on independence that shows that most of the leading figures in the Vincentian government sought to forestall independent status between the time it was launched in 1969 and finalized in 1979, because they considered independence viable only within a Caribbean federation (*Vincentian*, 1 February 1991). An editorial on the twelfth anniversary of independence called that status "utopian," "a cruel joke" played by the United Kingdom and a "clearly unviable economic option." The editor wrote that the essential course at present was independence within CARICOM, within the Organization of Eastern Caribbean States and within Windward Island political federation (*Vincentian*, 25 October 1991). The minority party leaders control many votes and the referendum on the new regional structure requires a two thirds affirmation. Although the general populace would probably seize readily on an enlargement of their identity, being an imaginative and innovative people, the educated group, who are more influenced by and sympathetic to ideological currents of pan–West Indianism, have career interests at stake and may think it is better to be a leader in a small country than no leader at all.

St. Vincent has not created nationalism. It has barely overcome the status of being owned by another country. Now an independent state, it seeks national identity. Vincentians talk to one another about their national identity and are becoming convinced of the idea that they have one. They would like to be recognized for their intrinsic qualities. In seeking over many years to find, identify, and enact a culture, and succeeding well, a momentum has set in. Movement from a past to a future has become part of the way of thought. This former slave society is still striving for a secure identity and for material security. Its people are not satisfied with themselves, their ways, and their leaders. Striving to identify why they are dissatisfied pervades the dialogues of the newspaper columnists, and the impeded energy of expressing dissatisfaction and seeking betterment pervades villagers conversations and letters. In this habituation to seeking change, a new entity of the Windward Islands Federation, offering an expanded identity, may win a referendum.

In recognition from other nations, Vincentians are able to overcome their sense of subjugation as a colony. Roles that their leaders have played or currently play outside the island are respected, and foreign appearances of government members are covered in the press. The newspaper that continually attacks the prime minister ran a jubilant editorial commending his speech to the United Nations in October 1990. Participation of their government with other governments is an affirming image. Still told by columnists and Calypsonians that they suffer from a slave mentality, Vincentians are ambivalent about pride and cannot approach the righteousness of nationalism. They are aware of being small and poor and of having been abandoned in attempted federation by the large West Indian nations. Again they are seeking federation with the only available partners, the other small, poor Windward Islands. The federal nation will not have common legends to legitimize it. It will be a union made for rational purposes, but it also will be a higher level of government and will represent the political skill and faith which the islands have excelled in. This is a compromise to the vision of becoming West Indian, but that vision will remain.

Notes

INTRODUCTION

1. Additional ethnographic works on St. Vincent are the unpublished Ph.D. dissertations of Betley 1976, Hourihan 1975, and Gearing 1988. A dissertation in historical geography of St. Vincent is also available by Spinelli 1971.

2. On development of national culture in the English-speaking Caribbean, see Macklin 1986 and Holzberg 1981. Segal 1988 presents Trinidadian national identity as an artifice without validity. He views the shifting references in national imagery as evidence of naïve confusion and false construction, failing to take into account the deliberate use of ambiguous reference and the skills of double meaning in West Indian speech traditions.

3. I agree with Mintz's observation, however, that homogeneity is not a condition of political integration (1974:321). A model of the construction of shared identity in multiethnic Guyana is presented by Drummond (1980). The "cultural continuum" interreferences symbols of different ethnicity and provides interchanges of imagery among groups. See also Crowley 1960.

CHAPTER I: COLONIZATION AND REBELLION

1. The document is extraordinary in that it declares the usurpation of land from the Caribs and is replete with vague ameliorative conditions. "That the com-

missioners shall survey and dispose of all the cultivated lands . . . [in] the Charaib country. . . . That no step shall be taken toward the removal of any Charaib, till the whole arrangement and design shall have been notified and explained to the satisfaction of their chiefs; . . . and that the plan be carried into effect with the gentlest hand, and in the mildest manner. . . . That the lands allotted for them in exchange be convenient for their habitation, sufficient for their support, and in point of situation, adapted to their manner of living. . . . They shall be permitted to remain in their former situation five years" (Young 1795:34–37).

2. This memorandum would not have reached the London office for a month. News of the initial Black Carib attack in March 1795 reached London in mid-April. The commander of British forces engaged in deterrence to the French in the Caribbean dispatched the troops, which quickly came to the aid of the weak Vincentian garrison, the news having spread quickly among the islands. These troops were embattled in their attempt to take St. Lucia from the French until the spring of 1796, when temporary victory there released the large force thrown into the Black Carib war in June of that year.

3. See Buckley 1979 on the Jamaica Island Rangers.

4. In Suriname the pacified Maroons delivered many fugitive slaves to the Dutch government after the treaty made with them in 1760, but the unpacified Boni did not do so and on the contrary accepted fugitives, thus acting in the same way as the Black Caribs. See Hoogbergen 1990.

5. A good description of houses of the surviving Carib community is found in Davy 1854:194.

6. Higman studied the records for three Jamaican plantations in 1825 and for Trinidad in 1813. He discusses the difficulties in interpreting these data, and his conclusions are complex and interesting. Household composition suggested that many of them were nuclear and extended families, polygynous families, and mother-child families of two and three generations. He found a greater incidence of nuclear families on large plantations and more mother-child households in towns. By the measure of stability that he developed, Higman judged slave families stable (Higman 1976:158; Higman 1978:168–71). Craton (1979:29) found in the slave registration records in the Bahamas a very high incidence of nuclear families on several plantations. See also R. T. Smith's cautions on interpreting the household pairing of a man and a woman as a nuclear-family relationship. He suggests that Euro-American assumptions about the nature of the family underlie this interpretation (R. T. Smith 1988:150, 159).

7. Both Mrs. Carmichael and William Young wanted to portray West Indian slavery as beneficent. They did so by describing gay holiday scenes, their own genial relationships with slaves, and slaves' amusing intrigues among themselves; and they deny that severe treatment was common. However, the many details and anecdotes, particularly in Mrs. Carmichael's volumes, and the acuity of many of her comments, afford much insight into plantation life in the colonies in which they lived. Mrs. Carmichael's knowledge of house slaves and supervisory slaves with whom she was in daily contact was far better than her knowledge of field slavery. In Chapter 2 I point out contradictions between her account and the testimony of a slave named Ashton Warner.

CHAPTER 2: CONSTRUCTING A SOCIETY

1. Riviere 1972:13. He notes also that in 1840 only six thousand were employed in sugar production and in 1845 only forty-five hundred were so employed. Thus the sugar labor force declined from fifteen thousand to forty-five hundred during the seven years after apprenticeship, leaving only 30 percent of the previous number.

2. A study of transfers of land titles in Jamaica from 1866 to 1900 has shown that Crown colony land policies in Jamaica followed the lead of estate profitability. At the beginning of the period when much estate land was abandoned because of decline in the sugar industry, division and sale to small settlers accounted for most of the land transfers recorded, although the tendency, even under depression conditions, was to attempt to sell estates intact. The renewed profitability of estates after 1870 in the production of bananas, coffee, and livestock, and in several parishes sugar, influenced the government sale of crown land, and land reclaimed from squatters and tax defaulters, to purchasers of large tracts, and the numbers of transfers of title to small acreages steeply declined (Satchell 1990).

3. Trouillot found in comparing plot ownership and tenancy that the income of tenant cultivators was not different from the income of plot owners, and that the amount of family labor that could be mustered mattered more in family income than whether land was owned or rented (1988:253).

4. See also Momsen 1988 and Lobdell 1988.

5. This description is based on DeBique 1982; Peters and John 1969; and Peacock 1986. See also Hart's description of the riot (1988). His account differs on several minor details. It is based on Ralph Gonsalves, "The role of Labor in the Political Process of St. Vincent," (M.Sc. thesis, University of the West Indies, Kingston, Jamaica, 1971).

6. Hourihan (1975) describes the Vincentian patronage system in the early 1970s. Betley's (1976) structural analysis of political cliques in 1969 in a Vincentian town places them in the context of the community status system. N. Price (1988) briefly describes patronage politics in 1980 in the Grenadine island of Bequia.

7. See also interviews with Mitchell by Brana-Shute, 1983 and 1985.

CHAPTER 3: VILLAGE CULTURE: WEST INDIAN ISSUES

1. *Lacatan* is "location" in standard English, a term used by the Banana Association to refer to one banana plant.

2. The middle class in Windward Valley corresponds with Fraser's category of lower middle class. He used a five-tier system: upper elite, lower elite, upper middle, lower middle, and lower (1975:204). In Betley's study of the town of Barouille, he used informants' ranking criteria for heads of all households in the town and distinguished five strata. By this method and by other analyses, he conveys very well the social characteristics of the town (1976:290ff.). Labels of middle class and lower class have little cross-national validity within the West Indies, and even within St.

Vincent problems of classification of strata would be encountered if town, rural, and suburban classes were compared. For instance, J. Alexander's middle class family, the Sears, as described by Raymond T. Smith (1988), has a higher standard of living than my middle class; the community in which Austin derived her definitions of the middle class is a suburban housing development, and it differs from my rural middle class, which is formed primarily out of local lower-class families (Austin 1984). Bordering Kingstown are several suburban, middle-class communities and numerous areas of poor residents, but the housing density of most of the town situates poor and affluent housing close together. Whether there are any stratified urban neighborhoods tied together by kinship as in Windward Valley, I do not know. See also Young 1991 for discussion of stratification.

3. In this connection, note research on attitudes of the Jamaican urban lower class toward middle and upper classes as perceived by Jamaican leaders and as actually expressed by lower-class persons. A survey of attitudes of sixty thousand Kingston slum residents in 1962 was compared with opinions expressed in interviews with Jamaican leaders. Among the leaders, 61 percent thought the lower class had hostile attitudes toward the middle and upper classes. The survey showed that among the lower class, 20 percent expressed hostility to the classes above them, "even counting relatively mild antagonism." Whereas 11 percent of the leaders thought the lower class emulated them, 56 percent of the lower class respondents said they emulated them (James Anthony Mau, "Social Change and Belief in Progress: A Study of Images of the Future in Jamaica," [Ph.D. diss., University of California, Los Angeles, 1963], as quoted in Bell and Oxaal 1964:67).

4. This technology is similar to that described by Jerome Handler as the earliest method for manioc processing. It was later adapted for arrowroot; "graters, perhaps based on Carib models, were simple metal sheets held stationary over wooden troughs." Handler found descriptions of rotary graters operated by hand or foot employed for manioc in the 1640s in Barbados, the French islands, and Brazil, and described in St. Vincent in 1840. "Cassava was used with such frequency, especially by European colonists, in the 17th and 18th centuries that it can be assumed they adopted mechanical rotary graters." The Windward Valley factory did not have a rotary grater and it used the Carib type grater (J. Handler 1971:88, 91).

5. Recent findings from Barbados on this issue "portray a far different picture from the stereotype of 'wandering stud.'" In interview research on male sexual behavior using a random sample of 185 men in age groups between eighteen and forty, the median number of relationships with women, past and present, of at least one month's duration, and involving sexual intercourse, was 2.11 (Dann 1987:72).

6. Two other ethnographers of St. Vincent interpret the payments as though for sexual services rather than for child support. They report that child support ceases when the parents end their sexual relationship, and if payments for the child continued they would represent the right of sexual access to the child's mother. I think this is a misinterpretation both on the ethnographers' part and in the statements of some informants. It derives from men's fear of women having multiple sexual partners and thus undermining the exclusive right of males to do so. Women may also muddle the principle out of fear of breaching the rule. This level of anxiety about former partners' claims is temporary, and most separated mates can distinguish between obligations to the child, which continue, and exchange of sexual

favors with the child's mother. To infer sexual rights after a relationship ceases imputes a degree of promiscuity and male dominance not ordinary here (cf. Rubenstein 1987; Gearing 1988).

7. This is one of several points where Carnegie's commentaries on social psychology add to our own observation on this subject. For instance, he writes: "It is common place to have several sources of income and systematically to maintain each one, even if some may bring in very little cash. Together they allow the household to meet its many obligations and to meet sudden and unexpected changes in economic conditions" (1987:38).

8. The town of Barouille was found to have the same percentages of male and female heads of house as in Windward Valley. Of 630 households in Barouille, 54 percent were male headed and 45 percent were female-headed (Betley 1976:114). In the Bequia community of Lower Bay, which had sixty-six households, 51 percent were male-headed and 48 percent were female-headed (Price 1988).

9. Gonzalez found in a restudy of household organization among the Garifuna in Belize that different types of households—those she had previously classified as consanguineal and affinal—were similar in a number of respects, and she concluded that as different types, they "exist only . . . in the minds of ethnographers" (1984:9). This research came to my attention after my own similar findings were made.

10. In her 1984 article Gonzalez confirmed the strong matrifocality of most households, which had been an emphasis of her earlier discussions (1969, 1970). It is important to note that the Garifuna households are more strongly matrifocal, as described in 1984, than the Windward Valley ones. With former male and female domestic production among the Garifuna abandoned in preference for increased migrant labor, the households are primarily caretaking groups and change frequently in membership. Windward Valley households are productive units, even though many of them receive remittances from a small number of absent members. Unlike Garifuna, Vincentian men's roles in local society contribute to traditional male dominance in gender relations. Christian family codes are more influential, the respect for enduring coresidence of couples is higher, male parental functions are more important. In these ways the cultural context of matrifocality is markedly different in Garifuna and Windward Valley. These differences suggest caution in generalizing about a "West Indian type" of domestic culture.

11. Wolf notes an increasing emphasis on cultural uniformity in Chinese studies and goes on to say: "Every study has found some new combination of family size, marriage forms, inheritance rules, or ritual usages. The discovery of basic uniformity has occurred in the midst of a surge of evidence reporting unimagined diversity. What I take this to mean is that Chinese domestic institutions are extraordinarily flexible. A few basic ideas provide coherence and continuity without interfering with people's ability to adapt to a wide variety of situations . . . How could such a combination of uniform ideas and diverse behavior endure? . . . How did elite ideas of marriage, for instance, survive the precedent of more than 60% minor marriage? How did communities with no or few joint families preserve the rules of joint estates, joint households and joint interests? That is, how did Chinese culture survive Chinese society?" (1981:357).

12. See also John O. Stewart: "Laughter is important. Humor is very impor-

tant. In the social sphere the aesthetic is experienced in the enactment of relations. Here, in Trinidadian culture, the comic makes its appearance as an ever ready antidote to uncomfortable meanings in the incongruous associations in history, or those evoked in argument and other disputatious discourse . . . here, where argument is as patent an activity as conversation, so too is humor, and probably for a balancing reason. If argument preserves our presence, laughter controls its value" (1989:220). Devisch writes on laughter among the Yaka people of Zaire: "Spontaneous laughter which is sparkling or jocund, or rejoicing, expresses inner delight. 'To feel delight in the heart,' and enchantment, may extend to lyrical self-praise, or joyful dancing. Laughter thereby intertwines, in a balanced way, inner and outer, centre (heart) and periphery (outward behavior), self and other" (Devisch 1990:129, Yaka words for each term in original text are omitted here).

13. Glazier's account of Spiritual Baptists in Trinidad emphasizes the worldly side of the sect, in struggles for rank, questioning the truth of visions, fund raising, and pragmatic leader-instigated adoption of rituals. He quotes a Baptist leader from St. Vincent who "complained of the excesses and commercialism of Spiritual Baptist churches in Trinidad. He asserted that Trinidad churches had 'traveled in the wrong direction'" (1983:128).

Works Cited

BOOKS AND PERIODICALS

Abrahams, Roger D.
[1964] 1971   Deep Down in the Jungle: Negro Narrative Folklore from the Streets of Philadelphia. Chicago: Aldine.
1977   The West Indian Tea Meeting: An Essay in Creolization. *In* Old Roots in the New World. Ann M. Pescatello, ed. pp. 173–209. Westport, Conn.: Greenwood Press.
1983   The Man-of-Words in the West Indies: Performance and the Emergence of Creole Culture. Baltimore: Johns Hopkins University Press.
Abrahams, Roger, and Richard Bauman
1971   Sense and Nonsense on St. Vincent: Speech Behavior and Decorum in a Caribbean Community. American Anthropologist 13:762–772.
Alexander, Jack
1976   A Study of the Cultural Domain of "Relatives." American Ethnologist 3:17–38.
1984   Love, Race, Slavery, and Sexuality in Jamaican Images of the Family. *In* Kinship Ideology and Practice in Latin America. Raymond T. Smith, ed. Chapel Hill: University of North Carolina Press.

Anderson, Alexander
1983   Alexander Anderson's Geography and History of St. Vincent,
               West Indies. Richard A. and Elizabeth S. Howard, eds. and
               transcribers. Cambridge: Harvard University and the Linnean
               Society of London.
Anderson, Benedict
1983   Imagined Communities: Reflections on the Origin and Spread
               of Nationalism. London: Verso.
Austin, Diane J.
1979   History and Symbols in Ideology: A Jamaican Example. Man
               14:497–514.
1983   Culture and Ideology in the English-speaking Caribbean: A
               View from Jamaica. American Ethnologist 10:223–240.
1984   Culture, Class, and Ideology: A study of Two Neighborhoods in
               Kingston, Jamaica. New York: Gordon and Breach.
Barrow, Christine
1986   Finding the Support: A Study of Strategies for Survival. Social
               and Economic Studies 35 (2):131–176.
Beachey, R. W.
1957   The British West Indian Sugar Industry in the 19th Century.
               Oxford: Basil Blackwell.
Bell, Wendell, and Ivar Oxaal
1964   Decisions of Nationhood: Political and Social Development in
               the British Caribbean. University of Denver Monograph Series
               in World Affairs, vols. 3–4. Denver, Colorado.
Belle, George
1988   The Struggle for Political Democracy: The 1937 Riots. In
               Emancipation III: Aspects of the post-slavery experience of Bar-
               bados. Lectures Commemorating the 150th Anniversary of
               Emancipation, Delivered in February and March 1987. Bridge-
               town, Barbados: University of the West Indies.
Besson, Jean
1988   Reputation and Respectability Reconsidered: A New Perspec-
               tive on Afro-Caribbean Peasant Women. Paper presented to the
               twelfth annual conference of the Society for Caribbean Studies,
               Hoddesdon, Hertfordshire.
Besson, Jean, and Janet Momsen, eds.
1987   Land and Development in the Caribbean. London: Macmillan.
Betley, Brian James
1976   Stratification and Strategies: A Study of Adaptation and Mo-
               bility in a Vincentian Town. Ph.D. dissertation, Department of
               Anthropology, University of California at Los Angeles.
Bolland, O. Nigel
1981   Systems of Domination after Slavery: The Control of Land and
               Labour in the British West Indies after 1838. Comparative
               Studies in Society and History 23:591–619.

Brana-Shute, Gary
1983   Interviewing James F. "Son" Mitchell: In the Center Looking for Change. Caribbean Review 12 (3):10–13.
1985   An Eastern Caribbean Centrist: Interviewing Prime Minister James F. "Son" Mitchell. Caribbean Review 14 (8):27–29.

Brathwaite, Edward
1971   The Development of Creole Society in Jamaica, 1770–1820. Oxford: Clarendon Press.

Braithwaite, Lloyd
1960   Social Stratification and Cultural Pluralism. New York Academy of Sciences, vol. 83, art. 5: 816–831.

Brodber, Erna
1987   Black Consciousness and Popular Music in Jamaica in the 1960's and 1970's. New West Indian Guide 6:145–160.

Bryce-Laporte, R. S.
1970   Crisis, Contra-Culture, and Religion Among West Indians in the Panama Canal Zone in Afro-American Anthropology. Norman E. Whitten, Jr., and John F. Szwed, eds. pp. 103–118. New York: Free Press.

Buckley, Roger Norman
1979   Slaves in Red Coats: The British West India Regiments, 1795–1815. New Haven: Yale University Press.

Cameron, Norman Eustace
[1929–34] 1970   The Evolution of the Negro. 2 vols. Westport, Conn.: Negro Universities Press.

Campbell, Mavis C.
1988   The Maroons of Jamaica, 1655–1796. Granby, Mass.: Bergin & Garvey.

Carmichael, A. C.
1833   Domestic Manners and Social Condition of the White, Coloured, and Negro Population of the West Indies. 2 vols. London: Whittaker, Treacher & Co.

Carnegie, Charles V.
1987   A Social Psychology of Caribbean Migrations: Strategic Flexibility in the West Indies. In The Caribbean Exodus. Barry B. Levine, ed. New York: Praeger.

Césaire, Aimé
1987   Paper presented to the Conference on Negritude, Ethnicity, and Afro-Cultures in the Americas, Florida International University.

Clarke, Edith
[1957] 1966   My Mother Who Fathered Me. London: Allen and Unwin.

Clarke, Roberta
1986   Women's Organizations, Women's Interests. Social and Economic Studies 35 (3):107–155.

Coke, Thomas
[1808–11] 1971   A History of the West Indies. London: Frank Cass and Co.
1816   Extracts of the Journals of the late Rev. Thomas Coke, compris-
                  ing of several visits to North America and the West Indies. Du-
                  blin: R. Napper.
Craton, Michael
1979   Changing Patterns of Slave Families in the British West Indies.
                  Journal of Interdisciplinary History 10 (1):1–35.
1982   Testing the Chains: Resistance to Slavery in the British West In-
                  dies. Ithaca: Cornell University Press.
Crowley, Daniel J.
1960   Cultural Assimilation in Multiracial Society. In Social and Cul-
                  tural Pluralism in the Caribbean. Vera Rubin, ed. Annals of the
                  New York Academy of Sciences 83:850–854.
Cust, Reginald J.
1865   The West Indies Incumbered Estates Acts. London: William
                  Amer. Supplement 1874.
Dann, Graham
1987   The Barbadian Male: Sexual Attitudes and Practices. London:
                  Macmillan Caribbean.
Davy, John
1854   The West Indies Before and Since Slave Emancipation. London:
                  W. and F. C. Cash.
DeBique, Lorna A.
1982   The 1935 Riots in St. Vincent and the Grenadines. B.A. thesis,
                  University of West Indies, Barbados.
Deere, Carmen Diana, Peggy Antrobus, Lynn Bolles, Edwin Melendez, Peter Phil-
lips, Marcia Rivera, and Helen Safa
1990   In the Shadows of the Sun: Caribbean Development Alterna-
                  tives and U.S. Policy. Boulder, Colo.: Westview Press.
Devisch, Rene
1990   The Human Body as a Vehicle for Emotion among the Yaka of
                  Zaire. In Personhood and Agency: The Experience of Self and
                  Other in African Cultures. Michael Jackson and Ivan Karp, eds.
                  Uppsala Studies in Cultural Anthropology 14.
Dirks, Robert
1972   Networks, Groups, and Adaptation in an Afro-Caribbean
                  Community. Man 7:565–585.
Drummond, Lee
1980   The Cultural Continuum: A Theory of Intersystems. Man
                  15:352–374.
Duncan, Ebenezer
[1941] 1970   A Brief History of St. Vincent with Studies in Citizenship.
                  Kingstown, St. Vincent, West Indies.
Edwards, Bryan
1807   The History Civil and Commercial of the British Colonies in the
                  West Indies. Vol. 1. 4th ed. London: John Stockdale.

Elder, Jacob D.
1964a   Color, Music and Conflict: A Study of Aggression in Trinidad
           with reference to the role of Traditional Music. Ethnomusicol-
           ogy 8:315–323.
1964b   Song games of Trinidad and Tobago. Publication of the Ameri-
           can Folklore Society, No. 16.

Epstein, A. L.
1992   In the Midst of Life: Affect and Ideation in the World of the
           Tolai. Berkeley and Los Angeles: University of California
           Press.

Fischer, Michael
1974   Value Assertion and Stratification: Religion and Marriage in
           Rural Jamaica. Caribbean Studies 14 (1):7–37; 14 (3):7–35.

Fitzpatrick, Robert V. W.
1976   Looking at a Community over the Years. St. Vincent: Graphic
           Printing.

Flambeau
1965–68   The Kingstown Study Group. Nos. 1–9. Kingstown, St. Vincent.

Fortes, Meyer
1983   Problems of Identity and Person. *In* Identity: Personal and
           Socio-Cultural. Anita Jacobson-Widding, ed. Stockholm: Alm-
           qvist & Wiksell.

Fox, Richard G.
1990   Introduction. *In* Nationalist Ideologies and the Production of
           National Cultures. American Ethnological Society Monograph
           Series, No. 2. Richard G. Fox, ed.

Fraser, Thomas M., Jr.
1975   Class and the Changing Bases of Elite Support in St. Vincent,
           West Indies. Ethnology 5:197–209.

Gearing, Margaret Jean
1988   The Reproduction of Labor in a Migration Society: Gender,
           Kinship, and Household in St. Vincent, West Indies. Ph.D. dis-
           sertation, University of Florida.

Geggins, David
1987   The Enigma of Jamaica in the 1790's: New Light on the Causes
           of Slave Rebellions. William and Mary Quarterly 44:274–
           299.

Georges, Eugenia
1990   The Making of a Transnational Community: Migration, Devel-
           opment, and Cultural Change in the Dominican Republic. New
           York: Columbia University Press.

Gibbs, Bentley
1987   The Establishment of the Tenantry System in Barbados. *In*
           Emancipation II: Aspects of the post-slavery experience of Bar-
           bados. Lectures Commemorating the 150th Anniversary of
           Emancipation, Delivered in February and March 1987. Bridge-
           town, Barbados: University of the West Indies.

Giddens, Anthony
1991   Modernity and Self-Identity: Self and Society in the Late Mod-
                 ern Age. Stanford: Stanford University Press.
Glazier, Stephen D.
1983   Marchin' the Pilgrims Home: Leadership and Decision-
                 Making in an Afro-Caribbean Faith. Westport, Conn.: Green-
                 wood Press.
Gonzalez, Nancie L.
1969   Black Carib Household Structure: A Study of Migration and
                 Modernization. Seattle: University of Washington Press.
1970   Toward a Definition of Matrifocality. In Afro-American An-
                 thropology: Contemporary Perspectives. Norman E. Whitten,
                 Jr., and John F. Szwed, ed. New York: Free Press.
1984   Rethinking the Consanguineal Household and Matrifocality.
                 Ethnology 23:1–12.
1988   Sojourners of the Caribbean: Ethnogenesis and Ethnohistory of
                 the Garifuna. Chicago: University of Illinois Press.
Gray, Obika
1991   Radicalism and Social Change in Jamaica, 1960–1972. Knox-
                 ville: University of Tennessee Press.
Green, William A.
1976   British Slave Emancipation: The Sugar Colonies and the Great
                 Experiment, 1830–1865. Oxford: Oxford University Press.
Gullick, C. J. M. R.
1985   Myths of a Minority: The Changing Traditions of the Vincent-
                 ian Caribs. Assen, Netherlands: Van Gorcum.
Hall, Douglas
1959   Free Jamaica, 1838–1869: An Economic History. New Haven:
                 Yale University Press.
1964   Absentee-Proprietorship in the British West Indies to about
                 1850. Jamaica Historical Review 4:15–35.
1971   Five of the Leewards, 1834–1870: The Major Problems of the
                 Post-emancipation period in Antigua, Barbuda, Montserrat,
                 Nevis, and St. Kitts. London: Ginn & Co.
Handler, Jerome S.
1971   The History of Arrowroot and the Origin of Peasantries in the
                 British West Indies. Journal of Caribbean History 2:64–93.
Handler, Richard
1988   Nationalism and the Politics of Culture in Quebec. Madison:
                 University of Wisconsin Press.
Hart, Richard
1982   Aspects of Early Caribbean Workers' Struggles. In Caribbean
                 Societies. University of London, Institute of Commonwealth
                 Studies, vol. 1.
1988   Origin and Development of the Working Class in the English-
                 speaking Caribbean Area: 1897–1937. In Labour in the Ca-
                 ribbean: From Emancipation to Independence. Malcolm Cross
                 and Gad Heuman, eds. London: Macmillan Caribbean.

Henney, Jeannette H.
1974   Spirit-Possession Belief and Trance Behavior in Two Fundamen-
               talist Groups in St. Vincent. *In* Trance, Healing, and Hallucina-
               tion. Felicitas D. Goodman, Jeanette H. Henney, and Esther
               Pressel, eds. New York: Wiley.
Herskovits, Melville J.
1937   Life in a Haitian Valley. New York: Knopf.
1941   The Myth of the Negro Past. New York: Harper.
Higman, B. W.
1976   Slave Populations and Economy in Jamaica, 1807–1834. Lon-
               don: Cambridge University Press.
1978   African and Creole Slave Family Patterns in Trinidad. Journal of
               Family History 3:163–180.
1984   Slave Populations of the British Caribbean 1807–1834. Bal-
               timore: Johns Hopkins University Press.
Hill, Errol
1972   The Trinidad Carnival: Mandate for a National Theater. Aus-
               tin: University of Texas Press.
Hobsbawn, E. J.
1990   Nations and Nationalism since 1780: Programme, Myth, Real-
               ity. Canto ed. Cambridge: Cambridge University Press.
Hoetink, Harmannus
1973   Slavery and Race Relations in the Americas: Comparative
               Notes on Their Nature and Nexus. New York: Harper and
               Row.
Holland, Dorothy, and Julia G. Crane
1987   Adapting to an Industrializing Nation: The Shango Cult in
               Trinidad. Social and Economic Studies 36 (4):41–66.
Holzberg, Carol S.
1981   The Cultural Context of the Jamaican National System. An-
               thropologica 23 (2):157–179.
Hoogbergen, Wim
1990   The Boni Maroon Wars in Suriname. Leiden: E. J. Brill.
Horowitz, Michael M.
1967a   Morne Paysan: Peasant Village in Martinique. New York: Holt
               Rinehart, Winston.
1967b   A Decision Model of Conjugal Patterns in Martinique. Man
               2:445–453.
Hourihan, John J.
1975   Rule in Hairoun: A Study of the Politics of Power. Ph.D. disser-
               tation, Dept. of Anthropology, University of Massachusetts.
Huang, Chieh-shan, and Arthur P. Wolf
1980   Marriage and Adoption in China, 1845–1945. Stanford: Stan-
               ford University Press.
Jackson, Michael, and Ivan Karp
1990   Introduction. Personhood and Agency: The Experience of Self
               and Other in African Cultures. Michael Jackson and Ivan Karp,
               eds. Washington D.C.: Smithsonian Institution Press.

Jacobson-Widding, Anita
1983   Introduction. *In* Identity: Personal and Socio-Cultural. Stock-
               holm: Almqvist & Wiksell.
James, Cyril L. R.
1977   The Future in The Present: Selected Writings. London: Allison
               & Busby.
John, Karl E. V.
1974   Policies and Programmes of Intervention into the Agrarian
               Structure of St. Vincent 1890–1974. Master's thesis, School
               of Urban and Regional Planning, University of Waterloo,
               Canada.
John, Kenneth
[1966] 1973   St. Vincent: A Political Kaleidoscope. *In* The Aftermath of Sov-
               ereignty. David Lowenthal and Lambros Comitas, eds. New
               York: Anchor Books.
Kapferer, Bruce
1988   Legends of People, Myths of State, Violence, Intolerance, and
               Political Culture in Sri Lanka and Australia. Washington and
               London: Smithsonian Institution Press.
Keizer, Norma
1967   A Short History of Education in St. Vincent During the Nine-
               teenth Century. Flambeau 8:16–20.
Kirby I. Earl, and C. I. Martin
1972   The Rise and Fall of the Black Caribs of St. Vincent. St. Vincent:
               Privately published.
Klomp, Ank
1986   Politics on Bonaire: An Anthropological Study. Translated by
               Dirk H. van der Elst. Assen/Maastricht, Netherlands: Van
               Gorcum.
Kondo, Dorinne K.
1990   Crafting Selves: Power, Gender, and Discourses of Identity in a
               Japanese Workplace. Chicago: University of Chicago Press.
Labat, Père
[1743] 1970   The Memoirs of Rène Labat 1693–1705. Translated and
               abridged by John Eaden. London: Frank Cass & Co.
Le Page, R. B., and Andrée Tabouret-Keller
1985   Acts of Identity: Creole-based Language and Ethnicity. Lon-
               don: Cambridge University Press.
Lewis, W. Arthur
[1939] 1972   Labour in the West Indies: The Birth of a Workers' Movement.
               Fabian Society Research Series No. 44. Nendeln/Lieschten-
               stein: Kraus.
1973   The Agony of the Eight. *In* After Sovereignty: West Indian Per-
               spectives. David Lowenthal and Lambros Comitas, eds. New
               York: Doubleday.
Lobdell, Richard S.
1988   British Officials and the West Indian Peasantry: 1842–1938. *In*

Labour in the Caribbean. Malcolm Cross and Gad Heuman, eds. London: Macmillan Caribbean.

Macklin, Catherine L.
1986   Crucibles of Identity: Ritual and Symbolic Dimensions of Garifuna Ethnicity. Ph.D. dissertation. Department of Anthropology, University of California, Berkeley.

Manning, Frank E.
1981   Campaign Rhetoric in Bermuda: The Politics of Race and Religion. *In* Politically Speaking: Cross-cultural Studies of Rhetoric. Robert Paine, ed. Philadelphia: Institute for the Study of Human Issues.
1985   The Performance of Politics. Anthropologica 27:39–54.

Marshall, Bernard
1973   The Black Caribs: Native Resistance to British Penetration into the Windward Side of St. Vincent, 1763–73. Caribbean Quarterly 19 (4):4–19.

Marshall, Dawn
1986   Vincentian Contract Labour Migration to Barbados: The Satisfaction of Mutual Needs. Social and Economic Studies 33 (3):63–92.
1987   A History of West Indian Migration: Overseas Opportunities and "Safety Valve" Policies. *In* The Caribbean Exodus. Barry B. Levine, ed. New York: Praeger.

Marshall, Woodville K.
1965a   Social and Economic Problems in the Windwards, 1838–1865. *In* The Caribbean in Transition. F. M. Andic and T.G. Mathews, eds. Rio Piedras: University of Puerto Rico.
1965b   Metayage in the Sugar Industry of the British Windward Islands, 1838–65. Jamaica Historical Review 5:28–55.
1968   Notes on Peasant Development in the West Indies since 1843. Social and Economic Studies 7:252–263.
1971   The Termination of the Apprenticeship in Barbados and the Windward Islands: An Essay in Colonial Administration and Politics. Journal of Caribbean History 2:1–45.
1972   Aspects of the Development of the Peasantry. Caribbean Quarterly 8:30–46.
1987   The Sugar Industry in Barbados. *In* Emancipation II: Aspects of the post-slavery experience of Barbados. Lectures Commemorating the 150th Anniversary of Emancipation, Delivered in February and March 1987. Bridgetown, Barbados: University of the West Indies.

Martinez-Alier, Verena
1974   Marriage, Class and Colour in Nineteenth-Century Cuba: A Study of Racial Attitudes and Sexual Values in a Slave Society. London: Cambridge University Press.

Mintz, Sidney W.
[1966] 1971 The Caribbean as a Socio-cultural Area. *In* Peoples and Cul-

tures of the Caribbean. Michael M. Horowitz, ed. Garden City, N.Y.: Natural History Press.

1974   Caribbean Transformations. Chicago: Aldine.

Mintz, Sidney W., and Richard Price

1976   An Anthropological Approach to the Afro-American Past: A Caribbean Perspective. Philadelphia: Institute for the Study of Human Issues.

Momsen, Janet

1987   Land Settlement as an Imposed Solution. *In* Land and Development in the Caribbean. Jean Besson and Janet Momsen, eds. London: Macmillan.

Murphy, Valerie Beach

1982   An Inquiry into Teenage Pregnancy in St. Vincent and the Grenadines. Master's thesis, Program in Public Health, University of the West Indies, Mona, Jamaica.

Nettleford, Rex

1988   Implications for Caribbean Development. *In* Caribbean Festival Arts. John W. Nunley and Judith Bettleheim, eds. Seattle: Saint Louis Art Museum in Association with the University of Washington Press.

Niddrie, David L.

1966   Eighteenth-Century Settlement in the British Caribbean. Transactions of Institute of British Geographers 40:67–80.

Olwig, Karen Fog

1985   Cultural Adaptation and Resistance on St. John: Three Centuries of Afro-Caribbean Life. Gainesville: University of Florida Press.

Peters, Oswald, and Kenneth John

1967   1935 Revisited. Flambeau 8:29–32.

Philpott, Stuart B.

1973   West Indian Migration: The Montserrat Case. London: Athlone Press.

Price, Neil

1988   Behind the Planter's Back: Lower Class Responses to Marginality in Bequia Island, St. Vincent. London: Macmillan.

Price, Richard

1971   Studies of Caribbean Family Organization: Problems and Prospects. Dedalo 7:23–58. Museum of Archeology and Ethnology, University of São Paulo, Brazil.

Ragatz, Lowell Joseph

1928   The Fall of the Planter Class in the British Caribbean 1763–1833: A Study in Social and Economic History. New York: Century.

Reisman, Karl

1970   Cultural and Linguistic Ambiguity in a West Indian Village, *In* Afro-American Anthropology. Norman E. Whitten, Jr., and John F. Szwed, eds. pp. 129–144. New York: Free Press.

Riviere, W. Emanuel
1972   Labour Shortage in the British West Indies After Emancipation.
               Journal of Caribbean History 4:1–30.
Roberts, George W.
1975   Fertility and Mating in Four West Indian Populations: Trinidad-
               Tobago, Barbados, St. Vincent, and Jamaica. Kingston: I.S.E.R.
               University of the West Indies.
Roberts, George W., and Sonja A. Sinclair
1978   Women in Jamaica: Patterns of Reproduction and Family. Mill-
               wood, N.Y.: KTO Press.
Rodman, Hyman
1971   Lower-Class Families: The Culture of Poverty in Negro Trini-
               dad. London: Oxford University Press.
Rubenstein, Hymie
1976   Incest, Effigy Hanging, and Biculturation in a West Indian Vil-
               lage. American Ethnologist 3:765–781.
1977   Economy History and Population Movements in an Eastern
               Caribbean Valley. Ethnohistory 24:19–45.
1980   Conjugal Behavior and Parental Role Flexibility in an Afro-Ca-
               ribbean Village. Canadian Review of Sociology and Anthropol-
               ogy 17:330–337.
1982   Return Migration to the English Speaking Caribbean: Review
               and Commentary. *In* Return Migration and Remittances: De-
               veloping a Caribbean Perspective. William F. Stinner, Klaus De
               Albuquerque, and Roy S. Bryce-Laporte, eds. pp. 3–33. Re-
               search Institute on Immigration and Ethnic Studies Occasional
               Papers, No. 3. Smithsonian Institution, Washington, D.C.
1983   Remittance and Rural Development in the English Speaking
               Caribbean. Human Organization: 42:295–306.
1987a   Coping with Poverty: Adaptive Strategies in a Caribbean Vil-
               lage. Boulder, Colo.: Westview Press.
1987b   Folk and Mainstream Systems of Land Tenure and Use in St.
               Vincent. *In* Land and Development in the Caribbean. Jean Bes-
               son and Janet Momsen, eds. London: Macmillan.
Safa, Helen I.
1987   Popular Culture, National Identity, and Race in the Caribbean.
               New West Indian Guide 6:115–126.
Sanford, Margaret
1974   A Socialization in Ambiguity: Child-Lending in a British West
               Indian Society. Ethnology 3:393–400.
Sargent, Carolyn, and Michael Harris
1992   Gender Ideology, Childrearing, and Child Health in Jamaica.
               American Ethnologist 19:523–537.
Satchell, Veront
1990   From Plots to Plantations: Land Transactions in Jamaica 1866–
               1900. Mona, Jamaica: Institute of Social and Economic Re-
               search, University of the West Indies.

Segal, Daniel
1988   Nationalism in a Colonial State: A Study of Trinidad and Toba-
                    go. Ph.D. dissertation, Department of Anthropology, Univer-
                    sity of Chicago.
Shephard, Charles
[1831] 1971   An Historical Account of the Island of St. Vincent. London:
                    Frank Cass & Co.
Smith, Michael G.
1962   West Indian Family Structure. Seattle: University of Washington
                    Press.
1965   The Plural Society in the British West Indies, Berkeley: Univer-
                    sity of California Press.
Smith, Raymond T.
1956   The Negro Family in British Guiana. London: Routledge &
                    Kegan Paul.
1967   Social Stratification, Cultural Pluralism and Integration in West
                    Indian Societies. In Caribbean Integration: Papers on Social,
                    Political and Economic Integration. Rio Pedras: Institute of
                    Caribbean Studies.
1970   The Nuclear Family in Afro-American Kinship. Journal of
                    Comparative Family Studies 1:55–70.
1973   The Matrifocal Family. In The Character of Kinship, Jack R.
                    Goody, ed. New York: Cambridge University Press.
1977   The Family and the Modern World System: Some Observations
                    from the Caribbean. Journal of Family History 3:337–360.
1988   Kinship and Class in The West Indies. New York: Cambridge
                    University Press.
Soto, Isa Maria
1987   West Indian Child Fostering: Its Role in Migrant Exchanges. In
                    Caribbean Life in New York City: Sociocultural Dimensions.
                    Constance R. Sutton and Elsa M. Chaney, eds. New York: Cen-
                    ter for Migration Studies.
Southey Thomas
[1827] 1968   Chronological History of the West Indies. Vol. 3. London:
                    Frank Cass and Co.
Spinelli, Joseph
1973   Land Use and Population in St. Vincent, 1763–1960. Ph.D. dis-
                    sertation, University of Florida.
Springer, Hugh W.
1973   Federation in the Caribbean: An Attempt That Failed. In After
                    Sovereignty: West Indian Perspectives. David Lowenthal and
                    Lambros Comitas, eds. New York: Doubleday.
Stack, Carol B.
1974   All Our Kin: Strategies for Survival in a Black Community. New
                    York: Harper and Row.
Stewart, John O.
1989   Drinkers, Drummers, and Decent Folk: Ethnographic Narra-

tives of Village Trinidad. Albany: State University of New York Press.

Stinner, William F., Klaus De Albuquerque, and Roy S. Bryce-Laporte, eds.
1982   Return Migration and Remittances: Developing a Caribbean Perspective. Research Institute on Immigration and Ethnic Studies Occasional Papers, No. 3. Smithsonian Institution, Washington, D.C.

Stycos, J. Mayone, and Kurt W. Back
1964   The Control of Human Fertility in Jamaica. New York: Cornell University Press.

Sutton, Constance, and Susan Makiesky-Barrow
1977   Social Inequality and Sexual Status in Barbados. *In* Sexual Stratification: A Cross-Cultural Perspective. Alice Schlegel, ed. New York: Columbia University Press.

Thomas, J. Paul
1983   The Caribs of St. Vincent: A Study in Imperial Maladministration, 1763–73. Journal of Caribbean History 18 (2):60–73.

Topley, Marjorie
1975   Marriage Resistance in Rural Kwangtung. *In* Women in Chinese Society. Margery Wolf and Roxanne Wilke, eds. Stanford: Stanford University Press.

Trouillot, Michel-Rolph
1988   Peasants and Capital: Dominica in the World Economy. Baltimore: John Hopkins University Press.

Valentine, Charles A.
1968   Culture and Poverty: Critique and Counter-proposals. Chicago: University of Chicago Press.

Verdery, Katherine
1990   The Production and Defense of "the Romanian Nation," 1900 to World War II. *In* Nationalist Ideologies and the Production of National Cultures. Richard G. Fox, ed. Washington, D.C.: American Ethnological Association.

Walker, F.
1937   Economic Progress in St. Vincent, B.W.I. Since 1927. Economic Geography 13:217–234.

Wedenoja, William
1989   Mothering and the Practice of "Balm" in Jamaica. *In* Women as Healers: Cross-Cultural Perspectives. Carol Shepard McClain, ed. pp. 76–97. New Brunswick, N.J.: Rutgers University Press.

Whitten, Norman E., Jr.
1965   Class, Kinship and Power in an Ecuadorian Town: The Negroes of San Lorenzo. Stanford: Stanford University Press.

Wilson, Peter J.
1969   Reputation and Respectability. Man 4:70–84.
1973   Crab Antics: The Social Anthropology of English-Speaking Ne-

gro Societies of the Caribbean. New Haven: Yale University Press.

Wolf, Arthur
1981   Domestic Organization. *In* E. M. Ahern and H. Gates, eds. The Anthropology of Taiwanese Society. Stanford: Stanford University Press.

Worrell, DeLisle
1987   Small Island Economies: Structure and Performance in the English-speaking Caribbean Since 1970. New York: Praeger.

Wright, G.
1929   Economic Condition in St. Vincent, B.W.I. Economic Geography 5:236–259.

Young, William
[1795] 1971   An account of the Black Charaibs in the Island of St. Vincent's with the Charaib Treaty of 1773 and other original documents compiled from the papers of the late Sir William Young. London: Frank Cass & Co.
1807   A Tour through the several islands of Barbados, St. Vincent, Antigua, Tobago, and Grenada in the year 1791 and 1792. Vol. 3 of The History Civil and Commercial of the British Colonies in the West Indies, by Brian Edwards. 4th ed. 241–284. London: John Stockdale.

Young, Virginia Heyer
1970   Family and Childhood in a Southern Negro Community. American Anthropologist 72:269–288.
1974   A Black American Socialization Pattern. American Ethnologist 1:405–413.
1990   Household Structure in a West Indian Society. Social and Economic Studies 39:147–179.
1991   Vincentian Domestic Culture: Continued Debate. Social and Economic Studies 40 (4):155–167.

OTHER SOURCES

Census Research Programme
1973   1970 Population Census of the Commonwealth Caribbean: St. Vincent and the Grenadines. Kingstown, Jamaica.
Carnival Development Committee of St. Vincent and the Grenadines
1984   Vincie 'Mas. Kingstown.
Digest of Statistics
1982   No. 32. Statistical Unit of the Ministry of Finance, Planning and Development. St. Vincent and the Grenadines.
Educational Forum of the People
1972   Forum. No. 6, St. Vincent in Focus: The Road Forward. Kingstown, St. Vincent.

St. Vincent Department of Agriculture
1975   Census of Agriculture for St. Vincent 1972–73. Agricultural
               Statistics Unit, British Development Division in the Caribbean.
               Bridgetown, Barbados.
Statistical Institute of Jamaica
[1981] 1980–81 Population Census of the Commonwealth Caribbean: St. Vincent
               and the Grenadines. Kingstown, Jamaica.
Vincentian. The National Newspaper of St. Vincent and the Grenadines. Kingstown: Vincentian Publishing Company.
World Bank
1985   Economic Situation and Selected Development Issues. Wash-
               ington, D.C.: The World Bank.

Index

Abrahams, Roger, 2, 8, 15, 26–47 *passim,* 78–80, 154, 160
Absentee land ownership, 46, 53
Africa: slaves from, 46; traditions in, 6, 91, 159–67 *passim,* 170, 173; percent of population, 8
Age: and gender, 154; and image of power, 177–78; and status, 153–55
Alexander, Jack, 112, 134, 204n2
Anderson, Alexander, 26–38 *passim,* 47
Anderson, Benedict, 7, 147, 195
Anglophilia, 43, 44, 91; and titles of office, 19
Antigua, 23, 46, 53
Arrowroot, 56–57, 59, 95; in Jamaica, 57, 59
Austin, Diane, 93, 203n2

Banana cultivation, 63, 95–98
Barbados, 24, 53–58 *passim,* 68, 71, 85
Barrow, Christine, 154
Beachey, R. W., 56, 60, 61

Bell, Wendell, and Ivar Oxaal, 204n3
Belle, George, 69
Berbice, 46
Besson, Jean, 112, 115, 154; and Janet Momsen, 94
Betley, Brian, 114, 122, 123, 201n1, 203n2, 203n6, 205n8
Biculturalism, 144
Black Caribs: arms, 25; colonial policy toward, 27–30; diplomacy, 18, 29, 36, 37; enticing slaves, 38, 39; hostilities preceding war, 29–30; origin, 23–24, population, 24, 25; presumed exoticness, 19, 20; relations with neighboring islands, 26, 31, 32; sale of land, 28; slave holding, 24, 28; society compared to slave conditions, 40; territory, 26–27, 82; trade and employment with colonists, 28, 82; treaty of 1773, 30. *See also* Caribs; Black Carib War
Black Carib War: actions, 33–36; casualties, 38; deportation, 36–37;

223

Black Carib War (cont.)
  meanings of, 15, 19, 20, 36–40;
  surrender negotiations, 36, 37
Bolland, O. Nigel, 53
Braithwaite, Captain, 24–25, 33
Braithwaite, Edward, 5
Braithwaite, Lloyd, 5
Brana-Shute, Gary, 203n7
British: colonial presence, 8, 18, 23–24;
  derived governmental institutions, 18,
  19, 20, 43, 196; land speculation, 28–
  29; percent of population, 8; titles of
  office, 19; values, 2, 91, 145, 147, 160
British colonial policy, 23, 27, 28, 29, 30;
  and Black Carib War, 15; and
  federation, 70; and independence, 4,
  71; and Shakerism, 162–63
British Guiana, 53, 55, 56, 70, 71
British Honduras, 71
Brodber, Erna, 7, 8
Bryce-Laporte, R. S., 6, 160
Buckley, Roger, 202n3
Byers, John, 23, 26, 27; map, 22

Calypso, 174–77 passim; themes, 180–82
Cameron, Norman E., 41, 48–52
Campbell, Mavis, 39
Caribbean: festivals and sports, 176;
  interisland relations, 13, 197;
  literature, rural knowledge of, 166;
  trade, 64
Caribbean Union of Teachers, 12, 66
Caribs: in nineteenth century, 43, 56,
  202n2, 204n4; opinions of, 19, 20, 43,
  44; in twentieth century, 20, 43–44,
  64, 99, 178. See also Black Caribs;
  Black Carib War
CARICOM (Caribbean Economic
  Community), 64, 198
CARIFTA (Caribbean Free Trade
  Association), 64; and festival, 170, 172
Carmichael, A. C., 41–52, 202n7
Carnegie, Charles, 205n7
Carnival: history, 173–74; national, 175–
  79; as representation of culture, 172,
  173, 184–85; rural, 179–85
Cassava, 99–100, 204n4
Cato, Milton, 71
Césaire, Aimé, 14
Chatoyer, 28–36 passim, 44, 76, 196; his
  brother, DuVallee, 28, 33; his son, 36

Childhood in St. Vincent: compared to
  Afro-American experience, 144–45;
  emotionality, 137–43; and erotic
  dance, 142; explaining one's self, 139,
  143; discipline, 138, 139–40;
  fostering, 147–49; individualism, 143;
  mother-child contests, 138–39, 144;
  and presentation of self, 140–41;
  tasks, 147. See also Schools
Christian and political ideas compared,
  166–67
Churches and sects, 16, 88, 161–67
Clarke, Edith, 122, 124, 131
Clarke, Roberta, 115
Clothing manufacture, 101
Coke, Thomas, 26–35, passim, 40, 42
Colonial government: Board of
  Commissioners, 28, 29; Colonial
  Assembly, 18; Committee of Planters
  and Merchants, 35; under Crown
  colony rule, 65, 66
Common-law marriage, 113, 116, 152. See
  also Union types
Contests, mother-child, 138–39, 144;
  political, 78, 81
Contraception use, 155, 156
Contract labor, 54, 104
Cotton cultivation, 59, 62, 63
Craton, Michael, 25, 33, 202n6
Creole language use, 88, 93, 170–72, 183–
  89 passim
Creolization, 5, 6, 103, 111, 192–93
Crown Colony rule, 65, 190
Crowley, Daniel, 201n3
Culture: and carnival, 172–73;
  distinguished from national identity,
  193; expressions of, 14, 187, 189, 199;
  government policy for, 14, 196; idea of,
  14; and identity, 196–97; and
  independence, 12
Cultural reification, 13
Cust, Reginald, 60, 61

Dance style: and children, 142; women's,
  142, 177; mas' band, 178–79
Dann, Graham, 204n5
Davison, Raphael, 175
Davy, John, 17–18, 43, 53–60 passim,
  202n2
DeBique, Lorna, 67, 203n5
Deere, Carmen, 63

Demerara, 46
Department of Agriculture, 62–64 *passim*
Devisch, Rene, 206n12
Diet in Windward Valley, 98, 99
District Council meeting, 80–81
Dirks, Robert, 133
Domestic culture, 113–35; and analysis of Chinese culture, 135–36; compared to Dominica, 135; and life cycle, 151; and political culture, 4; and values, 136
Dominica, 9, 54, 61, 94–98 *passim*, 135, 203n3
Drama, encouragement of, 185–86
Drummond, Lee, 6, 201n3
Duncan, Ebenezer, 19, 22, 43, 44, 52, 66–76 *passim*, 147
DuVallee (brother of Chatoyer), 28, 33

East Indians, 8, 9, 54, 90
Economic indices, 62–63
Educational Forum of the People, 169–70
Edwards, Bryan, 24, 25, 47; map, 21
Elder, Jacob, 142, 173
Elizabeth II (queen of England), 19, 138, 176
Emancipation: celebration of, 19, 52; and labor force, 54
Emigration: effects on sending societies, 4, 12, 94; remittances, 184, 193; returns and visits, 56, 86, 175–76; within Caribbean region, 56, 197
Emotion: in carnival, 184–85; in childhood, 137–43
Epstein, Alfred L., 195
Estates: absentee ownership, 53; division and sale, 60–61, 86, 203n2; and land ownership, 60–61, 62, 191; left idle, 60–61; managers, 53, 58, 85; mercantile ownership, 60; overseers, 107, 108; processing facilities, 57, 84, 85, 95
Ethnic diversity: in Caribbean, 9; and national identity, 201n3; in Windward Valley, 89–90
Exports, 63–64

Family: critique of research on, 111–12; labor, 95–98; as network, 132, 143; nuclear, 116, 136; research objectives and methods, 112–13. *See also* Households; Union types
Farming, small, 15, 52–61, 94–98, 190, 191–92. *See also* Banana cultivation; Family labor; Land ownership; Land reform; Land tenure
Father: role in family, 137, 141; relation to outside children, 118–19. *See also* Paternity: obligations of
Festivals: folk dance, 170, 172; rural, 179–84
Field methods, ix, x, 15, 112, 121
Fischer, Michael, 162
Fitzpatrick, Robert, 84–89 *passim*, 183
Flambeau, 48, 62, 65, 69, 168–69, 171
Fortes, Meyer, 141
Fox, Richard, 194
Fraser, Thomas, 123, 203n1 (chapter 3)
French: relations with Black Caribs, 24, 31–33; settlement, 8, 23, 31
Friendly Society, 85
Funerals: and village pride, 156, and grave diggers, 156–59; as resolution of values, 160

Garvey, Marcus, 12, 65, 66
Gearing, Margaret, 154, 201n1, 204n6
Geggins, David, 39
Gender: dichotomy of values, 154–55; and employment, 19, 95, 98; relationships, 136, 189, and "respectability," 115, 154; and union type, 115; and violence, 152
Geography and organization of space, 9–10
Georges, Eugenia, 94
Ghosts, 159, 164–65
Gibbs, Bentley, 55
Giddens, Anthony, 195
Glazier, Stephen, 206n13
Gonsalves, Ralph, 44, 76, 198, 203n5
Gonzalez, Nancy, 25, 33, 36, 37, 122, 205nn9, 10
Government: cultural policy of, 14; idea of, 191, 194, 196; respect for, 18, 19, 190; and self-esteem, 191; services in Windward Valley, 89; as signifier of national identity, 81; slaves' views of, 42, 190, 193
Gray, Obika, 68
Green, Edward, 61
Grenada, 32, 33, 54, 58, 59

Grenadine Islands, 6–7, 10
Gullick, C., 24, 25, 40, 43

Hackett, Jeff, 76
Hall, Douglas, 53–59 *passim*, 65
Handler, Jerome, 57, 204n4
Handler, Richard, 13
Hart, Richard, 67, 203n5
Henney, Jeannette, 163
Herskovits, Melville, 1, 2, 6, 15, 160
Hierarchy: absence from village and
    kinship organization, 141; closer
    relations across levels, 146, 149;
    respect for, 18; in teacher-pupil
    relation, 144–45; as vertical relations,
    195
Higman, Barry, 41, 46, 52, 202n6
.Hill, Errol, 173
Historical consciousness: and knowledge,
    19, 170; observed in nineteenth
    century, 17–18; in Vincentian thought,
    1, 4, 10, 12, 18–20
Hobsbawm, Eric, 196
Hoetink, Harmannus, 7, 103–104
Holland, Dorothy, and Julia Crane, 162
Holzberg, Carol, 201n2
Hoogbergen, Wim, 26, 202n4
Horowitz, Michael, 122
Hourihan, John, 201n1, 203n6
Households, 121–31, 137, 205n7;
    summary 134–35; during slavery,
    202n6
House ownership, 127, 130–31, 151
Huang, C., and Arthur Wolf, 136
Hughes, Victor, 32

Illegitimate child-bearing, views on, 149–
    50
Incumbered Estates Court, 60–61
Importation of contract labor, 8–9, 54, 104
Imported commodities, 64, 94, 101, 102
Importing companies, 19, 68, 69
Independence, political, 4, 71
Individualism, 3, 4, 15–16, 149, 189, 192,
    193; in childhood summarized, 143
Intelligentsia, 16, 19, 147, 169
Interracial unions: attitudes about, 107,
    109, 111; and creolization, 111;
    ideology of, 103–104
Island Rangers, 39
Iton, Clem, 76

Jackson, Michael, and Ivan Karp, 195
Jacobson-Widding, Anita, 141, 195
Jamaica, 5, 46, 57–68 *passim*, 71
James, C. L. R., 168, 174–75
John, Karl, 5
John, Kenneth, 66, 69, 70, 72–73, 74–75,
    76, 77, 78, 163, 186, 198, 203n5
Joshua, Ebenezer, 69–77 *passim*, 163, 196
Joshua, Ivy, 71, 75

Kapferer, Bruce, 195
Keizer, Norma, 60
King, Colin, 172
Kinship: attenuatedness of, 4, 188;
    demonstration of, 117; and nonlegal
    unions, 114; terms, 117
Kirby, Earl, and C. I. Martin, 34
Klomp, Ank, 73
Kondo, Dorinne, 195

Labat, Père, 24
Labor supply, post-emancipation, 53–58,
    203n1; and coercion, 53–54, 55; and
    housing, 54; and imported laborers, 54
Land ownership: and absenteeism, 53;
    small holdings, 56–62 *passim;* in
    Windward Valley, 86
Land reform programs, 62, 64, 78
Land sales. *See* Estates
Land tenure, 56–59, 61, 63, 203n3
Laughter, 138, 205n12
Leeward Islands, 54, 55, 65, 71
Le Page, R. B., and Andrée Tabouret-Keller,
    43
Lewis, Sheriff [pseud. Selassie], 67, 68
Lewis, W. Arthur, 67, 68, 69, 71
Life cycle, 15, 16; and gender dichotomy,
    154–55; of men, 152–54; of women,
    151–52
Lobdell, Richard, 203n4

McIntosh, Georges, 66–76 *passim*, 162–63
Macklin, Catherine, 37, 201n2
Madeirans: as contract laborers, 8, 54; and
    Portuguese as percent of population, 9
Manning, Frank, 8, 177
Manumission rates, 46
Margaret Rose, Princess (of England), 138
Marketing, rural, 92, 100

Maroons: in Jamaica, 25, 39; in St. Vincent, 20, 23–40; in Suriname 25–26, 202n4; slaves' relations with, 20, 37–40
Marriage, 91, 113, 116, 152. *See also* Union types
Marryshaw, T. A., 12, 66
Marshall, Bernard, 33
Marshall, Dawn, 56
Marshall, Woodville, 52, 53, 54, 55, 59, 65
Martinez-Alier, Verena, 103, 112
Martinique, 23, 24
Marxism, 7, 168
Masquerade marching (Mas'), 173, 174, 178–79
Matrifocality: in Windward Valley, 132, 133; compared to Garifuna, 205n10
Mau, James, 204n3
Media: and family, 140; foreign intrusion by, 14, 179, 186; newspapers, 79; prevalence of, 4, 13, 20
Mintz, Sydney, 3, 7, 50, 132, 133, 201n3
Missionization: of Caribs, 23, 26, 31; of slaves, 42–43
Mitchell, James F., 73, 74, 77–78, 177, 197, 199
Momsen, Janet, 203n4
Montserrat, 58
Mother-child relationship, 137, 138; with daughter, 127–29, 149–50; with son, 127–29, 151–53
Murphy, Valerie, 150

National culture, 1, 4, 8, 187, 194–95, 199; in Caribbean ethnographies, 201n2; and cultural reification, 13
National identity: and Christianity, 166–67, 197; comparative, 194–96; distinguished from culture, 193–94; and ethnic homogeneity, 201n3; and government, 81, 194; and personal identity, 166–67, 194–95; recognition of, 3, 4, 8, 10, 14; and schools, 8, 147; symbols of, 195–96; and West Indian identity, 16, 194–96
Nationalism, 7, 193–96
Nettleford, Rex, 14
Networks: and outside-father, 119–20; and households, 132–33; Afro-Caribbean, 132–33
Niddrie, David, 22

Nonlegal unions: and child support, 118; folk validity of, 156; and kinship, 117; opinions of, 155. *See also* Union types

OECS (Organization of Eastern Caribbean States), 64, 197, 198
Olwig, Karen, 50

Paternity: acknowledgment of, 156; and affection, 118; obligations of, 116–18; and outside-father, 118–19; and relation with mate, 117, 204n6; and child support, 120
Peacock, Nora, 70, 203n5
Personhood, 1, 15, 195
Peters, Oswald, and Kenneth John, 69, 203n5
Philpott, Stuart, 94
Plural Society model, 5, 6
Political contests, 78, 81
Political culture: attention to government, 12, 68; electioneering, 7–8, 78–81; government as symbol, 68, 81, 194; patronage, 73, 203n6; parties, 65, 66, 69–72, 73–74, 78; relation to domestic culture, 4; rural precedents of, 78–81; slaves' view of government, 42, 190; talking politics, 20, 79
Population, St. Vincent and the Grenadines, 9; by race, 9; sex ratio, 124; in Windward Valley, 89
Portuguese: percent of population, 9; in Windward Valley, 89, 90
Price, Neil, 6, 122, 203n6, 205n8
Price, Richard, 3
Preachers: and funerals, 157–58; and national identity, 13, 20

Race: as carnival theme, 180, 181, 182; and laughter, 138; and values, 91. *See also* Interracial unions
Ragatz, Lowell, 46, 47
Rastafarianism, 171, 177, 182
Regional Constituent Assembly, 197–98
Regisford, Beverly, 171–72
Reisman, Karl, 2, 6, 15, 166
Representative Government Association, 4, 65, 66, 88, 90
Riviere, W. E., 53, 54, 57, 58, 203n1

Riots: interpretation of, 69–70; in St. Vincent, 60–61, 66, 67–68, 173–74; targeting governors, 18, 62, 67, 174; in West Indies, 67–68

Roberts, George, 114, 118, 131

Rodman, Hyman, 111

Rubenstein, Hymie, 6, 94, 122, 133, 134, 144

Rural culture: in carnival, 189; and national culture, 8, 92, 189; and town, 179–80, 184–85

Safa, Helen, 7

St. Kitts, 46, 53, 58, 67

St. Lucia, 32, 54, 58, 197, 202n2

Sanford, Margaret, 148

Sargent, Carolyn, and Michael Harris, 52

Satchell, Veront, 203n2

Schools: and authority, 144, 145; culture of, 145; and national culture, 4, 147; nineteenth-century, 60; and performance arts, 172, 181; and social class, 146–47; teachers, 20, 85, 90, 146; and vernacular, 146

Segal, Daniel, 174, 201n2

Selassie, Haile. *See* Lewis, Sheriff

Self: assertion of vs. ritual defense of, 141–42; concept of, 15, 195; defense of 141, 150; definitions of, 141; presentation of, 166; respect for, 143; and self-consciousness, 161; sense of, 2, 3, 141

Sexual relationships: and child support, 117, 204n6; and promiscuity, 113, 204n5; and women's reputations, 120, 136

Shakers. *See* Spiritual Baptists

Share-rent system, 84, 86

Shephard, Charles, 23, 30, 35–39 *passim,* 45, 47, 52, 60, 84

Sinclair, Sonja, 114, 118, 131

Slavery: biases in accounts of, 47, 202n7; conditions of 48–52; conditions compared to Black Caribs', 39–40; in national imagery, 18; population characteristics, 46; provision grounds, 50, 51; as social status, 18. *See also* Slaves

Slaves: adaptation to plantations, 40–44; aid to Black Caribs, 37–38; attitudes to colonial society, 42, 190;

celebrations, 41; clothing, 41; described in contemporary accounts, 48–52; kinship groups, 40, 202n6; non-alliance with maroons, 20, 38; reproductivity, 51. *See also* Slavery

Smith, Michael, 5, 9, 111, 123

Smith, Raymond, 5, 112, 114, 123, 131, 202n6, 204n2

Social cleavages: and colonization, 8, 9; bridging of, 160–61, 193

Social distance: and ethnicity, 89–90; and social relations, 91–92; and yards, 91

Social stratification: compared to Jamaica, 93–94, 204n3; and creole society, 5; and lower-class values, 8, 93–94; and mobility, 93–94; and relations between statuses, 148–49; and signifiers of status 107, 109, 110, 160; in Windward Valley, 90–94, 123, 131, 203n2 (chap. 3)

Soto, Isa, 148

Soufriere, Mount, 10

Southey, Thomas, 42

Sparrow, Mighty, 174

Spinelli, Joseph, 57, 60, 201n1

Spiritual Baptists: and carnival, 179; history, 158–59; in Trinidad, 206n13; in Windward Valley, 161, 162–66

Springer, Hugh, 70

Stack, Carol, 133

State: and individuated relationships, 4

Steel bands, 175, 179

Stewart, John, 205n12

Stinner, William, 94

Strickland, S., 48, 49

Stycos, J. M., and Kurt W. Back, 118

Sugar, profitability of, 24, 46, 56, 60, 61, 63

Suriname Maroons, 25, 202n4

Sutton, Constance, and Susan Makiesky-Barrow, 115

Syncretism, 15, 159–60, 166, 170. *See also* Values

Tea meetings, 79–81, 182

Teenage pregnancy, 150, 155–56

Thomas, J. Paul, 29, 30, 39

Tobago, 47, 54, 55, 58, 59, 142

Topley, Marjorie, 136

Trade unions, 66–69 *passim,* 191

Transportation: buses, 92; canoes, 9, 28, 43; horse trails, 9, 26; roads, 9–10, 11,

47; sea-borne troops, 20, 34, 35; shipping, 10, 47; trucks, 85
Trinidad, 46, 54, 55, 56, 64, 67, 71, 142
Trouillot, Michael, 9, 66, 94, 97, 98, 203n3

Union types: and churches, 161; common-law, 113, 116, 152; compared, 113, 115–16, 122, 152, 188, 205n8; compared to Chinese marriage, 135, 205n11; duration of, 115–16, 150, 152; and gender, 115; and identity, 189; marriage, 91, 113, 116, 152; and morality, 135; and residence, 115–16, 149, 151, 152; and reputation, 149–51; as sequential, 117, 151; and social class, 114; visiting, 109, 110, 113, 115–16, 120, 152; and violence, 152
Universal Negro Improvement Association, 12, 66
University of the West Indies, 145, 146–47, 197

Valentine, Charles, 144
Values: conflict of, 1, 2, 15, 141; of domestic system, 135; as emblems, 192; European- and African-derived, 2, 91, 160, 165, 193, 196; of lower class, 93–94; and self-concept, 141; and status, 2, 91, 161

Verdery, Kathleen, 194
Village: continuity, 105, 106; density, 59
Visiting Unions. *See* Union types

Walker, F., 84
Warner, Ashton, 48–52, 190
Water: carrying, 102, 147, 148; piped, 102; use, 102
Wedenoja, William, 140
West Indian Federation: 4, 70–71, 196, 199; and independence, 198; and regional connections, 197
West Indian Regiment, 65
Whitten, Norman, 133
Williams, Anthony, 76
Williams, Eric, 168
Williams, Wheatley, 86–88, 171
Wilson, Peter, 115, 145, 154
Wolf, Arthur, 136, 205n11
Worrell, DeLisle, 63
Wright, G., 62

'Young man,' 153
Young, William (son of Sir William), 27, 29, 31, 32, 40, 41, 47, 173, 202n1, 202n7
Young, Sir William, 27, 35
Youth groups, 4, 85